The Unknown Self

George Frankl

OPEN GATE PRESS
LONDON

New, revised edition published in 2001 by Open Gate Press
51 Achilles Road, London NW6 1DZ

British Library Cataloguing-in-Publication Programme
A catalogue reference for this book is available from the
British Library.

ISBN: 1 871871 50 6

Printed in Great Britain by
Unity Print Limited, Corby, Northants

George Frankl was born in Vienna where he studied philosophy and psychoanalysis. The Nazi invasion of Austria forced him to emigrate and he eventually settled in London where he has been in psychoanalytic practice for over forty years. His work as a psychotherapist has attracted many followers, who consider his techniques to be a major breakthrough in the improvement of psychoanalytic treatment as well as in our understanding of the unconscious.

He has lectured on psychoanalysis, philosophy, prehistoric cultures and architectural psychology at several universities, and among his books, *The Failure of the Sexual Revolution* has been particularly widely acclaimed, both here and in the USA.

By the same author:

The End of War or the End of Mankind
  (Globe Publications, 1955)

The Failure of the Sexual Revolution
  (Kahn & Averill, 1974)

The Social History of the Unconscious
  (Open Gate Press, 1989)

  Paperback edition in two volumes:
Vol.1: Archaeology of the Mind
Vol 2: Civilisation – Utopia and Tragedy
  (Open Gate Press, 1992)

Exploring the Unconscious
  (Open Gate Press, 1994; new edition 2001)

Foundations of Morality
  (Open Gate Press, 2000; paperback edition 2001)

Contents

Preface

Many books have been written by psychoanalysts and by their journalistic interpreters on the psychological development of individuals, some of them of considerable value. The book I am presenting here is not a summary of the views either of the classic Freudian school or of the revisionist movements. While of course I am influenced by the writings of Freud, Reich, Karl Abraham, Melanie Klein, Fenichel, Glover and others, some of whom it was my good fortune to have known personally, the present book is based upon my own observations as a psychoanalytic therapist over a period of some forty years. While I began to work in what would nowadays be called the 'classical' mould of psychoanalytic theory and practice, I gradually formed conclusions which develop Freud's formulations and move on to new areas of the psyche which were not accessible to the pioneers. I was able to expand the boundaries of our understanding of unconscious processes with the help of a method of psychoanalytic therapy I developed over the years, which allows access to areas of the unconscious mind about which Freud could only make conjectures, however inspired they frequently were. He himself maintained that the unconscious cannot be directly observed, but could only be conjectured by means of interpretation of the material provided by free association. I have always considered this method cumbersome, and have attempted to overcome its vagaries and uncertainties by applying a form of hypnoid analysis which enormously increases a patient's awareness of his own sensations and feelings and makes it possible for him to remember and to relive periods in his life of which he was entirely unconscious but which nevertheless exercised an important influence upon his psyche, upon his body and his perceptions. Particularly the early infantile experiences were made accessible through this method, and perhaps for the first time made it possible to enter the unconscious directly. This produced an enormous amount of new material, and I can say that every day I learn new things about the psyche of people. In view of the mass of new data which emerge in my practice I have long hesitated to publish a summary of my findings, but I am reasonably confident that in this book the essential processes of people's psychological development are fairly presented.

However, I am not concerned merely with the psychic processes in individuals but equally with the psychological processes which occur in societies, their myths, beliefs, obsessions and conflicts.

Actually, this book is sandwiched, so to speak, between three others: the first two of this series, *Archaeology of the Mind* and *Civilisation: Utopia and Tragedy*, concerning the evolution of the psyche of our species, and the next, *Exploring the Unconscious*, which explains the clinical methods I have developed. Without the benefit of these methods I could not have arrived at the theories here presented, and without these theories I could not have written the previous books. There is no doubt that the experiences of our ancestors determine the genetic and cultural inheritance of the individual and provide the foundations for his psychological experiences. It is, therefore, difficult to say which of these books should be read first. I suppose it does not matter much, for the various realms of man's evolution are interconnected in a symbiotic unity. Nature does not know of these divisions, for they are merely conveniences we adopt to facilitate our intellectual pursuits.

I want to express my gratitude to the persons who helped me to formulate and test my ideas and who in various ways provided practical help in the production of this book. I am indebted to the editors of Open Gate Press and especially Jeannie Cohen and Elisabeth Petersdorff for their encouragement and support, and to my colleagues, in particular Sandra Lovell and Dr Peter Randell, whose comments and advice were most valuable. And as always I want to thank my wife Thelma, whose sensitivity for the English language prevented me from letting the habits of my Viennese German literary background intrude upon my writing, and who kept a critical eye on the linguistic misuse of scientific jargon.

The Unconscious

'The most important problem science has yet to face'
Erwin Schrödinger

1. BEFORE FREUD

'It is generally held,' writes Ernest Jones, 'that Freud's greatest contribution to science was his conception of the unconscious mind.' But he at once went on to note that Freud himself stated at his 70th birthday celebration: 'The poets and philosophers before me discovered the unconscious. What I discovered was the scientific method by which the unconscious can be studied.'

Long before Freud, attentive minds were drawn towards the exploration of that area of the mind beyond our consciousness which mocks the pretences of reason and morality and remains the real driving force of action. The nineteenth century produced thinkers who in a philosophical and sometimes poetic manner anticipated the discovery of the unconscious. Arthur Schopenhauer developed a system of philosophy that proclaimed the primacy of the will and of the instincts over mind and reason. He pursued reason to its ultimate source and found it to reside in the will, which he saw as the core and central foundation of all that lives. He constructed a concept of the will in nature, of which man is but an individuation, as he called it, to which the intellect is a secondary manifestation, its servant and its pale illuminant. He

1

used the concept of the will in a very wide sense, including drives and instincts as well as the libido. He recognised the will as being largely unconscious and the conscious mind as well as our reason as barely more than its tool. His pessimism had its foundation in his awareness that the claims of primacy which reason upholds for itself are an illusion. In his essay 'Transcendent Speculation on Apparent Design in the Fate of the Individual', he sets forth that: 'Precisely as in a dream it is our own will that unconsciously determines objective destiny, everything in it proceeding out of ourselves, and as each of us is the secret theatre manager of our own dreams, so also in reality there is but a single essence, the will itself that dreams with us our fate. We actually ourselves bring about what seems to be happening to us.' His whole complex of thought is, even to the presence of the sexual paradigm, a philosophical anticipation of psychoanalytic conceptions.

But it was Nietzsche who more than any other philosopher directed the attention of the European mind of the late nineteenth century to the psychic forces which lie beyond consciousness and reason. Thomas Mann considered him the greatest critic and psychologist of morals known to the history of the human mind. Contemporaries were impressed by the polemic character of his writings and by Nietzsche's vehement attacks against the current ideologies, the social order, established religion and conventional morality. It was Nietzsche's concern to unveil how man is a self-deceiving being, who is also constantly intent upon deceiving his fellow men. 'With all that which a person allows to appear, one may ask what is it meant to hide? What should it divert the eyes from? What prejudice should it conceal? How far goes the subtlety of this dissimulation? How far does he deceive himself in this action?' Nietzsche is inexhaustible in his attempts to show how every possible kind of feeling, opinion, attitude, conduct and virtue is rooted in self-deception or unconscious lie. 'Everyone is the furthest to himself, the unconscious is the essential part of the individual, consciousness being only a kind of ciphered formula of the unconscious, a more or less fantastic commentary on an unconscious, perhaps unknowable but felt text.'

Nietzsche conceived the unconscious as an area of confused thoughts, emotions and instincts and, at the same time, as an area of re-enactment of past stages of the individual and of the species. The obscurity, disorder and incoherence of our representations in dreams recalled the conditions of the human mind in its earliest stages. He thus laid the foundations for the historical approach of psychoanalytic theory which emphasises the importance of past events, often going back to earliest childhood for the disturbances and neuroses experienced by grown-up people. Moreover, he shared with Freud a preoccupation with the earliest stages of humanity. Dreams also remind Nietzsche of those collective hallucinations that seized whole communities of primitive man: 'Thus in sleep and dream we repeat once more the task performed by early mankind. Dream is a re-enactment of fragments of our own past and of the past of mankind. The same holds true for outbreaks of uncontrolled passion and mental illness.'

Under the name of inhibition Nietzsche describes what is today called repression, and applies it to perception and memory: 'Oblivion is not a mere force of inertia . . . on the contrary, it is an active and, in the strictest sense, a positive capacity for inhibition. 'I have done it', says my memory, 'I cannot have done it', says my pride, and remains inexorable. Finally, the memory gives way' (Friedrich Nietzsche: *Morgenrote*). Nietzsche had intuitively arrived at an insight that came to be central to psychoanalysis and which Freud discovered gradually and laboriously in his work with his patients. The concept of repression allows us to understand how emotionally important experiences, which for various reasons are unacceptable to consciousness, are pushed back into the unconscious, where they continue to influence the psyche and emerge in distorted and often incomprehensible forms, apparently devoid of meaning. Neurotic symptoms, dreams, bizarre fantasies, obsessive thoughts or compulsive behaviour are some of the ways in which the unconscious attempts to find expression, by-passing, so to speak, the censorship of the ego. These manifestations of the unconscious are not confined to neurotic symptoms, but we can trace them to a wide range of experiences which are common to mankind.

Moritz Benedikt, another of the influential precursors of psychoanalysis, taught the importance of the secret life, daydreams, fantasies, suppressed wishes and ambitions, the importance of the sexual element in the life of ordinary people as well as in hysteria and other neuroses. He also described how he achieved brilliant psychotherapeutic cures by relieving the patients from their pathogenic secrets. In 1868 he published four cases of male hysteria that he blamed on mistreatment in childhood, and proclaimed the necessity for psychotherapy. He described what he called the second life, the existence and importance of a secret life in many persons, and the pathogenic role of a secret which almost always concerns some aspect of the sexual life of the patients.

It is worth mentioning here that already in the eighteenth century the philosopher Leibniz maintained that an important part of psychic life escapes man's conscious knowledge, and he proposed the first theory of the unconscious. He pointed to the small perceptions, that is, those that are under the threshold of conscious perception, even though they play a great part in our mental life. J. F. Herbart took the concept of small perceptions and the threshold from Leibniz. He thought of the threshold as a surface where an ever-changing multitude of perceptions and representations constantly fight against one another. The stronger ones push the weaker ones down under the threshold, the repressed representations strive to re-emerge, and for that reason often associate themselves with other representations. Under the threshold, the obscure representations constitute a kind of chorus that accompanies the drama being played on the conscious stage. Herbart gave mathematical formulations of the relationships of forces between perceptions. Although his theory of the unconscious was a largely speculative one, it exerted a great influence on German psychology throughout the nineteenth century, providing an intellectual milieu which no doubt stimulated Freud's thoughts and made it possible for him to persevere in his researches.

There is no need here to delve further into the history concerning the speculations and investigations of the unconscious areas of the mind, but it is necessary to remind ourselves that Freud did not simply invent it – as many of our contemporary philosophers and psychologists seem to assume. He made it possible for the most subjective and private of all human experiences to become the field of scientific investigation. This can be considered the most outstanding of all Freud's achievements; it can be called the Freudian revolution in science.

2. PSYCHOANALYSIS AS THE SCIENCE OF INTERNAL DATA

It is well known that Freud received a thorough training in the physiology and anatomy of the nervous system and that he achieved recognition as a brilliant neurologist. What may be less well known is the deep influence which a classical education exercised upon him, his profound admiration for the great writers and humanists, and his identification with them. In his consulting room hung the pictures of his scientific heroes and teachers, Brücke and Charcot, and between them a painting of Montaigne, the humanist. He never allowed his love for scientific research to obliterate his interest in the subjective experiences of men. Indeed, the problem of the interrelationship between subjective experience and objective phenomena, between mind and the physiology and chemistry of the nervous system as two dimensions of the same thing continued to fascinate him all his life, and he never claimed that either one or the other could demand a psychologist's exclusive attention.

In his last work, written in London shortly before his death, he wrote: 'We know two kinds of things about what we call our psyche (or mental life): firstly, its bodily organ and scene of action, the brain (or nervous system), and, on the other hand, our acts of consciousness, which are immediate data and cannot be further explained by any sort of description.' (Sigmund Freud: *An Outline of Psychoanalysis*)

Not only did Freud combine the two dimensions of mind – its physical as well as its psychical manifestations – in his own studies, but he bridged the major traditions of European thought and co-ordinated them into a unified concept. In doing so he managed to overcome the apparent opposites which have split European thinking into two opposing camps: the introspective tradition of the humanists, starting during the Renaissance with

Pico della Mirandola through Montaigne to the great poets like Shakespeare, Goethe and Schiller, and representatives of the scientific tradition like Galton, Wundt, Helmholtz, Pavlov and Brücke, among others.

It is of course true that during the course of his development one or other of the two sides tended to predominate. But even in Freud's choice of medicine and his decision to devote himself to the natural sciences he was influenced by Goethe's *Essay on Nature*.

In his schooldays Freud read much of Ovid's *Metamorphoses*, with its poetic rendering of many of the Greek myths, Sallust, Cicero's orations, Virgil's *Eclogues* and the *Aeneid*, Horace's poems and Tacitus' *Histories*. In Greek, Xenophon's *Anabasis* and *Cyropaedia* familiarised Freud with the Greek struggle with the Persians and with the character and education of Cyrus. He read Herodotus on the death of Darius, Xerxes' invasion of Greece and the battle of Thermopylae, Demosthenes' orations, Sophocles' *Ajax* and *Antigone*, Homer's *Iliad* and *Odyssey*, and Plato's *Apology* and *Crito*. (John E. Gedo & G. H. Pollock: *Freud: The Fustion of Science and Humanism*)

Freud's library, now in London, documents his lifelong fascination with the history, archaeology, art and literature of classical antiquity. He had an extensive collection of archaeological objects, subscribed to archaeological journals, and indeed boasted that he had read more books on archaeology than on psychology. It is not surprising that the founder of psychoanalysis should be interested in glimpses of an extinct civilisation; archaeology and psychoanalysis have obvious links with one another; both value the understanding of the past through present day remnants (S. S. Bernfeldt, 1951). His love for the literature of antiquity as well as the archaeology of primitive peoples of different cultures provided an opportunity to authenticate the universal nature of psychoanalytic findings. All through his life he was sustained by the awareness that discoveries made in specific clinical situations had a general applicability and had already been hinted at in ancient cultures as well as the great dramatic writings of Western civilisation. His frequent references to classical myths, the use of Greek names such as Oedipus, Electra, Thanatos, Narcissus, for psychological concepts testify not only to his familiarity with classical antiquity but to his need to give wider significance to his clinical findings.

Through his interests in literature and drama and particularly the writings of Goethe, he became acquainted with the Romantic movement and its emphasis upon the irrational and the unconscious. However, his desire to control his urge for speculation and to direct it towards disciplined observation was encouraged by the high regard in which science came to be held in the second part of the nineteenth century, which pointed to science as being the supreme path by which he could fulfil his ambitions. He writes: 'The theories of Darwin, which were then of topical interest, strongly interested me, for they held out hopes of an extraordinary advance in our understanding of the world; and it was hearing Goethe's beautiful "Essay on Nature", read aloud at a popular lecture by Professor Karl Brühl, that decided me to become a medical student.

"Nature!' (Goethe exclaimed). 'We are surrounded by her, embraced by her – impossible to release ourselves from her and impossible to enter more deeply into her. Without our asking and without warning she drags us into the circle of her dance and carries us along until exhausted we drop from her arm . . . She has a purpose and broods continuously . . . She reserves to herself an all-embracing intention which no one discovers . . . She has set me within. She will also lead me without; I commit myself to her. She may command me. She will not hate her work. I have not spoken of her. No, what is true and what is false, it is she who has spoken it. Hers is all the blame, hers is all the praise. (1780)

Goethe's essay may be seen as a romantic picture of nature as a beautiful and bountiful mother who allows her favourite children the privilege of exploring her secrets. It is interesting to note that it was the 'holy spark of curiosity', as Einstein called it, which activated many scientists towards the exploration of nature, even though they transformed the romantic impulse into a controlled discipline. Brücke and Dubois-Reymond, the great exponents of the mechanistic school of biology, 'swore a solemn oath' in their youth pledging them to investigate nature and matter as being reducible to the forces of attraction and repulsion, thus showing the romantic foundation of their subsequent teachings.

In the nineteenth century, the belief in scientific knowledge as the prime source for an understanding of the world as well as for solving the world's ills – the belief which Freud retained to the end – began to displace the hopes that had previously been built upon religion, political action and philosophy in turn. 'In my youth, I felt an overpowering need to understand something of the riddles of the world in which we live and perhaps even to contribute something to their solution. The most helpful means of achieving this end seemed to be to enrol in the medical faculty.'

As a medical student, his ambition to understand something about the riddles of the world came to focus upon the riddles of living things. He was drawn towards biology, and through biology to zoology and the study of the nervous system, gradually arriving at the destiny of his intellectual pursuits, the study of the mind. His leaning towards biology became pronounced in the third year of his medical studies; he spent ten hours a week on zoology proper, besides the normal courses on anatomy and physiology, but he also continued to attend lectures on philosophy under Professor Brentano. At the end of that semester, he began the first of his original researches. The task assigned to him concerned the sexual structure of the male eel, which had remained a puzzle since the days of Aristotle as no one had yet been able to examine the testes of mature male eels due to their extraordinary migrations before the mating period. While his researches were considered satisfactory by his professor, he himself was not pleased with the results he had obtained. Despite his own sense of dissatisfaction with his first original research work in scientific investigation, he was accepted as a member of the Institute of Physiology, which had already attracted considerable acclaim and attention from foreign scientists. Professor Brücke, the head of this institute, set Freud to work on the histology of the nerve cells. He managed to prove that the cells of the nervous system of lower animals showed a continuity with those of the higher animals and that the sharp distinction previously accepted was unfounded. The paper which he published as a result of his experiments was, as

Ernest Jones has pointed out, well above the beginner's level. Any zoologist would have been proud to have made these discoveries.

In his next research project he undertook to examine the life tissues of nerve cells microscopically, and made important discoveries about the relationship between the structure and functions of nerve cells, anticipating the future concept of neuron theory. Many scientific biographers of Freud have remarked that by being too careful in the presentation of his findings he narrowly missed world fame for his neurological researches in his early life.

He worked at Brücke's institute from 1876 to 1882, and it was generally thought that he would be appointed 'Assistent' as soon as the post fell vacant. The various branches of medicine proper, apart from psychiatry, had little attraction for him. He relates that he was negligent in pursuing his medical study, and it was not until 1881 at the age of 25 that he took his medical degree. He repeatedly pointed out in his memoirs that the pursuit of scientific studies was of far greater interest to him than the practice of medicine. To discover something new, and thus to add to our stock of knowledge, was perhaps the strongest motive in his nature. However, in 1882 at the age of 26 his teacher advised him to abandon his theoretical career in view of his bad financial position. He left the physiological laboratory and became a Junior Resident Physician at the General Hospital, working in various departments. 'Nevertheless, I remained faithful to the line of work upon which I had originally started. The subject which Brücke had proposed for my investigations had been the spinal cord of one of the lowest of the fishes; and I now passed on to the human central nervous system. The fact that I began by choosing the medulla oblongata as the subject of my work was another sign of the continuity of my development.'

Freud became an active worker in the Institute of Cerebral Anatomy, and Professor Meynert was sufficiently impressed with the quality of his work to propose to him that he should fully devote himself to the anatomy of the brain, and offered to hand his teaching work over to him. Although Freud became increasingly interested in the study of nervous diseases, he realised that brain anatomy did not contribute very much to an understanding of the subject, nor did it offer an opportunity for practical work with patients. There were at the time few specialists in that branch of medicine in Vienna and there was no satisfactory opportunity of studying it. Meynert was a brilliant brain anatomist but a poor psychiatrist. He considered all psychoses to be due to diseases of the forebrain (the anatomical pathology of which, however, was unknown) and catatonia to be caused by meningitis at the base of the brain. Psychiatry at that time was, as Zilboorg has remarked, 'anatomic-physiological cerebral mythology'. (G. Zilboorg: *Freud's Fundamental Psychiatric Orientation*, 1954) In the distance, however, glimmered the name of Charcot, the great French neurologist, and Freud decided to find a way of going to Paris, in order to continue his studies under him. He formed a plan of first obtaining an appointment as lecturer on nervous diseases at Vienna University, as this would provide him with an opportunity of going to Paris. Meanwhile he continued his work as a junior physician and his studies in neurology, and published a number of clinical observations on organic diseases of the nervous system. These publications gave him recognition as a neurologist, and in 1885 he was appointed 'Privatdozent' in neuropathology, a highly prized position that allowed him to lecture on nervous diseases. Shortly afterwards, he was awarded a Travelling Fellowship, mainly due to Brücke's 'passionate intervention' on his behalf, and in the autumn of the same year he made the journey to Paris. When Freud set off to Paris his interest in brain anatomy was still uppermost in his mind, and in fact one of the chief purposes in visiting Charcot was to learn more about neurology. But there was something else at the back of his mind which he hoped to clarify with the help of the famous French professor.

While Freud greatly treasured and enjoyed his clinical work in neurology and physiology and achieved considerable acclaim as a researcher, he did not find these studies entirely satisfactory from a theoretical point of view. His deep-lying interests in the psychological motivations of human behaviour and its disturbances could not be satisfied by neurophysiological investigations. Even while he was for long periods entirely absorbed by his clinical work, the humanist in him prompted him to ask questions about the relationship between mental processes and physiological phenomena. These interests were powerfully aroused by an important event that occurred in 1882 while he was still working in Brücke's laboratory; it was the day that Dr. Breuer told him of the case of Anna O., whom he had been treating for nearly two years. The details of this case captured Freud's imagination, particularly the observation that Anna O.'s hysterical symptoms could be made to disappear permanently when, under hypnosis, the circumstances surrounding their origin were unravelled and thus discharged.

Breuer's treatment, which would have been considered peculiar at that time, had enabled him to penetrate deeply into the causation and significance of hysterical symptoms; they uncovered mental processes, forgotten ideas and memories which were shown to have a direct bearing upon her physiological disturbances. Breuer's account of his experience with Fräulein Anna O. was unquestionably a major determinant in arousing Freud's attention and interest in the problem of the psychoneuroses, although the incident apparently lay dormant in his mind for the next few years.

As it turned out, his visit to Charcot brought these interests to the foreground again and proved pivotal to his shift from neurophysiological to psychopathological investigations. As Ernest Jones has observed: 'It was assuredly the experience with Charcot in Paris that aroused Freud's interest in hysteria, then in psychopathology in general, and so paved the way for resuscitating Breuer's observations and developing psychoanalysis.' Most of all, however, it was his discovery of hypnosis at Charcot's clinic which had a powerful impact upon Freud's mind. Many years later he wrote that he always liked to refer anyone who doubted the existence of the unconscious to the extraordinary processes that take place under hypnosis. There is no doubt that the phenomena of hypnotic suggestion made him recognise the power of unconscious ideas upon the organic as well as psychological functions.

Charcot, who was a specialist in organic diseases of the nervous system, had become increasingly interested in patients suffering from hysteria. Before he began to investigate these symptoms, physicians had felt that hysteria did not deserve their attention, and patients with this diagnosis were often considered to be malingerers, or worse. (Walter A. Stewart: *Psychoanalysis: The First Ten Years*) Charcot was one of the most brilliant observers and classifiers in all psychiatric-neurological history. In keeping with his extraordinary capacity to connect apparently disparate symptoms into coherent syndromes, he pieced together the various components of hysteria into a single syndrome. Freud observed that: 'The whole trend of his mind leads me to suppose that he can find no rest until he has correctly defined and clarified some phenomenon.' But he added: 'He can sleep quite soundly, however, without having arrived at a satisfactory explanation of that phenomenon.' Charcot recognised hysteria as a mental phenomenon but, while he was aware of certain mental and emotional factors relevant to the disease, he simultaneously leaned heavily upon a concept of an inherent neuropathic tendency. This vacillation between psychological and organic determinants was paralleled by his vacillation between a recognition of the sexual factors and his attempt to show that the neurosis is not necessarily connected with the genital system, as had been thought before. While in most cases he recognised the linkage between sexuality and hysterical neurosis, he did not take the next step, namely, to implicate sexual feelings or drives in his theoretical formulations, although he took them for granted in his clinical descriptions and case histories. His chief contribution to the study of hysteria, besides his detailed descriptions of its manifestations, was to show that the symptoms of the disease could be induced by suggestions given to a patient while he was in an hypnotic trance, and that, furthermore, the symptoms induced in this manner, as well as genuine hysteric symptoms, could be removed by hypnotic suggestion.

Freud recollected that he was particularly impressed by the fact that Charcot could produce paralyses and contractions by hypnotic suggestion and by the fact that such artificially produced symptoms showed, down to the smallest detail, the same features as spontaneous attacks.

Despite Charcot's adherence to the physical-neurological approach to hysteric manifestations, as a clinician he assumed the role of a psychotherapist. He used hypnosis, suggestion, exhortation and environmental and transference manipulation: that is, he frequently used his charismatic personality on patients. He was, as we have remarked, perfectly aware of psychological factors and described them in clinical papers, which Freud heard and which he remembered when he came to develop his own ideas. Thus the visit to Paris helped Freud significantly to break out of the neurophysiological strait-jacket in his approach to psychiatry – a straitjacket which at that time was equated with sound science and which, in our own time, once again claims exclusive dominion in 'empirical psychiatry'. It was not Charcot the neurologist but Charcot the psychotherapist who helped Freud towards a clearer understanding of the factors responsible for neurotic diseases. He wrote: 'Monsieur Charcot was the first to teach us that to explain the hysterical neuroses we must appeal to psychology.'

Although Charcot had no systematic way of conceptualising or explaining the facts of emotional traumas, he had a startling perception of their importance in hysteria, whatever his theoretical statements about the neurophysiological predispositions may have been. By 1885 he seemed convinced that hysteria required mental treatment: 'We have here a psychical affliction; it is therefore by a mental treatment that we must hope to modify it.'

The many similarities between Charcot's hypnotic methods and Breuer's treatment of Anna O. prompted Freud to mention the case to Charcot, but much to his disappointment Charcot seemed unimpressed and failed to share his enthusiasm about Breuer's discovery.

In the autumn of 1886 Freud returned to Vienna and settled down as a specialist in nervous diseases. He turned once more to Breuer's observations and made him tell him more about the case of Anna O. This patient had been a young girl of unusual education and gifts who had fallen ill while she was nursing her father, of whom she was devotedly fond. When Breuer took over her case it presented a variegated picture of paralysis, with contractions, inhibitions and states of mental confusion. A chance observation showed him that the patient could be relieved of these clouded states of consciousness if she was induced to express in words the affective fantasy by which she was at the moment dominated. From this discovery, Breuer arrived at a new method of treatment. He put her into deep hypnosis and made her tell him each time what it was that was oppressing her mind. After the attacks of depressive confusion had been overcome in this way, he employed the same procedure for removing her inhibitions and physical disorders. In her waking state the girl could no more describe than other patients how her symptoms had arisen, and she could discover no link between them and any experiences of her life. In hypnosis she immediately revealed the missing connection. When the patient recalled certain situations which were highly emotionally charged, under hypnosis with a free expression of emotion the symptom was abolished and did not return. By this procedure Breuer succeeded, after long and painful efforts, in relieving his patient of all symptoms. The immediate question came to Freud's mind whether it was possible to generalise from what had been found in a single case. The state of things which Breuer had discovered seemed to Freud to be of so fundamental a nature that he could not believe it could fail to be present in every case of hysteria if it had been proved to occur in a single one. But as he observed: 'The question could only be decided by experience.' He began to repeat Breuer's investigations with his own patients. After observing for several years that Breuer's findings were invariably confirmed in every case of hysteria that was accessible to hypnotic treatment, and after having accumulated a considerable amount of material in the shape of observations analogous to his, he proposed to him that they should issue a joint publication. In 1893 they issued a preliminary paper, 'On the Psychical Mechanism of Hysterical Phenomena', and in 1895 there followed the book, *Studies in Hysteria*. Breuer called their method 'cathartic'; its therapeutic aim was explained as making it possible that the accumulated affect used for maintaining the symptom which had got onto the wrong lines and had, as it were, become stuck there, should be directed onto the normal path, along which it could obtain discharge. Their book laid stress upon the significance of the life of the emotions and on the importance of distinguishing between mental acts which are unconscious and those which are conscious; it introduced a dynamic factor which supposed that a symptom arises through the damming up of an affect, and an economic factor regarding that same symptom as the product or equivalent of a quantity of energy which would otherwise have been employed in some other way.

Although Breuer recognised the sexual factor in hysteria, he was extraordinarily ambiguous about admitting its theoretical importance. Yet for a long time Breuer seems to have been quite convinced of the sexual aetiology of neurotic disorders; in fact, he appears in some of his writings almost casual and matter-of-fact about it. Thus, in his chapter in the *Studies in Hysteria*, he writes: 'The sexual instinct is undoubtedly the most powerful source of continued increases of excitation and, consequently, of neuroses.' However, he became increasingly reluctant to follow Freud in his investigation of his patients' sexual lives and the far-reaching conclusions Freud was beginning to draw from it. There have been many studies about the reasons for Breuer's extraordinary vacillations and his anxiety about admitting the sexual factor in hysteric patients, but, whatever the reason, it is a vacillation he shared with many other neurologists and psychologists who found it difficult to overcome the deep-seated taboos which civilisation imposes upon sexuality.

In his rapidly increasing experience, Freud learnt that it was not any kind of emotional excitation that was in action behind the phenomena of the neurosis but habitually one of a sexual nature – whether it was a current sexual conflict or the effect of earlier sexual experiences. As he recalled: 'I was not prepared for this conclusion and my expectation played no part in it, for I had begun my investigations of neurotics quite unsuspectingly.'

Under the influence of his surprising discoveries, Freud took a momentous step. He went beyond the domain of hysteria and began to investigate the sexual life of the so-called neurasthenics, who used to visit him in numbers during his consultation hours.

Having become convinced of the importance of sexuality as a precipitating factor in the development of hysteria and neurasthenia, he increasingly came to ask by what mechanism the sexual memories came to be forgotten and repressed from discharge, thus being transformed or converted into symptoms. While hypnotism had been of immense help in the cathartic treatment by widening the field of the patient's consciousness and putting within his reach knowledge which he did not possess in his waking life, he found the method restricting as it showed obvious limitations in the degree to which it was applicable to various patients. Freud visited Bernheim in Nancy in order to improve the method and to learn more about it, and there witnessed an experiment which proved to be of great importance in the clarification of the problem of forgetting or of the problem of why patients managed to forget some of the most powerful emotional experiences. When one of Bernheim's subjects awoke from the state of somnambulism, he seemed to have lost all memory of what had happened while he was in that state. Bernheim maintained that the memory was present all the same; and if he insisted on the subject remembering, if he asserted that the subject knew it all and only had to say it, and if at the same time he laid his hand on the subject's forehead, then the forgotten memories used in fact to return, hesitatingly at first but eventually in a flood and with complete clarity.

Freud decided that he would act in the same way as Bernheim when he made his patients recall memories they had forgotten after their hypnosis. He reflected that his patients must in fact 'know' all the things which had hitherto only been made accessible to them in hypnosis, and he drew an analogy between events forgotten after hypnosis and the forgotten events that play an important part in hysterias. Assurances and encouragement on his part, assisted perhaps by the touch of his hand, would, he thought, have the power of forcing the forgotten fact and connections into consciousness. By one of those insights which enables genius to go beyond the plodding experiments of ordinary talent he came to equate in his mind the events under hypnosis which afterwards appeared to be forgotten with the traumas of neurotics that are normally forgotten or repressed from consciousness. So he abandoned hypnotism, only retaining his practice of requiring the patient to lie upon a sofa while he sat behind him, seeing him but not being seen himself. It is interesting to note how jubilant he felt when he was thus set free from the limitations of hypnotism.

His expectations were fulfilled; but along with the change in technique the process of catharsis took on new complexions. The new method which he used allowed a much wider range of observation into the function of the human psyche. Again he asked how it had come about that the patients had forgotten so many of the facts of their internal and external lives but could nevertheless recollect them if a particular technique was applied. Observation supplied an exhaustive answer to those questions. Everything that had been forgotten had in some way or other been painful; it had been either alarming or disagreeable or shameful by the standards of the subject's personality. In order to make it conscious again the physician had to overcome a resistance on the part of the patient. It was only necessary to translate into words what he had observed, and he was in possession of the theory of repression.

In neurotic cases, an instinct or drive or an emotive situation is debarred from access to consciousness and motor discharge but at the same time the impulse retains its full charge of energy. He named this process repression. As he remarked: 'It was a novelty, and nothing like it had ever been recognised in mental life.' It was obviously a primary mechanism of defence, comparable to an attempt at flight. The repressed impulse, which was unconscious, was able to find means of discharge and substitute gratification by circuitous routes and thus to bring the whole purpose of the repression to nothing. In the case of conversion hysteria, the circuitous route led to the nerve supply of the body, the repressed impulse broke its way through at some point or other and produced symptoms. The symptoms were thus the results of a compromise, for although they were substitute gratifications, they were nevertheless distorted and apparently meaningless, and in this way acceptable to the Ego.

The theory of repression became the foundation stone for the psychoanalytic understanding of neurosis. A different view had now to be taken of the task of therapy. Its aim was no longer to 'abreact' an affect which had got onto the wrong lines, but to uncover repressions and replace them by conscious judgments which might result either in the acceptance or the rejection of what had formerly been repudiated. In other words, certain memories and impulses which the Ego refused to acknowledge had to be recognised and understood as well as discharged. Freud ceased to call this new method of treatment catharsis, and decided to call it psychoanalysis.

The study of repressions and other phenomena compelled psychoanalysis to take the concept of the 'unconscious' seriously. Freud came to consider everything mental as being in the first instance unconscious; the further quality of 'consciousness' might also be present or again it might be absent. This of course provoked a vehement denial from philosophers, for whom 'conscious' and 'mental' were identical and who protested that they could not conceive of such a monstrosity as the 'unconscious mental'. Freud did not let this objection, which he called an idiosyncracy of the philosophers, deter him. Experience gained from pathological material, of which the philosophers were ignorant, left no alternative open. Anyone who argued that those hidden processes discovered in pyschoanalytic work actually belonged to a second consciousness would be faced with a concept of a consciousness of which one knew nothing, an 'unconscious consciousness', and this would scarcely be preferable to the assumption of an 'unconscious mental'.

Freud's investigation of the precipitating and hidden causes of the neuroses led him more and more frequently to the conflicts between the subject's sexual impulses and his resistances to sexuality. In his search for the pathogenic situations in which the repressions of sexuality had set in and in which the symptoms as substitutes for what was repressed had their origin, he was carried further and further back into the patient's life and ended by reaching the first years of childhood. The impressions of that period of life, though they were for the most part buried in amnesia, had left ineradicable traces upon the individual's growth and, in particular, laid the foundations of any nervous disorder that was to follow.

As Fenichel observed many years later: 'The more thoroughly the psychogenesis of a system is explored, the more definitely do the associations of the patient lead back into the past and ultimately to early childhood.' But since these experiences of childhood were almost always concerned with sexual excitations and reactions against them, Freud found himself faced by the fact of *infantile sexuality,* once again a novelty and a contradiction of one of the strongest of human prejudices. Few of the findings of psychoanalysis have met with such universal opposition or aroused such an outburst of indignation as the assertion that the sexual function starts at the beginning of life and reveals its presence by important signs even in childhood. And yet no other finding of analysis can be demonstrated so easily and so completely. Freud, however, had come to realise that the neurotic symptoms were not necessarily related to actual events which patients remembered but to fantasies representing desires, and that, as far as the neurosis was concerned, psychic reality and its fantasies are of more importance than material reality.

Under the technical procedure which he used at that time, the majority of his patients reproduced from their childhood scenes in which they were sexually seduced by some grown-up person. With female patients the part of the seducer was almost always assigned to the father. 'I believed these stories,' he reports, 'and consequently supposed that I had discovered the roots of the subsequent neurosis in these experiences of sexual seduction in childhood. When, however, I was at last obliged to recognise that these scenes of seduction had never taken place and that they were only fantasies which my patients had made up, I was for some time completely at a loss.' The period following this shock relating to his apparent gullibility and subsequent wrong theoretical conclusions turned out, however, to be one of the most fruitful aspects of his development, for he had in fact stumbled for the first time upon the *Oedipus complex,* which was later to assume such overwhelming importance but which Freud did not at first recognise in its disguise of fantasy. When the mistake had been cleared up, the path to the study of the sexual life of children lay open.

The analysis of his patients' childhood memories showed that sexuality is not limited to genital sexuality, that children are not sexless as had been assumed, but that there exists in the child a wide spectrum of sexual drives and that at certain periods of the child's development certain sexual drives become dominant: that is, attain primacy over the others. He found that the sexual function is in existence from the very beginning of the individual's life, but it is connected to a wide range of vital functions and does not become independent of them apparently until a later stage; it has to pass through a long and complicated process of development before it becomes what we are familiar with as the normal genital sex life of the adult. Freud recognised that sexuality is not an instinct that manifests itself in a particular form only, but is more like an energy that undergoes many transformations in a person's life and that, furthermore, these transformations developed with considerable regularity in all the individuals he analysed.

The regularity of developmental transformations emboldened Freud to formulate a *law of sexual development,* which has since found ample confirmation in the psychoanalysis of children and adults. However, Freud also discovered that the processes of sexual development can be disturbed, that a person may be arrested in his sexual development and, in consequence, may suffer from a fixation upon a certain sexual primacy.

The most remarkable feature of the sexual life of man is that it comes on in two waves, with an interval between. The first genital primacy is attained in the fourth or fifth year of a child's life. But this early development of genital sexuality is nipped in the bud before it can reach physiological completion; sexual impulses towards the parent of the opposite sex become repressed, and a period of *latency* follows which lasts until puberty. During this period the reaction formations of morality and conscience are built up. Of all living creatures man alone seems to show this double onset of sexual growth, and it may perhaps be the most important determinant of man's predisposition to neurosis. At puberty the impulses and object relations of a child's early years become reanimated, and amongst them the emotional ties of his Oedipus complex. The sexual life of puberty is a struggle between the impulses of early years and the inhibitions of the latency period.

In his many supplements to his book *Three Contributions to the Theory of Sexuality,* Freud increasingly emphasised that it is necessary to separate sexuality from its too close connection with the genitals, and to regard it as a more comprehensive energy having pleasure as its goal and only secondarily coming to serve the ends of reproduction. It was one of Freud's greatest achievements to discover that sexual energy, or libido, is involved in all the major bodily functions and is not confined to the genitals; that all the important bodily processes have a sexual dimension, and that sexual disturbances can create disturbances of the bodily functions. Looked at from the psychoanalytic standpoint, Freud said, even the most eccentric and bizarre perversions are explicable as manifestations of infantile forms of sexuality to which the libido has regressed. They continue in the pursuit of pleasure on their own account as they did in the very early days of the libido's development.

Freud's surprising discoveries as to the sexuality of children were made in the first instance through the analysis of adults. But later it became possible to confirm them in the most satisfactory way and in every detail by direct observation of children. 'Indeed, it is so easy to convince oneself of the regular sexual activities of children that one cannot help asking in astonishment how the human race can have succeeded in overlooking the facts and in maintaining for so long the legend of the non-sexuality of children.' This surprising circumstance must be connected with the amnesia by which the majority of adults hide their own infancy.

The theories of resistance and of repression, of the unconscious, of the aetiological significance of sexual life and of the importance of infantile experiences came to form the principal constituents of the theoretical structure of psychoanalysis. However, alterations gradually took place in the technique of the analytical method and culminated in the process of *free association*, which came to be the fundamental method of psychoanalytic therapy. Instead of urging the patient to say something on a particular subject Freud came to ask him to say whatever came into his head while ceasing to give any conscious direction to his thoughts. It was essential that the patient should bind himself to report literally everything that occurred to his mind and not give way to critical objections, which sought to put certain associations on one side on the ground that they were not sufficiently important or that they were irrelevant or that they were altogether meaningless. This was called the fundamental rule of psychoanalysis. This method made it possible to study the processes of *resistance* or *censorship* and of *displacement* which play an important part in dreaming.

With the help of the method of free association, and the closely related art of interpretation, psychoanalysis succeeded in showing that dreams have a meaning which could be discovered. Dreams are constructed like a neurotic symptom; they are compromises between the demands of a repressed impulse and the resistance of a censoring force in the Ego. Since both dreams and symptoms have a similar origin, they are equally unintelligible and stand in equal need of interpretation. The interpretation of dreams became an essential aspect of psychoanalytic therapy as it was shown that dreams have access to forgotten material of childhood, and that *infantile amnesia is* for the most part overcome in connection with the interpretation of dreams.

In the same way that psychoanalysis makes use of dream interpretation, it also profits by the study of numerous slips and mistakes which people make – symptomatic actions, as they came to be called. In his book *The Psychopathology of Everyday Life* Freud pointed out that these phenomena are not accidental, but that they have a meaning and can be interpreted, and that one is justified in inferring from them the presence of restraint or repressed impulses and intentions. Previously, psychoanalysis had only been concerned with solving pathological phenomena, but when it came to dreams psychoanalysis was no longer dealing with the pathological symptom but with the phenomenon of normal mental life which occurs in any healthy person. If dreams turned out to be constructed like symptoms, if their explanation required the same assumptions – the repression of impulses, substitute formation, displacement, compromise formation, the dividing of the conscious and the unconscious into various psychical systems – then psychoanalysis was no longer a subsidiary science in the field of psychopathology; it was rather the foundation for a new and deeper science of the mind which would be equally indispensable for the understanding of the normal. Its postulates and findings could be carried over to other regions of mental happening; a path lay open that led far afield into spheres of universal interest.

3. WAS FREUD RIGHT?

Largely due to Freud's pioneering investigations, it is now generally acknowledged that there are areas of the mind of which we are not conscious but which nevertheless influence our behaviour and our thoughts and, moreover, are responsible for many psychological and even physical disturbances. The idea that forgotten experiences and traumas, unconscious desires, fears and hatreds influence our mind is commonly accepted, while many psychoanalytical terms, such as repression, inhibition and frustration, guilt complex, Superego, Oedipus complex, penis envy, sublimation, identification, sexual symbolism, have become part of our language.

There is also no doubt that psychoanalysis has had a profound influence upon modern art, literature and anthropology. Schoenberg, Mahler, André Breton, Paul Klee, Picasso, and in literature, Thomas Mann, James Joyce, Franz Kafka, Virginia Woolf, Ernest Hemingway, Stefan Zweig, Hermann Hesse and many others, cherished the hope that this new science would provide a path towards a new humanism, and a quality of human relationships, more free and more tolerant than any that had been possible in our fear-ridden, hate-ridden, neurotic world. As Thomas Mann has expressed it: 'Call this, if you choose, a poet's Utopia, but the thought is after all not unthinkable that the resolution of our great fears and our great hates, their conversion into a different relation to the world of our unconscious may one day be the great healer, going beyond the therapy of individuals towards a wiser and freer humanity.'

But now, some sixty years after Freud's death, it is inevitable that questions have arisen about some aspects of psychoanalytical theory and therapeutic methods. The most obvious question repeatedly asked, often in a critical manner, is whether the discoveries Freud made from the analysis of neurotic individuals can be applied to normal, healthy people generally, whether he discovered universal laws which govern man's psychic processes or whether his discoveries only apply to neurotics; furthermore, whether the disturbances he observed were typical only of people living in a certain cultural environment, namely, members of the middle and upper classes caught in the sex-repressive morality of the bourgeois culture of the late nineteenth and early twentieth century. Does the analysis of people in our time, when sexual taboos are no longer as powerful as those which prevailed in Victorian times, give us reason to believe that they suffer from the same traumas and repressions, and are Freud's theoretical concepts still relevant for an understanding of the psychological processes and disturbances prevalent at the beginning of this new century?

There is no doubt that the cultural milieu of our time has undergone considerable changes. The sexual taboos which exercised a tyrannical power over people's minds have lessened considerably, to some extent due to Freud's own pioneering work. There is nowadays even an emphasis upon the need for sexual gratification, and Victorian prudery has become a source for general amusement. Even the 'sexual perversions' which in the last century were viewed with horror, a source of intense shame for anyone who experienced their urges, are encouraged to show themselves openly and are considered as equal in value and dignity to so-called normal sexuality. Children are taught at an early age about sex, about homosexuality and lesbianism, and woe to anyone who harbours prejudices about these forms of love and expresses his distaste for them. Sexuality in all its manifestations is considered normal in the same way as male and female gender, all classes, races, religions and cultures are considered equal, and any claim for superiority of one over the others is condemned with various degrees of passion. Sexual, racial and religious prejudices are regarded as the ultimate sin in the demonology of the early twenty-first century. We might say that we have indeed arrived at a psychological Utopia, and assume that the battles of Freud, Reich, and the army of psychoanalysts, libertarians and humanists have been truly won.

However, even a cursory glance at the behavioural disturbances, drug addiction, violence, hooliganism and psychopathic aggressiveness which one encounters in urban areas, as well as the undiminished numbers of psychotic and neurotic individuals who need professional help, shows that the sexual liberation of the last thirty years or so has not in fact fulfilled the hopes of its pioneers. We may also be inclined to view the sexual liberation movements as a kind of ideological posturing, often serving political interests which have little impact upon the deeper, more permanent layers of our psychic structures. It seems that the old taboos, inhibitions and complexes have remained basically unchanged. The manifestations of our psychic conflicts have only shifted from one area to another. The drive for sexual gratification, which in previous centuries was largely blocked under the impact of a Christian patriarchal culture and found expression in a wide range of neurotic symptoms, is now more readily discharged, and sexual anxieties no longer play the same predominant role in the aetiology of neuroses, even while sexual taboos and conflicts are by no means resolved in our permissive age. But here we find a paradox: while the new permissiveness has no doubt to a great extent liberated sexuality from its old inhibition among adolescents and adults, infantile sexuality is still shrouded in a maze of confusions, anxieties and taboos. The intimate, instinctive, erotic relationship between mother and child has in many ways undergone profound disturbances. Scientific tracts and instructions, which mothers feel they have to study, are evidence for their increased insecurity rather than for a sense of confidence and enlightenment. At the same time we experience a profound change in the nature of the Superego, both on the individual as well as cultural level. Many books have been written concerning the 'waning of the fathers' or the 'fatherless society' as well as the 'identity crisis', particularly among young people. The role of a culture to provide a model upon which young people can fashion their identity has swung from being too authoritarian and repressive to being too vacuous in its permissiveness. In their own insecurity the fathers fail to provide the necessary guidelines for their children's Ego formation, and, indeed, appear to be indifferent or uncaring in their responses to them.

People feel that their real needs are not acknowledged and are estranged from the world around them. They then tend to express themselves in aggressive, sadistic forms, in the arts, in technology, in the hard-nosed, unemotional and impersonal fact worship of science as well as in business and politics. Competition and self-assertiveness are prime movers for establishing a lost sense of personal relationships. Ever greater numbers of people are deprived of their narcissistic needs, and it is largely narcissistic neuroses, a sense of isolation and estrangement in various degrees of desperation which the therapist encounters.

It is noteworthy that the prevalent feeling of narcissistic deprivation has had an effect upon contemporary theories of psychoanalysis and other therapeutic schools. Their attention has turned away from the libido theory and has tended to focus upon the importance of relationships. The sense of isolation of the modern individual rather than sexual repression has (probably unconsciously) motivated psychologists to emphasise the narcissistic needs, giving prominence to the Ego functions and to the patient's personality. Among the initiators of this movement, the most important were Alfred Adler, H. S. Sullivan, Heinz Hartmann, Erich Fromm, Karen Horney, Carl Rogers, and more recently, W. R. D. Fairbairn and Harry Guntrip. Anna Freud too is often seen as an important contributor towards this movement, which goes by various names, such as Ego psychology, interpersonal relationship theory and object relations therapy. Recent psychoanalytic theory is particularly preoccupied with the problem of self and the need to emphasise the subjective processes as the true field of psychoanalytic therapy. They pride themselves in various degrees upon having brought Freud up to date and improved upon him, and Guntrip states that: 'Quoting Freud in psychoanalysis is beginning at last to be like quoting Newton in physics.'

Now, I am all in favour of bringing psychoanalysis up to date and of improving its techniques and theories in the light of new discoveries. But I see no good reason for the attacks upon what these writers call Freud's 'biological orientation'. I have found no evidence to justify the patronising attitudes towards Freud's fundamental concepts, such as the libido theory, infantile sexuality, the unconscious and the transformations of sexuality in the psychological evolution of individuals. It is true that the concepts of sexuality and its transformations into a number of stages of primacies can be applied too mechanically, and no doubt many of the early psychoanalysts can be held guilty in this respect, but such shortcomings do not justify attempts to reject the instinctual foundations or, rather, deep-seated drives in the operation of the human psyche. Freud's discovery of infantile sexuality, and its transformations into a sequence of primacies, are the very foundation upon which subsequent observations in clinical experiences have been built. He did not neglect Ego psychology, but he considered the clash between what he called the Id and the Superego as a truly new discovery which he introduced into psychology. That the Ego itself is part of the development of the libido and operates largely unconsciously is an important part of his later teaching which the innovators tend to forget. It is the constant interaction between the sexual energy, or libido, with the objects of its needs, the vicissitudes of being accepted, denied, encouraged, thwarted, punished, frustrated or ignored in a thousand ways, which is the life experience of every individual in an almost endless multiplicity of ways. The libido is directed inwards towards the self, and outwards towards mother, father, siblings, authority figures, community and society; the introjection of external objects into internal presences plays an important part in the transformations of the libido and in the formation of character, personality or neurotic symptomatology.

The way these modifications of the libido occur is the subject of psychoanalysis as a science. In my own work, I have never hesitated to question any part of Freud's theories or to subject his observations to the test of my own empirical experiences. And I have found confirmation of the basic soundness of his libido theory, and an abundance of evidence to confirm and enlarge upon it. If in our time the narcissistic or Ego libido is particularly deprived, and many patients who come to us suffer from narcissistic injuries, then we must take this as a sign of changed cultural and social conditions and their influence upon the psyche. By showing the influence of new cultural conditions upon the conscious as well as unconscious self, we can also throw some light upon the psychic forces which operate in our culture. The transfer from the social to the personal and from the personal to the social remains one of the major fields for psychoanalytic investigation.

4. WHAT DO WE MEAN BY LIBIDO?

Here we should say a few words about the libido theory, for it is the most fundamental concept of psychoanalysis and probably the most easily misunderstood. When we use the word sexuality or libido we mean the desire for a person of the other sex, and in particular, the genital longing that occurs between the sexes and draws them together irrevocably, often in face of the most powerful obstacles and difficulties. We can also mean the sexual desire for another person of the same sex. This is the linguistic and conceptual usage of the term which is appropriate to the adolescent or grown-up individual who has repressed the earlier functions of sexuality, which have been centred not so much on the genitals but on a much wider region of bodily needs such as oral incorporation, the eroticism of the skin periphery, its caressing and protection, and urethral and anal functions, among others.

Psychoanalysis has shown that the activities of the lips and the mouth, the functions of the musculature, the sensations of the skin and of the body periphery, the urethral functions, the anal activities, even looking, listening, touching, tasting and thinking, all have an erotic component, and genital sexuality is only one of the many aspects of the libido, albeit one of the most important. We can thus conceive of libido as an energy or drive which permeates the living organism, and seeks discharge or expression in a wide range of psychic and organic activities. In the development of an individual one form of expression after the other seeks primacy. That the other areas of sexual interest do not disappear during the reign of genital primacy, for instance, is shown by the fact that in normal adult love-making the earlier erotic activities such as sucking, kissing, looking, smelling, touching, play an important part, and genital pleasure and fulfilment is the culmination of the sexual needs of an individual. Every fulfilling sex act of a mature individual is, as it were, a recapitulation of his sexual development.

However, by giving libido such a wide-ranging definition Freud created much confusion, not only for himself but also for his followers, and the debate about the actual meaning of libido still preoccupies psychoanalysts and their opponents. Certainly,

Freud was determined not to allow the sexual drive to be reduced to a vague metaphysical concept; this would make it more palatable to popular prejudice and the repressive forces operating in our civilisation, but would undermine his findings about the significance of sexuality in the aetiology of neuroses as well as in the life of ordinary, normal people. His arguments with Adler, Jung, and more recent revisionist schools centred around this issue.

In his early attempts to arrive at a definition of 'instinct' as it operates in man's psychic life, Freud followed the then popular assumption that there must be two basic instincts which dominate the life of all living organisms, including man, namely, the instinct of self-preservation and the instinct of procreation, the preservation of the species, and that they are made manifest in the two great needs: hunger and love. They represent a fundamental duality, and while their needs often conflict they nevertheless exist independently of each other. He at that time thought that any attempt to trace them to a common source had remained futile. In accordance with this view, Freud introduced the concept of Ego instincts in contradistinction to the sexual instincts. Under the former, he placed everything that had to do with the preservation, maintenance and advancement of the individual; to the latter he ascribed the rich content of adult as well as infantile and perverse sexual life. His investigations into the neuroses led him to regard the Ego as the restrictive and repressive force and the sexual instinct as the restricted and repressed force which frequently could only find an outlet by means of neurotic symptoms. As in his analyses of his patients he found the sources of most neurotic disturbances to lie in the repressed sexual drive, he came to formulate the nature of man's frequently unconscious sexuality, and arrived at his theory of the libido. In his investigations of man's sexuality, Freud came gradually to realise that the sexual instinct is devoted not only to the aim of reproduction but also to the affirmation and preservation of the individual. Thus libido energy is devoted both to the narcissistic Ego functions as well as to genital sexuality, and, moreover, is involved in all major bodily functions. It is, as he has put it, impossible to have any understanding of people's fantasies or of aspirations which occur under the influence of the frequently unconscious erotic drives, or of the language of symptoms, if one does not know of these deep-lying connections. He continues: 'Thus, when we began to study the Ego in greater detail, we came to understand the idea of narcissism, and the contrast between the Ego instincts and sexual instincts lost much of its validity.'

However, these discoveries presented Freud with a dilemma: if the two, namely, the Ego instincts and the sexual instincts are not different from each other, and if there is no point in distinguishing the energy of one from that of the other, one would be inclined, as he said, to use the word 'libido' as meaning the same as psychic energy in general. But if one begins to equate libido with a general psychic force, perhaps an *élan vital*, life force, etc., one enters into a world of meanings which escapes scientific or concrete definitions, and, as we have pointed out, he strongly resisted this trend. But, nevertheless, Freud had to admit the existence of a universal, biological drive which operates in all living organisms, and he came to call it Eros.

But then another problem arose: what role is one to ascribe to the aggressive instinct, which, without doubt, plays an important part in the life of organisms, human and animal? If Eros is seen as the life-affirming drive or instinct, how can one define the aggressive instinct but as the powerful adversary of Eros, introducing hate and destruction into the psychic and biological universe? As the reality of aggression cannot be denied, Freud found a simple solution: he reintroduced the duality, which he originally posited as sexual instinct and self-preserving instinct or Ego drive and sexual drive, with his grand theory of the universal conflict between Eros and Thanatos, the instinct of life affirmation versus the death instinct. However, while he spoke of these two forces as being in a constant state of antagonism, I shall show that this antagonism, although real enough in the actual psychological as well as political experiences of man, is not fundamental, for aggression is itself a manifestation of Eros. There are certain conditions under which Eros, the life force, has to fight against barriers it encounters which present a threat to its self-affirmation and even to its very existence. Without a doubt, aggressiveness can in many respects be seen as the promoter and protector of Eros, and it finds expression in work, in creativity, and serves the need to protect life in the battle for survival. As such, as we shall see, it is different from the destructive drive. However, we find a further paradox in that destructiveness as such can be a source of satisfaction, manifested in sadism, the pleasure of causing harm and death, of denying everything that is expansive and joyful; but even here we find a fusion between libido and destruction, and it certainly is a surprising fact that libidinous gratification can be obtained under certain conditions by the expression of destructive as well as self-destructive urges.

It is one of the tasks I have set myself in my work as a therapist to find how the erotic urge can find expression by turning against itself, how libido denied can evoke a destructive urge, how the expansive drive of the living can turn into the constrictive drive of life denial. And, indeed, we can see in the way these transformations occur how neurotic or psychotic symptoms occur, as well as the way in which nations can be overtaken by a fury of hate devoted to the urge to kill and destroy, and how human beings can annihilate everything they have created. For there is no doubt that self-destructive drives have played and continue to play an important part in human history, as they play a part in the life of individuals.

If we refuse to accept Freud's simplistic explanations of these tragic paradoxes, which have dominated man's existence since time immemorial, by his concept of the universal and inevitable duality between Eros and Thanatos, we are forced to search again for their causes and be more painstaking and thorough in our investigations than before. It is in this way that scientific progress occurs.

The psychoanalytic method, and its constant refinement, makes it possible for us to gain access to the hidden world of the mind, more rich and dramatic than any dramatist – or comedian – has ever been able to present.

Earliest Experiences

1. THE UNKNOWN MIND OF THE INFANT

It is one of the paradoxes of human evolution that parents remain largely ignorant of their children's emotional experiences and their mental activities. The dichotomy between the parents' perception of the child's behaviour and their inability to understand 'what really goes on in its mind' is a reflection of our general inability to understand other people and even to understand ourselves. While animals develop signalling systems which members of the same species recognise and instinctively comprehend, we rely on language and symbolic gestures which frequently fail to make others understand what we mean.

Before the child can speak it relies on pre-verbal forms of communication such as bodily movements, sounds, gestures and facial expressions to express its needs. While some of these evoke instinctive responses in parents, it is obvious that a wide range of children's emotions and actions remain incomprehensible and leave parents anxious and perplexed.

The child also develops behavioural patterns which are invisible from outside: it may tense its jaw and neck muscles, suck its tongue, or endlessly explore the roof of the mouth with it, make choking movements and tense up the throat, hold its breath, turn its eyes inwards or upwards, tighten its abdominal muscles, squeeze its urethral muscles and its anal sphincter, pull in the vaginal walls, or pull the legs upwards, make the pelvis immobile, or imagine itself to be invisible or non-existent – just to mention a few of the large number of very puzzling activities which remain invisible to the onlooker. They only communicate themselves to the parents through some vague sense of disturbance or unease which cannot be explained in a conscious manner. Even a number of manifest activities like obsessive postures, repetitive acts and rituals, represent a kind of pre-verbal signalling which remains inaccessible to our conscious understanding. Indeed, even with the acquisition of language only a narrow spectrum of experiences, feelings or thoughts can be communicated.

This applies not only to our relationship with infants and children or to grown-up individuals, but equally to the behaviour of societies and their cultures, their myths, rituals and religions. All of these express emotions, feelings and conflicts which are only inadequately expressed by the words they use. Indeed, the words themselves are used to intimate meanings which frequently elude common understanding. Language is of course only one form which cultures use to express collective emotions; dance, music, painting, sculpture, architecture and ritualistic observances express cultural and religious meanings, but there is no doubt that the more advanced cultures become, the more they attempt to communicate themselves through language. Drama, poetry, fables and novels, theological systems as well as philosophical and ideological concepts attempt to communicate to the world a part of what men experience.

Even the gods, insofar as they are represented by painting, sculpture or words, remain mysterious, often only made accessible in part by shamans and priests, by a complex hierarchy of magicians and diviners. The squabbles of the theologians and the systems of the philosophers must remain inadequate for a full comprehension of the meaning of the gods whom they try to define. In other words: what is made conscious by word or gesture, symbol and artifice remains only a small part of what occurs in our minds. But the quest to comprehend the areas of mind which have remained hidden from consciousness remains an irresistible challenge, a constant stimulant for our curiosity. A few words here about psychological time. In the nine months of gestation the embryo undergoes a process of development which recapitulates to a considerable extent the development of his species from a unicellular organism to a fish, a reptile, a mammal, a human being. This is called the biogenetic law which was made popular at about the turn of the century by the German embryologist Ernst Haeckel, and was widely accepted at that time. Since then there has been a reaction against this concept among biologists, who could not reconcile certain observed details of embryonic development with the evolution of the species, but more recently this 'law' has been given renewed attention. While it may contradict many details of evolutionary processes, it nevertheless provides a useful view of embryonic development. Without discussing the merits or demerits of the 'biogenetic law' here, let it suffice to say that for the embryo the intra-uterinal state must appear to last a long time indeed. (One is justified in speaking of the psychological experience of an embryo, certainly during the last two months of its development).

The psychological experience of time is, so to speak, relative. A day of an infant appears infinitely longer than the day of a grown-up; while even for a grown-up time seems to stand still at moments of intense danger or joy. We can say therefore that in states of increased attention and heightened sensory input time passes more slowly than usual.

Infants respond much more intensively, much more single-mindedly to sensations; their experiences are much more absorbing; the now seems to be forever, and awareness is not diluted by a sense of proportion where one moment is seen as one amongst others relating to a wider sequence of events.

The older we get the less intensely do we tend to respond to experiences and the shorter in terms of time they become. An infant's day is a little eternity, and its moments major events.

These considerations are of some importance if we wish to understand the impact of infantile experiences upon the psychology of an individual. If we understand that the human being is an infant for a very long time, as it were, we may appreciate that although repressed and usually forgotten, the experiences of infancy and childhood play a very large part in our emotional lives. The child continues to live inside the grown-up to a far greater extent than we can consciously realise, and infantile dependencies and infantile fixations exert a major influence upon our adult orientations. On the social level, as we shall point out, the grown-up person retains many infantile aspects in his thinking and remains dependent upon the social equivalent of parental protection and security. The attitude of the child towards his parents, his reactions to them and his conflicts with them, will be carried over to the grown-up individual's relationship to his social environment and influence his ideological, political, social and religious attitudes.

2. THE EARLIEST STAGES: THE ORAL LIBIDO AND ITS TRANSFORMATIONS

We must consider the enormous length of psychological time spent in the womb if we wish to understand the shock of birth, which many writers have equated with an experience of death or, at least, with a major trauma. In birth the infant is expelled from the safe and protective world of the womb, to which it had become accustomed during its long evolution, to confront an entirely unfamiliar and strange existence. However, nature provides the new-born being with a crucial link with the new world by the libidinisation of its lips. As the child is expelled from its accustomed universe, large amounts of libido flow into its lips, and they become highly sensitised. It is important to realise that the infant is not merely a passive recipient of the mother's milk when the nipple is put into its mouth, but that it is imbued with an instinct to reach out towards the nipple as soon as it feels its contact. Its lips are an orientation and explorative organ, similar to that of a monkey or ape. As soon as it feels the sensations of the mother's body, and, in particular, as it receives the libidinous sensations of the breast, its lips reach out towards the nipples and the sucking reflex emerges. It is no exaggeration to say that the new-born infant sees with its lips, that they are the centre of all attention, orientation and gratification, and very quickly it becomes aware of the mother's feel and of her libidinous responses through the nipple. Just as much as the infant's centre of attention and orientation lie in its lips, the most highly libidinous part of its body, so the mother's nipples become the centre of its world, the focus of its needs. And furthermore, the mother's nipples are not only the main object for the child, but the mother's central area of communication with the child. The mother's breast becomes indeed the baby's whole universe.

It seems that nature has provided us with a signalling system for the communication of libido in the form of pleasure sensations. We reach out with desire for warmth and libidinous experience, and we are made aware of it by a feeling of pleasure. But we also want to give out libido to another person whom we love, and one of the most important of these giving urges is that of the mother to the child. In the interaction between mother and child (as indeed in the interaction of two people who love each other), the child feels pleasure upon receiving the mother's libido, but it also perceives the mother's pleasure which it has stimulated; if we perceive that the object responds with pleasure to our desire and feel that we give pleasure to the object upon whom we depend, then we are important and wanted and our desire is good. Then we incorporate the other person's pleasure into ourselves and are pleased with ourselves. The object then is a good object and we are good subjects, and we have a good feeling of ourselves. There is also no doubt that the sensations of pleasure we feel also have an erotic or sexual component. The pleasure sensation aroused by the baby as it stimulates the mother's nipple also stimulates a wider range of erotic sensations in her, often accompanied by vaginal sensations, and conversely, one can frequently observe genital sensations with erections in male infants, and this also occurs in the form of vaginal sensations in baby girls.

However, these fundamental processes can be easily disturbed, particularly by mothers who suffer from erotic inhibitions and various degrees of pleasure anxiety. The basic and apparently simple act of mothering can undergo an enormously wide range of disturbances and complications among human beings, with important repercussions in the psychological development of the child.

Melanie Klein has repeatedly stressed the overriding importance of the infant's relationship to its mother's breast as the foundation for a person's character development. In her pioneering work on child analysis she has shed much new light on the remote and forgotten periods of our life: 'Throughout my work I have attributed fundamental importance to the infant's first object relation – the relation to the mother's breast and to the mother – and have drawn the conclusion that if this primal object, which is introjected, takes root in the Ego with relative security, the basis for a satisfactory development is laid. Innate factors contribute to this bond. Under the dominance of oral impulses the breast is instinctively felt to be the source of nourishment and therefore, in a deeper sense, of life itself. The mental and physical closeness to the gratifying breast in some measure restores, if things go well, the lost pre-natal unity with the mother, and the feelings of security that go with it. This largely depends on the infant's capacity to cathect sufficiently the breast or its symbolic representative, the bottle; in this way the mother is turned into a loved object. It may well be that having been part of the mother in the pre-natal stage contributes to the infant's innate feeling that there exists something outside him, something that will give him all he needs and desires. The good breast is taken in and becomes part of the Ego, and the infant who was first inside the mother now has the mother inside himself.

'I would not assume that the breast is to the child merely a physical object. The whole of his instinctual desires and his unconscious fantasies imbue the breast with qualities going far beyond the actual nourishment it affords. We find in analysis of our patients that the breast, as the good object, is the prototype of eternal goodness, inexhaustible patience and generosity as well as of creativeness. It is these fantasies and instinctual needs that so enrich the primal object that remains the foundation for hope, trust and belief in goodness.' (Melanie Klein: *The Psychoanalysis of Children*, Hogarth, 1954)

We notice that Melanie Klein draws attention to the fact that it is not only the nourishment, the milk, which is all important. It is the sensation of the libido, the mother's pleasure sensations, which the infant needs to feel in order to experience a secure and joyful relationship to the mother and with it, later, to the outside world.

Karl Abraham, whose researches have contributed enormously to an understanding of the early development of the individual, posits two stages in the development of the oral libido: the sucking, lip-centred libido, which he holds to be free from aggressiveness or hostility, and the dental, cannibalistic stages, whose chief qualities are aggression and object destruction. This schema of development is too rigid, however, for it ignores a great variety of responses and libidinous development already in the sucking stage. To quote Abraham: 'On the primary level of the oral phase, the libido of the infant is attached to the act of sucking. This act is one of incorporation, but one which does not put an end to the existence of the object. The child is not yet able to distinguish between its own self and the external object. Ego and object are concepts which are incompatible with the level of development. There is as yet no differentiation made between the sucking child and the suckling breast. Moreover, the child has as yet neither feelings of hatred nor of love. Its mental state is consequently free from manifestations of ambivalence at this stage. The secondary level of this phase differs from the first in that the child exchanges its sucking activity for a biting one.

'We must bear in mind the close association of sadism with the muscular system. But there is no doubt that in small children far and away the most powerful muscles of the body are the jaw muscles. And besides, the teeth are the only organs they possess that are sufficiently hard to be able to injure objects around them.' (Karl Abraham: *A Short Study in the Development of the Libido*, Hogarth)

Whereas Abraham states that there are as yet neither feelings of hatred nor of love at this stage, there is indeed, as Melanie Klein pointed out, a capacity for conflict in the experience and the awareness of the good or bad breast, good or bad feelings, and a great capacity for anxiety and anger. There is a great variety of experiences in the process of suckling, owing to the enormous variety of physical and psychological characteristics of the mother or whether bottle-feeding has been selected from the outset or introduced at some later stage. My work with depth analysis has shown that the infant not only experiences intense sensations in its contact with the breast but is made dramatically aware of mother's reactions to its needs, whether she feels pleasure in contact with the baby or whether she withholds her libido, whether she is tense, unyielding, resentful, or loving and excited by it, whether the baby is wanted or rejected or regarded with indifference. The mother who loves the child experiences the child as a source of pleasure, feeling pleasure in the child's pleasures. She, in turn, is experienced by the child as a good mother, and the child feels itself to be good. The mother who suffers from pleasure anxiety, from sexual conflicts and libidinous repressions, will feel anxiety in her own and the child's pleasure sensations; the child will be a source of anxiety to her, her anxiety will be transmitted to the child, who will feel her to be a bad mother and will feel itself to be bad and anxious. In order to illustrate the intensity and complexity of the infant's oral experiences, I shall give some examples provided by the analysis of individuals.

During my psychotherapeutic practice I have developed a method of hypnoid depth analysis, which enables the patient to go back to the earliest periods of his life and relive his infantile experiences of the first weeks and months of his existence. The patient, in the state of hypnoid regression, feels himself to be the infant, and he not only experiences his sensations as a baby but also communicates them by sounds and movements appropriate to that age.

However, while I could respond with a certain measure of empathy to these forms of pre-verbal communication, I found them, as a grown-up, to be insufficient for a proper understanding of what is going on in the mind of the patient as an infant. I therefore developed a technique by which the pre-verbal experiences of the infant could be communicated to the patient's speech cortex and reported or communicated in terms of language. The grown-up patient is able to receive the messages of his infantile experiences and communicate them in verbal terms. In short, the patient not only learns to relive infantile experiences of which he long ago ceased to be conscious (although they continue to operate in the unconscious layers of his mind) but also to communicate them in words. (See my book *Exploring the Unconscious*, Open Gate Press, 1994.)

Having regressed the patient to infancy, I ask him to feel his lips and, after a while, to describe their sensations in words. By directing all his attention to the lips, and by becoming aware of sensations and urges in them, he also becomes aware of the nipple, its feel, its pleasure output, its libido. He invariably connects from the nipple to the mother, and feels her attitude, her state of mind, her resentment towards the child or love for it.

Here are a few extracts from patients' communications of their infantile experiences with mother's breast:

Mr J.D., age 32 – treated for acute depression and inability to pursue any work activity. Mother a medical practitioner, unstable relationship with her husband.

I feel the nipple – very good, deep pleasure; mouth, throat and stomach feel marvellous. But I can't feel my mother's mind, she doesn't relate to me, she is not with me, she thinks of other things. She says, 'That's enough, that's all – so much and no more'. I can't understand it; I am confused and very distressed. Why can't I have more? Why stop it? I am not hungry, but I want to enjoy the pleasure feeling. Why don't people say it out loudly that this pleasure communication is absolutely essential; mother should have the pleasure of my pleasure, the unrestricted pleasure of libido exchange. Baby resents the person who deprives him of pleasure. Now contact disappears – I can't make contact, and next time she makes contact I can't trust her any more. It would be a marvellous feeling if the breast would come to meet me. Women are silly creatures, cruel creatures.

Miss R.G., age 34 – long-lasting depression, chronic indecision, paranoid tendencies and obsessive rumination.

I don't like it. I don't like the material. It's got a bad, unyielding feel. I can't get the milk the way I want it. It squirts out at me, I can't control it. It makes me annoyed. It's so uncompromising, one has not got a choice over it. I seem to have a memory of one that was better. This is too large, it does not take account of my size. I don't feel that my surroundings take any account of me; I find it very frightening. I feel alone-sort of separate. I am always angry; it's cold, the whole atmosphere is cold, everything around me is cold. Milk comes out of it but I can't get any; it is always taken away. If at least I could get a hold on it. This big one, it makes me anxious; I am very tense; I lose the sense of having a body. Stomach is very small. I don't feel anything around me. I withdraw from the outside to the inside – I am all cooped in. I can't expand. I feel angry and want to kill everybody.

Mr T. P., age 35 – treated for sexual sadism, unreality feelings, inability to take initiative, overriding feelings of passivity.

Nipple does not do much for me – not much excitement. Sucking reflex. Not much desire to suck – as if I don't really want to suck – as if I don't really want the milk – tastes thick, not sweet. It's real but not sweet. Not much sensation in mouth; there is not enough taste there; it does not satisfy me; I always want something else. I want to bite the nipple. The pleasure to be got from the milk does not satisfy me, I can't get involved in this. Biting would energise the whole body, sucking does not mean anything.

Mother is lacking in warmth. We are not one, we are separate. She can't allow herself, she can't respond to the child's needs. She could not let herself go, she is too matter-of-fact. I have this feeling of emptiness – it's all empty inside me. Oh, dear! I don't know what to do.

Miss H. P, age 31 – long-standing anorexia nervosa, depression and symptoms of retreat.

Nipple feels like an impersonal object, a thing like foam-rubber with a lump on it. I am disgusted. It is like being forcibly fed. It is offensive. It tastes spongy like a lump of sponge. It's like a piece of rag, it's like sucking a piece of sponge-rubber. Somebody shoves it into my mouth to pacify me. Like nothing real there. When is it going to leave? One can only react with indifference. It seems to exist in a vacuum. Sometimes it seems more attractive, but I don't like to admit it. Maybe I could enjoy it sometimes but I'm not going to. Mother is busy – she has not got any time for me – she has lots of troubles. I don't think she wants me there.

Mrs C. N., age 42 – psoriasis, periodic depressions.

Nipple is no good – it's disgusting. I like to cuddle the breast but I don't want the nipple; it's terrible if my life depends on it. I don't like sucking the nipple. I don't like the taste nor the smell of it. It's not sweet and not warm, and it's not good. It tastes real bad. Baby does not want to swallow it, it does not like it. What is the matter with mother? She feels terrible – she is imposed upon – she wants to be left alone. She does not want the baby to suck her – she is forced to do so – she is forced to have the baby. It's an imposition. She has got to give her body to it, her body does not like the baby, the baby is a vulture sucking her dry. Not a good relationship going on between mother and me.

Mr M. N., age 32 – paranoid anxiety states, aggressive rejection particularly towards the other sex, and intense sense of isolation.

Breast feels quite natural, but if I like it she has me in her power – then we are inseparable. At first it was all right. I don't want to think anything good about her, it makes me so angry. Terrible anger against the mother. She gives out too freely – then she is dependent on me. She needs someone to give her libido – then I am responsible for giving her libido. I don't want to be responsible. My mother assumes that she has got me. It is like sinking into her mouth. I sort of masturbate her. I don't want to be there to masturbate her, I want to be independent. She is too pleased now, she is in a swoon of delight. My mouth is a masturbatory mouth , the mouth goes very tense. I hate her. Body angry to get away. Don't want to be a masturbatory lap-dog. My shoulders are rigid with rage; I am not going to be people's lap-dog. I would feel sick and horrible if I let myself want. I can't move now.

These are just a few examples of the verbalised reports of primary experiences, but they give us a glimpse of the enormously rich and varied responses of the baby to the mother's breast and its awareness of her responses to it. One has, of course, to bear in mind that the infant's awareness of its mother does not occur on a conceptual-verbal but on a pre-verbal, pre-conceptual level of experience, and that the sensations reported are experienced physically, so to speak, in its body. In other words, the infant reacts somatically to the libido stimulation which it receives. This makes it also understandable that the pre-verbal responses have a particularly powerful impact on the somatic structure and thus, in turn, on the character structure of an individual. Posture, muscular tensions, organ and hormonal functions, the character of narcissistic feelings as well as object relationships find here their first determination.

All these patients, in fact all patients who suffer from various forms of depression, anxiety or disorientation, had very early developed a deep layer of aggressiveness whose fate is determined by later modes of repression or control.

Let us now consider in more detail how the primary libido, the need for love comes to be transformed into the many different forms of aggressiveness, rage, tension and anxiety.

In the beginning there is no urge for destruction, for the annihilation of objects. There is only an overwhelming desire to re-establish a living contact. There is only life or non-life, unfulfilled hunger or satisfaction, the horror of isolation or the reassuring warmth of a life-giving substance.

The infant, who experienced the 'death of birth', the horror of separation at the moment of birth, must re-establish contact with life. As it has been cut off from the umbilical cord and the living universe of the womb, so it must re-establish the umbilical cord with the new world outside by its new relationship with the mother, and it feels its mouth groping for a new fountain-head of life. The mouth and especially the lips feel the instinctive drive to make contact with the breast, which sets in motion the sucking reflex established pre-natally. (We can now observe that many children in the womb suck their finger, usually the thumb, during the last six weeks of their intra-uterinal existence, and some are even born with their thumb in the mouth.) If the mouth cannot feel the sensations of libidinous warmth coming to its lips it will feel anxiety, a reappearance of the primary separation anxiety which Reik called the trauma of birth, while it will feel reassurance, pleasure and release from anxiety through the sensation of a warm and flowing life-giving substance, which it perceives to emanate from the breast.

With the good sensations, due to a satisfactory flow of libido, the inherent natural rhythms of contraction and expansion of the primary organs of contact, the lips and mouth, take place in a vigorous and rewarding sucking action, followed by rhythmic swallowing, breathing, digestion and defaecation. (In this context

I wish to draw attention to the fundamental significance of the natural rhythm of contraction and expansion, tension and relaxation, which is basic to all organic life and which manifests itself in the sucking reflex.) The infant's lips, embracing and sucking at the mother's breast, are meant to stimulate libidinous response from the mother which, in turn, stimulates in the child sensations of satisfaction and pleasure. This primary, libidinous exchange we can call expansive-contact libido. If, however, the child does not sufficiently receive the mother's libidinous response to its lips, then the expansive-contact libido will gradually be transformed into contractive-aggressive libido. In the first instance, the muscles of the mucous membrane of the lips expand and soak in, suck in, so to speak, the libidinous sensations, whereas in the second instance, the muscles contract and evoke an aggressive response. If the breast appears rejective, cold, non-giving, hostile or anxious, it arouses anxiety in the lips, and a tightening of the muscles of the upper and lower lips – the incisivus superiori and the incisivus inferiori – occurs. These are the most superficial muscles underneath the skin of the lips, and when they contract the lips tend to make a biting movement, as the name of the muscle implies. Anxiety creates tension – a tensing-up of the musculature – and this can happen in the very first days of the sucking process.

Tension of these muscles will provide for more energetic movement, the sucking will become more forceful, the mouth will press and squeeze the nipple with extra power. If through the tightening of the lips a better libido emerges from the nipple – that is, the mother responds and is able to yield to the baby's needs – then the baby will relinquish its tension and start sucking again with an expansive lip libido. This can happen, but if it finds that with the untensed lips an affect block again occurs in the mother, i.e., the libido from her ceases to flow again, then the infant's tension will come back and become chronic. The tensing of the lip musculature and the more aggressive application of the mouth in the sucking process will then be the only form of satisfying contact. Out of the aggressive function of the lip musculature an aggressive structure emerges. (All structure is basically the result of repeated or fixed function – this is of primary importance for an understanding of psychosomatic processes.) We must remember that without receiving libido from the breast, the child feels itself denied, empty and non-existent, indeed, its very existence is threatened. So we can see that primary aggression is a way of getting access to libidinous response, breaking across a barrier, a 'coming together' with the object, exercising mastery over it in order to make it respond. (I should point out here that the sense of taste is the primary signal by which the quality of the mother's libido is transferred to the child. It would not be an exaggeration to say that the infant can taste the mother's attitudes and reactions towards it. A tight, unyielding libido will manifest itself in the nipple and in the milk, and will make both taste bitter, sour, empty or tasteless, unpleasant or, indeed, horrible, as we have seen in the examples of infantile experiences quoted earlier; a happy, loving and responsive, expansive breast will feel and taste sweet and satisfying. It can be readily appreciated that a sour or bitter taste evokes a reflex of tightening of the lip musculature, whereas a sweet taste evokes an expansive reflex. Of course, smell and touch sensations are also allied to taste sensations. The psychological and physiological significance of taste deserves a more thorough investigation than it has hitherto received.)

If the lips and mouth continue to experience lack of gratification or feelings of being rejected, or if the mother responds with anxiety or even resentment and anger, the contractions of the musculature will spread from the lips to the important and powerful muscular system of the jaw and mastoid muscles, and these will become the focus for oral activity. Increased energy is accumulated in the mouth, the cheeks and jaws will require powerful discharge; thus biting and chewing movements will be necessary to replace tension long before dentition occurs.

It often happens that at this stage the child is transferred to the bottle. If the bottle gives a good flow of milk, both the mother and child may be relieved, and the child may experience a release from anxiety and tension. But the bottle is only a partial substitute for the breast; the feel of the mother's body is still very important and the bottle only provides a satisfactory breast substitute if the mother lavishes affection, love and attention on the child, and gives it plenty of opportunity to feel the warmth of her body and her satisfaction with the child's activities. If, however, such com-

45

pensatory gratification factors fail to emerge, then the child's anger will not subside, it will be directed towards the bottle, the child will transfer resentment, hostility and aggression towards it. If aggressive and angry feelings were very powerful prior to the transfer to the bottle, they may give rise to fantasies of the child having caused the breast to disappear or having mutilated it or killed it by angry squeezing. Thus primitive, vampiristic feelings associated with guilt may emerge, and the process of sucking itself may create anxiety. Tensions around the mouth may re-emerge, the lips and jaws become rigid, the lips become dry, sore, painful, etc. Rhythmic sucking movements may disappear to give way to awkward, forced, tense sucking. The child may often be unable to suck with its lips, but will try to do so with its tongue or with its jaws. The milk from the bottle may often spill over its mouth and face; the rigid mouth may create a general sense of distress, and awkward, disorientated movements will appear.

While it is said that the infant is not able to conceive of an outside object, it is certainly aware of a stimulus creating certain sensations in its mouth and body. It may hate those sensations and recoil from them. It can happen that the infant attempts to deny rejective or cold sensations by minimising all sensations. It can do this by negating and minimising the awareness of vegetative processes in its own body; in other words, it has already at a very early stage the capacity to make itself unfeeling. It may do this by stopping breathing, refusing to swallow, making the lips rigid, tightening up the stomach and producing rejection: that is, vomiting symptoms. While we cannot here speak of object destruction, we can notice a form of self-destruction in the shape of denial of its sensations. These rejections of the object and of the sensations aroused by it can take the form of convulsions and breathlessness, sometimes endangering the child's life. If the early convulsions, which represent a muscular rejection of vegetative sensations and self-negation, become an important pattern in a person's mechanisms of defence, they can under certain circumstances lead to catatonic rigidities.

The infant's refusal to breathe, that is, to take in or incorporate the outside world, is another form of self and object rejection, and can lead to schizophrenic fantasies of having destroyed –

negated – the world, from which follow manic fantasies of re-creating the world by exhaling breath. Indeed, as I shall show, the process of exhalation represents a form of self-acceptance and self-feeling and also a trust of the world outside. The blowing of breath is an important image of restitution in religious imagery – the creation of life in the form of the divine breath which produces and gives life in the primeval emptiness. Jehovah's original name was probably Ja-Jo, which means breath. Jove: the wind. Ruach Hakodesh: the Holy Spirit, the Holy Breath. Oral anxiety and tension usually extend to the swallowing process, creating anxious and tense swallowing reflexes, which is commonly designated as being 'choked', affecting the oesophagus, the stomach and anus as well as the whole peripheral musculature of the body. (I shall describe these processes in more detail in the section on narcissism.)

When the teeth emerge they will absorb the already established aggressive libido. The teeth do not, as has been suggested by Karl Abraham and others, initiate the aggressive urge but give it a new dimension of intensity. Aggressive sucking will be transformed into a cannibalistic type of aggression. While the aggressiveness of the pre-dental stage is characterised by tense holding on and squeezing movements, dental aggression is characterised by biting, piercing, cutting and penetrating processes. I would, however, prefer to call the dental, cannibalistic drives penetrating-aggressive rather than destructive, as they were termed in the past, for the urge of destructiveness has not yet emerged at this stage of the child's development.

The early penetrative-aggressive urge wants to cut and tear at the life-denying surface of the breast, not to destroy it but to open it up, liberate it from its constrictive surface layer. The infant literally wants to penetrate the cold or indifferent periphery of the primary object in order to release the libido hidden beneath the cold surface. Far from wanting to destroy the breast or breast substitute, which are for the infant the fountain-head of life, he wants: (1) Release from tensions through the violent and aggressive use of the jaws and teeth. This we may call the subjective release from muscular contraction and anxiety in order to experience vasodilation and relaxation. (2) To attack the object

47

which is felt to be constricted, tense and depriving, and by cutting it open, to penetrate it, so to speak, make it expansive, make it give warmth and libido. It is as if the instinct realises that if living responses do not occur on the surface of the desired objects, they must be hidden below and beyond the periphery.

The importance of these impulses for the development of character structure as well as for the evolution of culture patterns are quite obvious. Intense, effort-making attitudes, of going beyond the surface of things, both in the intellectual sphere as well as in the area of work activity, are of great significance for the development of human labour and the attempts of transforming the environment. Erich Fromm has called these forms of aggression benign, in contradistinction to the malign forms of aggression, namely, destructiveness. (Erich Fromm: *The Anatomy of Human Destructiveness*, Jonathan Cape, 1974)

We can summarise the sequence of behaviour in the infant described above as a psycho-biological process: (1) hunger and deprivation trigger off anxiety, which acts as a signal of danger; (2) anxiety creates tension and accumulates energy, in turn creating (3) the need for aggressive and forceful discharge of the energy accumulated by attacking the depriving object with jaws and teeth and claws in order to penetrate its negating periphery and to release the potentials of warmth and libido beneath.

In many individuals jaws and teeth can become the centre of libidinous activity and, in some cases, the only source of pleasure. The urge to bite is the original form of the sadistic impulse and it can remain, throughout life, a focal point for excitement and pleasure. I have had ample opportunity to observe in such people distinctive sexualisation of their teeth, a sexual feel associated with them and a desire to use them, to bite hard, to penetrate flesh and draw blood, which often is imagined to be the very elixir of life, even evoking orgastic responses. However, if the biting impulse and the forceful squeezing of the breast with lips and gums evoke an anxiety or anger reaction in the mother, then the child introjects or becomes aware of the mother's anger or fear: it will feel the mother's reflex of withdrawal and will be afraid that the breast disappears, that it does not want the child, that mother does not want to give her libido to it. Then fear will be followed by an aggressive and forceful sucking, a tight holding on to the nipple in order to feel its presence. The child cannot relinquish the object if it is not satisfied and feels that it does not want to give itself to the child. It is only there if it is forcefully held on to, and if it is gone it would not come back again. Then the child is always restless, cannot relax, and has no sense of permanence of the needed object; it does not feel that it will return again, there is no continuum of its presence. Thus I have found that the aggressive drive is a compensatory response of the life-seeking instinct to the dangers of loss or negation of libidinous flow, an attempt to regain it by attacking the depriving object and breaking through its inhibitions, and to release the tensions, both in the object as well as in the self. The life-seeking instinct becomes aggressive in order to restore contact with life by breaking through the barriers which the primary object has erected against the fufilment of its needs.

However, the question whether the aggressive drive is an instinct or a secondary drive continues to preoccupy psychoanalysts; and the resolution of this question is of considerable importance, not only for the therapy of disturbed individuals but also for an understanding of our cultural conflicts. No one can doubt the importance of this drive, not only in the human individual and his private fantasies, but also in man's behaviour in society and in the behaviour of societies, states, religions and races towards each other. The ubiquitous urge to tear things apart, to break things up, is very evident when people feel they must free themselves from the confines of an environment that stifles their lives and keeps them in a state of emotional and material oppression. It is no doubt true that society frequently deprives people of their emotional needs, and just as the infant attacks the depriving breast, so the masses will often attack the social establishment which appears to them as hostile and indifferent. It is quite extraordinary, however, how groups of people who commit acts of extreme brutality regress to an infantilistic state of mind and are emotionally unaware of the suffering they cause – they only feel the exhilaration of gaining access to libidinous excitement through their acts of aggression.

I have become well aware of the powers of the aggressive

drive in man's individual and social behaviour; I regard the emergence of intense aggressiveness among the hominid of the ice ages, the development of the killer ape, as the factor chiefly responsible for the development of the genus *homo*. I have stressed that this process did not, however, arise as simply a biological phenomenon but as a psychological superimposition upon biological evolution. In the analogy I have drawn between man's earliest history and the earliest development of the individual, we can see that it is the cold, denying breast which produces aggressive, sadistic drives in just the same manner in which the cold and denying environment of the ice ages produced aggressive-sadistic urges and fantasies in man's hominid ancestors and transformed them into Primitive Man. (See my book *Archaeology of the Mind*, Open Gate Press, 1992)

The polarisation of Eros and Thanatos appear to me merely a superficial résumé of complex processes. I wish to show that the destructive urges do not exist as an independent instinct in opposition to Eros but emerge out of it. They represent a transformation of Eros insofar as aggression can be seen as a discharge of tension and a release from anxiety. Gratification denied creates tension, anxiety and aggressiveness.

3. THE ORIGINS OF THE DESTRUCTIVE URGE

Whereas the human infant has no instinctive urges to destroy the object on which it depends (even though the human infant is capable of aggressiveness which far exceeds that of any other animal species), we know that human beings are capable of violent, destructive behaviour, culminating in psychopathy, or in its socialised forms, terrorism, wars and genocide.

How then does aggression become associated and equated with destruction? If our contention that at the early oral stage of the libido the infant has no destructive urge is true, then destructive fantasies must occur at a later stage. The image of destruction usually occurs at the late 'oral-cannibalistic' stage when the baby begins to eat. Upon starting to eat solid food he notices, usually with some alarm, that it disappears. Object incorporation is for the first time accompanied by the actual disappearance of the object. It is therefore at this stage that incorporation and biting becomes associated with the annihilation of the object. But even at this stage children experience a wide variety and difference of sensations. These will be over-determined by the disposition and attitude of earlier stages, which determine whether the eating incorporation of food is angry-aggressive or not. Aggressive incorporation accompanied by the physical disappearance of food will be associated with its destruction.

Thus the biting and mastication of food is frequently associated with fantasies of biting and attacking the breast. To quote Melanie Klein: 'In the anxious, aggressive child we can speak of bad incorporation of food objects, the food, like the breast before, has hostility projected upon it; eating it is aggressive, and the disappearance of the food and the eating process is experienced as a form of destructive annihilation.'

While in many infants the urge to bite the breast produces intense anxiety that it would be hurt or mutilated or that it would disappear, the baby now faces a situation where it is encouraged to exercise its biting urges, to attack the object and make it disappear. No wonder that a large number of babies confront the eating process with a feeling of confusion and anxiety, and will be unable to eat or swallow food offered to them. This phenomenon has frequently been interpreted as a symptom of defiance, but while this factor plays a certain role in eating difficulties, the anxiety caused by what appears to be an act of ultimate destruction of the primary object has not been fully appreciated. In the analysis of anorexic patients, traumas relating to the fear of destroying the breast can be observed quite clearly, if one can regress the patient to that time, and they also play a decisive part in individuals who manifest intense food fads and obsessive anxieties about eating meat. The important role of food and eating rituals in most cultures have their origins in these infantile conflicts.

But what of the urge to kill, to tear an object to pieces, harm it and cause it to suffer and make it disappear? These are undoubtedly aggressive urges, associated with the sadistic libido, but are also destructive. But how can the destructive urges be considered as a need to produce life or life-giving sensations if the urge consists in making the object dead – unliving? It does not seem feasible to connect it with eating incorporation. Indeed, it must relate to an urge to reject the object. While in the aggressive form of the libido we depend upon the object ('aggression' deriving from the Latin 'aggredi' – to get close to), the destructive urge obviously wants to eliminate the object and make it disappear. However, we cannot at the same time depend upon and incorporate the object and make it disappear. But here we have a clue to the problem. We encounter the phenomenon of incorporation-rejection of which I shall speak later, but which also at this early stage plays a fateful role in the psychic apparatus. The bad, hurtful, painful, frustrating and denying object which we have to take in, incorporate, makes us at the same time want to reject it. We want to be rid of it, annihilate its existence, as it causes us to suffer pain. We want to rid ourselves of the pain it causes by inflicting it upon the object. The incorporation is reversed by projective elimination. It is significant here to notice that every rejective anger, that is, destructive urge, produces tensions in the stomach and the solar plexus, as they tighten up in order to reject the bad internal object. We want to deny the existence of the object which has denied our needs, we want to hurt it as it has hurt us, to deny its right to exist as it has denied the right to our existence, we want to remove it as a stimulus and take pleasure in its destruction.

There is another point: if the infant does not experience responsiveness from the parents towards its own needs and feels helpless to influence them by aggressive manipulation, the aggression turns into rage – helpless rage. The fear and tension which cannot be discharged and find relief by means of aggressive manipulation, the squeezing, biting and pulling aggression, turns into rage. Rage is a kind of explosion of aggressive libido which cannot find an outlet by channels available to the child. The object which we cannot manipulate or master in any way acquires the image of an all-powerful, dangerous object, which we have to eliminate from our sensorium by destroying it, so that it can no longer threaten and destroy us.

At a very early age images of monsters, with frightening teeth and claws, will appear in the child's fantasies, invading its sleep and taking possession of its dreams as well as its waking dreams, making it re-experience our ancestors' battles with wild and dangerous animals; and what was reality to our ancestors reappears in the imagination of the child, particularly so, when its own aggressive drives are profoundly aroused and cannot find adequate discharge. The important point here is the sense of helplessness, the inability to draw life from a rejective object, to transform a negative object into a giving object, which make the child and, indeed, the grown-up, want to destroy. In some character types this urge for destruction, which Fromm calls necrophilia, is a dominant form of gratification, and we find it also in certain socio-cultural situations, when the destruction of an enemy or a hated social system appears to be the only way of dealing with it and making it disappear, when the capacity of creating an alternative, of transforming a dangerous into a life-enhancing situation appears to be unimaginable and therefore impossible.

I must mention that we cannot attribute fantasies and images of monsters and dangerous objects to the minds of infants, but this does not preclude their disposition to experience them in their bodies, in their senses and in their nervous responses. Fear may not at first produce images of dangerous objects but certainly evokes responses of danger and anxiety and rage. Later, when the narcissistic Ego begins to develop, these sensations and reflexes are transformed into images and fantasies. Now let us return to the eating – incorporation of food and the internal awareness of the good or the bad object.

4. INTROJECTION AND IDENTIFICATION

If eating is not associated with angry, aggressive urges, then incorporation is not associated with object destruction. The disappearance of the food will not be associated with its annihilation insofar as in the experience of the good breast there is a feeling of continued supply, of a periodic replenishment and an anticipation of the repetition of gratification. Thus even in eating-incorporation the further availability of food is anticipated. Like the good breast it is there, it exists, however lustily the mouth and even the teeth apply themselves to the food. In this case it will be noticed that the child is not afraid of using its teeth. They produce pleasure, they do the right thing, their activity is approved of. Just as the food is a transformation of the breast, so the teeth are a transformation of the sucking and pleasure-giving lips, gums and mouth. Incorporation becomes good activity, it becomes pleasurable and rewarding – indeed, biting and chewing become creative, and the exercise of the dental musculature will not be destructive in such children but productive. Indeed, a loving relationship is established between the eater and the eaten.

We can say, therefore, that incorporation is not to be simply equated with a concept of destruction but can be characterised by a great variety of feelings and experience. This brings us to a process which provides the foundations for the individual's acquisition of identity. To put it into simple words: the feeling of the object incorporated becomes the feeling of the self.

On the unconscious and infantile level, the individual derives his identity from the primary object which he incorporates and feels inside himself. Just as the breast and nipple can be experienced by infants in a variety of ways, so the internalised object can have many different qualities. The point is: the feeling of self largely depends on the feeling of the object inside – within one. The ceremony of eating the totem in the totem feast and acquiring its qualities by eating it, thereby deriving identity from it, exemplifies this process of identification through incorporation. Primitive man actually eats parts of his ancestors in order to acquire their powers and to preserve his links with them. While in civilised man this affirmation of the unity with ancestors is carried out in many symbolic ways, the infant derives his identity in the same way as primitive man.

Incorporation, putting the object inside oneself by eating it, is an extension of the activity of the oral libido – the lips and mouth – and the quality of the incorporated object is largely determined by the quality of feeling experienced in the sucking process. The incorporation of the unsatisfactory, depriving or bad object will differ from the incorporation of the satisfactory or good object. We have seen that in pleasurable sucking it is the milk and its libido which is incorporated, and the breast will continue to exist, providing a continued and recurring source of gratification. In aggressive sucking the infant attacks the breast and will become afraid of destroying it or of causing it to disappear.

He is forever concerned with his internal self, with his bad, introjected object and, as it does not provide him with gratification, he has to attack it. The anger towards the breast which he has taken in is now directed inside himself. His capacity of looking outwards for object-cathexis and gratification is hampered, as he is forever concerned with the bad feeling inside him. The outside world appears empty and devoid of warmth, there is little empathy of feeling towards the things around him; everything seems distant as it were, and there is no optimistic expectation of the good things in the outside world to give him periodically renewed gratification or a sense of continuum.

As we have stressed, the child will squeeze or attack the depriving object in order to force life-sensations from it, so when the child feels the object inside him his aggressive urges will be turned towards the internal object and, consequently, against himself. He will squeeze himself and tighten up inside in the same way as he tightened his lips and mouth to the outside object.

In short, the internalised object demands the same treatment as the primary external object and its substitutes. Aggression towards the object becomes, through the process of internalisation, aggression against the self. While the experience of pleasure through aggression is the basis of sadism, the internalisation of the object of aggression turns sadism into masochism. This urge, or rather, system of urges, usually becomes strongly repressed and turns into fears of being attacked and is the foundation for paranoic fantasies and feelings of anxious apprehension, often in the form of free-floating anxiety, that is, a feeling of anxiety the sources of which seem to be indeterminable. Before we speak of the important process of projection, the other side of internalisation, we must say a few words about the emergence of narcissism and the psychology of Ego formation.

The Emergence of the Ego

1. NARCISSISM: THE SELF AND THE OTHER

Towards the later stages of the oral primacy, usually with the beginning of eating and weaning from the breast, a shift takes place from the mouth towards the libidinisation of the periphery and the skin of the body. The peripheral area becomes the focus of libidinous sensitivity, and the child becomes aware of the quality and feel of objects through skin and peripheral sensations. Tactual contact becomes of primary importance, for a new kind of awareness not only of his environment but of his own bodily identity. A body image begins to develop and with it the foundation of a primitive Ego. The peripheral libido, therefore, is the basis of self-awareness as a distinct and separate self. This narcissistic Ego needs to be fed by bodily contact with the mother and the feeling of her attention through contactual gratification. (I want to draw attention here to a problem of translation which has caused a lot of bother in English speaking countries. Freud has repeatedly been accused of 'objectifying, depersonalising' intensely subjective, personal experiences with his terms 'Ego, Superego and Id'. However, we must remember that he never used these words, but the words 'Ich' or 'selbst', which mean 'I' or 'self', and 'Über-Ich' – above self', and 'das Es' – 'the it', which he took from Groddeck. The Latin words are an Anglo-Saxon invention, in keeping with the tradition of Latinising medical terms.

The child will be able to have a good feeling of itself and of its own body if it experiences the mother's embrace, her affectionate touch and her attention. In fact, we can speak of a narcissistic hunger and an undernourishment of the peripheral libido due to insufficient contactual stimulation. There is no doubt that the narcissistic libido is an extension of the sensitivity of the lips over the whole surface of the body, and the child in consequence will experience a sensation of itself as a distinct and separate being. Its need for affection and warmth will be felt in its whole body, and its attention will be focused on its sense of self. It will develop a new interest in itself, and explore the many libidinous areas which gradually emerge on its bodily surface. The child will need large amounts of whole body contact to feel its expansive peripheral libido, a sense of pleasure and a feeling of self. The whole body periphery needs to soak in, as it were, the libido of the mother, and it replaces the lips or rather presents an extension of the lips as the centre of libidinous hunger.

The important change which takes place at this stage is a discovery of the whole body and a new sense of self. Just as the child becomes aware of itself as a separate and whole entity, so it is aware of the mother's whole body; inasmuch as it develops its own body image (and this appears to be the purpose of the libidinisation of the periphery), so it develops an image of the mother's body and, gradually, of the bodies of other people. One cannot, at this point, speak of an awareness of the mother's personality but certainly of a body awareness of her. The child will begin to distinguish objects, take an interest in them, learn to know them by their shape and feel. In short, it acquires an awareness of externality. However, in the same way as the nipple or breast can be felt as depriving or cold, so the body of the mother can be felt to be cold or indifferent, with the result that the child's own body will be taut or restless, or cold and unfeeling.

As a description of psycho-biological processes which occur at various stages of a child's development cannot possibly convey to us the intense and often very dramatic experiences to which it is subjected, I shall quote more or less verbatim from part of a session with a patient suffering from severe narcissistic deprivation.

Mr T. E., 36 years of age at the time, had suffered for something like twenty years from a condition of acute mental and emotional paralysis, a state of alienation insofar as he did not feel himself to be real and could feel neither his body and skin, nor his hands, legs and genitals. Furthermore, people around him did not appear real, and he had no sense of meaningful continuity of time and space. He could not connect situations with a sense of permanence or interrelatedness, to such an extent that whatever he may have done or whatever may have happened one or two hours earlier, or the day before, seemed to have no relationship at all with what happened to him at the present moment; when he was not at home, the idea of home appeared meaningless and quite unreal, and vice versa.

The session represented a typical example of the unconscious processes behind an extreme affect and orientation block. Most of the session was carried out under hypnosis.

Patient: 'My stomach is hard, encased, metallic. It's hard and very stubborn, it feels as if it is surrounded by thick, hard metal. I am stuck with it all my life.'

Upon my asking him how this hard metal came to be in his stomach, and directing his attention to his mouth, he first felt that he was swallowing a frog. I then asked him to associate to this frog, and he spontaneously regressed to infantile imagery and sensations.

'Mother is hard and stony; she is a hard, stony figure; she is a marble figure like a tombstone – it is too hard for existence. I cannot make any impression upon her – like a figure in a church on a tombstone. Her breast feels empty and useless – all dried up. Mother is cold and ill and remote. She is suffering. There is a sense of utter, terrifying weakness. She is so limp all over her body. She is lying on the bed, I am looking out of the cot. She is so grey; she is a stone-dead figure, she feels quite unreal to me. I feel frightened and isolated'.

After some more descriptions of her in this vein, he reflected:

'Mother was so frequently ill. Agonies in her head, she has to

58

soothe her head. I can smell the stuff on the bandage on her forehead. I feel her breast now. It is cold and miserable. It feels wooden – quite wooden – devoid of reality. Teeth want to bite hard, want to bite the nipple, I want to attack her. Terrible! What's the use!' Later in the session he spoke of wanting to mutilate the body of his mother and the bodies of women, wanting to cut them open, get into their stomachs and draw blood. At another session, he developed fantasies of attacking and dismembering men, cutting off their limbs, their heads and penes. This frequently led to pre-conscious fantasies and desires to mutilate himself, which had resulted in an actual attempt of self-castration with a knife at the age of twenty.

In this patient very powerful cannibalistic urges extended from the teeth to body-destructive fantasies. His sexual urges were on the phallic-sadistic level, which created intense anxiety because the phallus was regarded by him as a knife, a dangerous weapon, cutting and mutilating women, ripping open their vaginae and tearing their legs apart. These fantasies, understandably enough, had to be strongly repressed from consciousness, so that he literally could not think of sex at all; it was absolutely unthinkable to him, and he was quite impotent to the extent that he had no sexual feelings in his genitals. When he touched his genital organs they felt to him to be wooden, strange and lifeless. It is, of course, interesting here to observe the similarity of his penis to his experiences of the mother's nipple. Having cut himself off from any erotic contact with the outside world, having thus withdrawn all cathexis from it, it seemed unreal to him, and women, as sex objects, seemed meaningless, or at other times, despicable. The whole world became to him de-libidinised, unreal and meaningless.

2. THE PERCEPTION OF REALITY

It is particularly interesting here that the sensation of meaninglessness of the external object was related to an inability to comprehend time and space relations. With the emergence of libidinous sensations on the periphery of the body a sense of self emerges, and also an awareness of body boundaries which are in direct proximity to the outside world. The self develops an awareness of objects, an awareness of external objects which are cathexed with libido and relate to the libidinous sensations of the self. Out of the narcissistic peripheral libido, which we can call a primitive Ego, an Ego proper emerges with its complex system of information devoted to the integration of stimuli and responses, and with it a creation of a reality system, a reality testing. While the narcissistic system is originally part of the Id, it develops gradually into a protective layer between the primary or Id impulses and the demands of reality, to become the Ego proper. It is its function to interpose between desire and action the delaying and selective functions necessary to protect the self. Eventually the Ego creates the reality principle. In order to cope with the stimuli from within and from without, and to integrate them into a sense of order within which perception and consciousness of reality can develop, the Ego creates the concepts of time and space.

This is shown by the fact that if severe deprivation of the narcissistic libido occurs, both the sense of self and that of externality become meaningless, and the experience of time and space is disturbed. However, the most frequent result of impaired narcissistic libido is the accumulation and blocking of energy in the periphery, a tightening up of the musculature and a sense of isolation. Sado-masochistic urges frequently accompany these processes insofar as the only way the dead and painfully tense feelings can be relieved and a sense of aliveness produced is by means of attacking objects and by being attacked.

The above case illustrates the processes by which severe deprivation of the narcissistic libido can lead to an impairment of self-awareness and also of space and time awareness. One can indeed say that the experience of space, perhaps we should say the sensation of space, depends on the sensation of body boundaries. Spatial awareness is thus dependent upon the sensation of one's own periphery as a spatial determinant, and we may even say that if there is no peripheral self-feeling, there is no feeling of objects, and no feelings of space. It is, therefore, the libidinisation of the body periphery which is the foundation for the emergence of the category of space and extension.

Equally we can say that the experience of time has its foundation in the sensation of movement, the movement of the body and the body periphery, the perception of activity and therefore of sequence of events. If there is no sensation of bodily movements then there is no awareness of time. Movement, energy and action create an awareness of events, and the sequence of events produces a sense of time. In other words: without narcissistic libido there is no sense of body, no sense of space, and without the discharge of energy into bodily action producing events there is no sense of time. No body – no space; no movement – no time. The categories of time, space, extension, causation, which, as Kant has observed, provide the framework for perception and for understanding, are therefore made possible by the development of the narcissistic libido. These considerations of the impact of libido functions upon the sensations of space and time are fundamental not only for philosophical considerations but also for the development of personality; they play a large role in psychological disturbances which are especially obvious in catatonic schizophrenia. Catatonia can be considered as the perfect example of the almost complete obliteration of time and space awareness due to the blocking of movement and the gross impairment of the narcissistic sensations of self. An analysis of catatonia and in particular the recollections of patients who have recovered from this disease show that in states of catatonia patients do not experience a sense of time. In chronic catatonia as well as in catatonic periods, there is a feeling of timelessness, and events which occur are perceived as being opaque and isolated, as it were 'mere happenings' (if perceived at all) without any sense of continuum or time relationships.

The impairment of narcissistic sensations is always accompanied by a tautness of the peripheral musculature which hides an underlying body anger and aggressiveness. In exactly the same way in which lips and mouth tense up and develop aggressive drives if deprived of libido, so the periphery of a child which is subjected to deprivation of peripheral contact tenses up. Indeed, its own periphery will appear as a kind of barrier to sensations. One encounters many individuals suffering from an impairment of narcissistic sensations, whose movements are stiff, rigid and angular and who, at the same time, unfailingly knock and bump into things wherever they go. I had one such patient who whenever he sat down managed somehow or other to knock a table over, or bang into things, frequently breaking them, and after prolonged apologies managed to knock into something else. The patient mentioned earlier repeatedly fell off his chair and knocked it over. He walked into furniture and even into walls, and it was not difficult to see behind this awkwardness many aspects of destructiveness.

With all such persons the rage of the body, though carefully hidden, never fails to manifest itself behind the mask of restraint. Indeed, catatonia can be seen as the ultimate repression of a profound rage, and analysis, without exception, reveals fantasies of destructiveness aimed at attacking and maiming people, dismembering them and cutting them into pieces. It is indeed an ultimate repression of ultimate destructiveness.

3. THE TASKS OF THE EGO

Up till now we have spoken of narcissism as a primitive Ego, insofar as it produces a measure of self-awareness, a body image and an image of other bodies. The integrative factor of body boundaries very soon, however, develops into an orientation system which is related not only to sensations or impulses but to a much wider range of awareness of the self as a causative entity, i.e., as being possessed by a will that makes things happen, and which is responsible for things happening. From the capacity of registering and perceiving events, that is, the sequence of actions in time, and perceiving objects in spatial relationships, an awareness of the self as a causative agent emerges.

There is a veritable explosion of muscular skills as well as information systems during the narcissistic stage from about eighteen months onwards. The most important of the new information systems is without doubt the visual sense. Vision represents a dimension of peripheral recognition which goes beyond the periphery and transcends its boundaries. The eyes are a specialised organ providing a much wider and accurate dimension of contact and communication. They are an extension of the skin, just as the skin of the body is an extension of the lips. While, however, the eyes take over from the skin, so to speak, and vastly extend the child's field of information, they do not eliminate the sensorium of the skin. The skin remains a medium of contact as well as information, but it will be relegated to a secondary position, and its sensitivity and its capacity to provide information will become pre-conscious. Even so, it will continue to exercise its sensitivity and frequently provide information or understanding of events in terms of intuition and sometimes telepathic awareness. Telepathic awareness of external events or of the state of mind of other individuals is quite pronounced in animals, whereas in humans it has atrophied with the emergence of specialised sense organs. But even amongst man, peripheral sensitivity plays a much larger role than we realise. It is usually responsible for feelings of empathy, for attraction or distaste, and plays an important, albeit pre-conscious role in our object choices; it comes into pre-eminence in erotic relationships when body contact is once again of first importance. While, therefore, visual contact acquires primary importance, it is influenced by skin sensations and other senses, such as smell and sounds. (Our disposition to look at certain objects and ignore others, our choice of what we are looking at or looking for is over-determined by deeper layers of the psyche, and our interpretation of visual experiences largely depends on pre-conscious motivations.) Our emotions are manifest in the eyes, and they will expand with pleasure, or tense with anxiety – they become taut in states of anger, just in the same way as the lips of the infant or the whole periphery. They will pull back in states of inhibition or fear, producing a visual sensation of darkness, and they move forward and expand in states of pleasurable excitement, creating brightness and light. No wonder people say that the soul of a person is reflected in his eyes.

The eyes also introduce a new dimension of body image – a new dimension of self-awareness – the child acquires a visual image of itself largely dependent upon the reflection in the mother's eyes of her image of the child.

As the senses become increasingly specialised and a multiplicity of information and communication centres develop, the individual needs a new agency which integrates their activities in order to keep a sense of self intact, and this integration system we call the Ego. It is the Ego's chief function to co-ordinate the manifold of sensations and impulses into a unity of self to which all sensations and experiences relate. The Ego becomes the psychic structure that enables the narcissistic self to form a coherent organisation of mental processes to which all sensations refer. The Ego controls and co-ordinates not only the sensory inputs but also the approaches to motility – that is, the discharge of excitations into the external world. It is the mental agency which supervises all its own constituent processes, as Freud has put it. It is the organisation which transforms sensations into perceptions and impulses into acts of will. It develops the images and concepts of purposeful anticipation and of interests. The Ego transforms the self, as I have said above, into an active willing being that has an image of itself as a goal-seeking individual. In other words, through the agency of the Ego, a person becomes conscious of his desires, of his attitudes to the environment, and also of the attitudes of the environment towards him; he becomes self-conscious.

It is the task of the Ego to safeguard the sense of continuity of the self; it is the centre to which everything relates and that experiences itself as permanent in the flux of sensations. Even while an individual's own body changes and his feelings and his state of mind undergo many transformations, even while the Ego can be aware of these changes, it perceives itself as constant. Out of the thousands of stimuli pressing for discharge from within and the thousands of stimuli from outside demanding responses, the Ego selects those that are in keeping with its own self-image. The Ego is not only the co-ordinating but also the selective apparatus endeavouring to keep a measure of psychic equilibrium.

It is important, however, to remember the law of multiple layers of the psyche which operates in individuals. The Ego does not respond quite autonomously, as it were, to stimuli and impulses, but its modes of operation are constantly influenced by the activities of more primitive levels; its responses will be fed by earlier layers, and it will be its task to provide them with a measure of discharge or satisfaction, or to repress them and to modify them in a manner acceptable to its self-consciousness and its awareness of reality. Once the Ego is established, the activities of the earlier levels of the psyche are conveniently called pre-Ego responses, and the Ego attempts to control or restrain their entry into consciousness. Thus they become pre-conscious, entering, as we said earlier, only fleetingly into consciousness and always subject to the repressing, selective agency of the Ego. There are, furthermore, so-called archaic or primitive impulses which are quite unacceptable to the self-consciousness of the Ego, and they will be repressed, and then we speak of them as being unconscious, as belonging to the Id. Those drives, which from the point of view of Ego consciousness we call primitive or archaic, are nothing more than infantile responses which the Ego inherits but which it has to exclude from its new system of self-awareness. From a genetic point of view the Ego is that part of the psyche which has developed from the narcissistic libido – the peripheral libido – and takes over the task of presenting the external world to the self and to the Id, and so protecting it. It serves the task of receiving stimuli and protecting the organism, like the cortical layer with which living things surround themselves. And like the skin of an organism, it is the task of the Ego to safeguard the sense of identity and coherence of the self.

While this is the primary function of the Ego, it develops many ways of reinforcing its sense of identity.

Anal Libido and Projection

1. THE MAGIC SELF

The task of identity acquisition is particularly important in human beings as their responses and orientations are not fully determined by instincts. Indeed, we can speak of a psycho-biological void which must be filled by a constant quest for identity.

During the oral primacy of the libido, identification takes place through the introjection of the primary object, when the child is what he incorporates; in the narcissistic phase, his libido is centred upon his own body; he produces a self-image determined by the awareness of his own periphery. During the anal primacy, he identifies with what he produces, i.e., he projects himself outside, makes himself into an object and then identifies with the object he has produced.

There are fundamentally two types of projection: one can be called primary or self-affirmative projection, and the other can be called splitting projection. In the first, the child succeeds in identifying himself with his own product, whereas in the other, identification with it is denied. He will split himself off from his externalised self, and the projected object will appear to have a life independent and separate from the self.

Whereas the impulses of the oral primacy centre around the intake and incorporation of external objects, the main impulses of the anal primacy centre around the externalisation of what is inside. When a large proportion of the libido is transferred to anal functions, the child becomes aware of the pleasure sensations connected with defaecation and will be much preoccupied and interested in his anal product. The object that comes out of him and which he can see in the pot will arouse his curiosity and fascination. He will feel it to be part of himself, part of his being that emerges into the outside world from some hidden and previously secret part of himself. His anal products appear to him as precious, exciting and very much alive.

I have on many occasions been able to observe how during states of regression to childhood, patients re-experience the child's intense fascination with its faeces, describing them as golden, shiny, shimmering and exciting substances. It is interesting to note how proud the child tends to be when he observes the magical substance that comes out of him. He wants to touch, feel and smell his golden treasure, play with it, put it in his mouth and, frequently, smear it over himself to establish contact with what has emerged from inside him. The child is curious to discover himself in the faeces; he will wish to mould them, shape them into representations of the self – the manikin – the primary representation of a person's spirit. (Plato was more perceptive than people realise when he placed the seat of the soul in the stomach, for it is not unreasonable to feel that we are what is in us – what we have introjected and identified with.) If love and trust towards the mother are well established, the child will offer his product to her as a very intimate and precious part of himself. Most mothers will instinctively be prompted to make exclamations of praise and pleasure with the child's gift offering. The libido, which was first embodied in the milk which it received from the mother, is now embodied, materialised, as it were, in the faeces, and the child will feel its own identity reaffirmed in presenting them and having them accepted by the mother; he will expect her to be pleased with his gift offering.

However, needless to say, a great many disturbances occur in the process of anal projection. We may divide these disturbances into three categories:

1 Those which are inevitable and universal among human beings, indeed, characteristic of the human species and, in many respects, decisive for man's evolution.

2 Disturbances due to deprivations and tensions of the oral and narcissistic libido which are displaced upon the anal projective libido.

3 Disturbances due to parental anxiety or panic when faced with the child's anal activities. Such responses of anxiety can be traced to the mother's own complexes and inhibitions, which derive from the taboos to which she has been subjected; she expresses the taboos of her culture in a wide range of neurotic reactions, which she then reproduces in her offspring.

There is no doubt that the taboo upon contact with faeces is universal among human beings; unlike man's ancestors, the apes, who are vegetarians and frequently touch their faeces and put them into their mouths – just like a child wishes to do – man, being a carnivore, produces faecal matter which is poisonous and harmful. The child's fascination with his anal product, and his urge to handle and introject it, generally evokes a sharp denial response and threat of punishment from the parents. In consequence, exciting and pleasurable anal sensations will become frightening to the child – the good product, the representation of the narcissistic Ego, becomes nasty and bad, and its magic is transformed into revulsion. The faeces of a baby who is being fed exclusively on the mother's milk are rarely disgusting to its mother. Only when the baby starts to eat solid food, including meat, do its faeces become repellent.

The universal taboo and consequent transformation of the good anal product into a nasty and threatening object does not, however, eliminate the libidinous interest in anal matter but necessitates its displacement upon natural material, the most common being earth, that is, soil. The child will instinctively turn toward soil material and re-discover in it the libido that was first manifest in its faeces. He will play with the earth, or mud, handle and shape it and will attempt, this time more successfully than before, to form a manikin, a material self-representation of his soul. But still the taboo on anality continues to operate, creating in the child the need to control and discriminate between acceptable and non-acceptable objects. Ferenczi remarks that the child's interest in its anal products experiences its first disturbance through the disagreeable, disgusting smell of faeces. There is no evidence, however, that the child by itself considers the faecal smell unacceptable or disgusting. Indeed, there is much evidence that this smell is highly fascinating and, indeed, does not cease in later life but becomes displaced on to other odours that in any way resemble it. Children continue to show a liking for the smell of sticky materials with a characteristic odour, as, for instance, the cast-off epidermic cells which collect between the toes, the smell of nasal secretion, ear-wax and the dirt from finger nails, and many children do not content themselves with the moulding and sniffing of these substances but also take them into the mouth. The passionate enjoyment of children in moulding putty and smelling it is well known. The smell of stables and country odours generally, the smell of fresh earth greatly pleases children, and it is not by chance that popular belief considers places having these smells as being healthy, even as being a cure for diseases. Ferenczi points out that a special path of sublimation branches off from anal eroticism towards the enjoyment of perfumes of all kinds by means of which the development of a reaction formation – representation through the opposite – is concluded. Disgust turns towards refinement, and people with whom this kind of sublimation occurs powerfully develop into aesthetes, and there can be no question that aesthetics in general have their principal root in repressed anal eroticism. The aesthetic and playful interest springing from the enjoyment of playing with mud and experiencing its odours no doubt plays a large part in the development of sculpture and painting.

The tactile attributes of faeces, such as moistness and stickiness, are first displaced on mud, clay and putty, and for the time being these attributes do not offend the child. As the child's taboos and subsequent notions of cleanliness increase, mud also becomes objectionable. Substances which on account of their stickiness and moistness and their colour are apt to leave traces on the body and clothing become despised and avoided as dirty things. The symbol of filth must therefore undergo a further distortion, a dehydration, so to speak; the child turns its interest to sand, a substance which, while having the colour of earth, is cleaner and dry. The instinctive joy of children in gathering up, massing together and shaping sand is subsequently rationalised and sanctioned by the adults, whom it suits to see the child playing with sand for hours, and they declare this playing to be healthy.

Nonetheless, sand as well as putty are nothing more than faecal symbols – deodorised and dehydrated filth, so to speak. Already at this stage of development, however, there occurs a 'return of the repressed'. It gives children endless pleasure to fill the holes they dig with water, and so to bring the material of their play nearer to the original watery stage. Boys not infrequently employ their own urine for this irrigation, as though in this way they wish to emphasise quite clearly the relationship of the two materials.

The enjoyment which children derive from shaping objects out of mud and sand and other materials is well known and provides a major contribution for the advancement of the narcissistic self-image. However, with the development of manipulative skills and the advance in anal repressions, narcissistic self-representation is overtaken by activities devoted to imitation of real objects. Symbolic presentations (often similar to what we call abstract art) will give way to imitative activities, and children will produce castles, mountains and valleys, or motor cars, articles of diet such as tarts, rolls, and so on. It is interesting to note that, having built edifices by the sea-shore, children watch with mounting excitement how the encroaching tide gradually engulfs their realistic artefacts, transforming them once more into wet mud, resembling the material which all along provided the motivation for their play. The excitement of children represents the resurgence of the repressed primeval substance; the urge of the primitive overwhelms the sublimated activity, the Id breaking over the veneer of the Ego.

Progress in the sense of cleanliness gradually makes even sand unacceptable to the child, and the 'infantile stone age' begins; a higher stage of displacement formation is attained in the collection of stones and pebbles. The attributes of colour, moisture and softness are replaced by materials which are characterised by absence of odour, by dryness and also hardness.

Stones, being 'clean objects', are most suitable for collecting into heaps, and they symbolise in this way a mass of faeces in which the child can take great delight. Just as the child feels its internal self, his essence becoming manifest in his faeces, so the stones he gathers and builds up into heaps represent to him the magic of his soul made manifest in reality. Stones, moreover, are indestructible, and soon become symbols of permanence and of eternity. Time stands still in the stone monuments, the souls petrified become immortal; birth and death, the gulf between generations is obliterated by these symbols of perpetual existence, and they soon come to represent not only the soul of the individuals who have produced them but also that of the ancestors made timeless and immortal. Time is obliterated, the past is made present, and eternity becomes real. He who worships the stone is in communion with his soul and with the souls of his ancestors, and in such worship members of a group acquire a common identity, a common heritage; they discover their collective identity and are bound into a community. The heaping of stones into pyramids of all kinds – from the stone mounds which proliferated during neolithic times all over Europe and the Middle East to the great pyramids of Egypt – provided a focus of common worship and the affirmation of collective identity. The gigantic edifices of Ancient Egypt, which demanded the lifelong labours of tens of thousands of workers and the most ingenious technique devised by its architects, represented the first manifestations of large-scale industry, the 'mega-machine' as Lewis Mumford called it. And they represent man's age-old quest to capture immortality for their collective as well as individual souls. The spirit of the dead lives on, no longer merely in the imagery of the pre-conscious mind but in common places of worship, which since time immemorial have drawn individuals together and given them a name and intimations of immortality.

The stone circles and megaliths of the English countryside were worshipped for the psychic powers which were believed to be locked up in them. They were not merely astronomical observatories but more significantly the abodes of mysterious forces emanating from the souls hidden in them. 'Thou art Peter (Petros – Greek for rock), and upon this rock I will build my Church';

71

and the spiritual embodiment of Christ was to be founded upon the symbol of eternity. He who reveals the soul hidden in the stone is the first magician, the idol maker, the builder of the altar, the temple, the church.

At a later stage of development, the magician-priest emerges as the lawmaker-prophet, to whom the thoughts of the ancestral god, his will and his meaning, are revealed in words which are inscribed on the tablets of stone. The law, engraved on stone, is the authentic, eternal essence of God's will. Or he who opens the Book (the later symbol of the tablets of stone) and makes its contents known and interprets it to the people becomes the messenger of the divine thought – the sage, the rabbi, or the alchemist who understands magical formulas hidden in ancient books and transforms the inert stone into living gold, which was all the time hidden in it. The writings of the prophets, be they Isaiah or Marx, are enshrined in ancient books which bear the authority of magic tablets.

While the ideas or laws engraved on tablets of stone and inscribed in books belong to the most mature achievements of the human intellect, they have a tendency to regress to the level of idol worship. The thoughts of the living thinker and of the prophet become petrified and made eternal in order to acquire the authority and power of ancient stones. The play of ideas and the investigation and recommendations of the intellect can be subjected to regressive forces, which transform them once again into worship of ancient authority, immutable and sacred. The constant eruption of regressive forces upon the forces of progress is well known and has made the best intellects despair about the educability of mankind.

It is not only the mystery of the soul and the eternal spirit of the ancestors which are ascribed to the stones and engraved on them, but also the idea of beauty. The quest for the immortality of youth that remains immune to the ravages of time and decay finds the most exalted expression in poetry as well as in sculpture.

The victory of eternity over the transitoriness of time, the pleasures of beauty presented by a Grecian urn, can they be more convincingly shown than in Keats' poem, which is itself a timeless monument of the intellect?

Heard melodies are sweet, but those unheard
Are sweeter; therefore, ye soft pipes, play on;
Not to the sensual ear, but, more endear'd,
Pipe to the spirit ditties of no tone:
Fair youth, beneath the trees, thou canst not leave
Thy song, nor ever can those trees be bare;
Bold Lover, never, never canst thou kiss,
Though winning near the goal – yet, do not grieve;
She cannot fade, though thou hast not thy bliss,
For ever wilt thou love, and she be fair!

Ah, happy, happy boughs! that cannot shed
Your leaves, nor ever bid the Spring adieu;
And, happy melodist, unwearied,
For ever piping songs for ever new;
More happy love! more happy, happy love!
For ever warm and still be enjoyed,
For ever panting and for ever young;
All breathing human passion far above,
That leaves a heart high-sorrowful and cloyed,
A burning forehead, and a parching tongue.

O Attic shape! fair attitude! with brede
Of marble men and maidens overwrought,
With forest branches and the trodden weed;
Thou silent form! dost tease us out of thought
As doth eternity; Cold Pastoral!
When old age shall this generation waste,
Than ours, a friend to man, to whom thou say'st
'Beauty is truth, truth beauty, – that is all
Ye know on earth, and all ye need to know'.

Or Yeats calling upon the images of Byzantium in order to evoke
the eternal presentation of human passion:

Before me floats an image, man or shade,
Shade more than man, more image than a shade;
For Hades' bobbin bound in mummy-cloth
May unwind the winding path;

A mouth that has no moisture and no breath
Breathless mouths may summon;
I hail the superhuman;
I call it death-in-life and life-in-death.

Miracle, bird or golden handiwork,
More miracle than bird or handiwork,
Planted on the star-lit golden bough,
Can like the cocks of Hades crow,
Or, by the moon embittered, scorn aloud
In glory of changeless metal
Common bird or petal
And all complexities of mire and blood.

And we can wonder at the timeless images in the caves of Lascaux, where Magdalenian man 20,000 years ago celebrated the hunt, and enshrined the pleasure and certainty of his success for eternity. For only in the artistic representation of the deed is its success assured and the identity of man made permanent through eons of time. In the beginning was the imagination projected upon the rock, the magic that inspired the deed. The stone sculpted or inscribed, the cave walls painted by ancient hunters and the canvas painted by modern artists represent to man the embodiment of his identity and the affirmation of his desires. They compensate for man's existential insecurity, created by his inadequate instincts, or, rather, instincts upon which the thousand possibilities for cortical experiment and choice have been super-imposed. The certainty of instinct which man has lost with the emergence of the dominant role of his cortical brain is redis-covered by his symbolic projections, from the primitive manikin made in the mud to the highest creations of religious and artistic imagery.

But we are racing ahead; or rather, we are moving from past to present, from infancy to maturity, from disturbance to normalcy without proper regard to the stages of evolution. But it is one of the pleasures of psychoanalytic thinking to throw a bridge across time and to discover the unity of past and present, the primitive and the sophisticated, their mutual interrelation and coexistence.

Before the child can sculpt or make things out of stone he moves on from the fascination which stones hold for him to the collection of shiny objects. Glass marbles, colourful pebbles, beads, fruit pips and, the most cherished of all, diamonds, pieces of gold and silver, are eagerly collected, not only for the sake of the intrinsic fascination they provide but as a measure of value. While ancient man would sculpt and paint probably from the earliest times, he would also pursue the more 'mundane' task of collecting 'objects of value'.

The collecting, counting, comparing, measuring and weighing of such objects becomes a dominant preoccupation among children and primitive and not so primitive men. Besides the recognition and representation of man's soul in material objects and their worship as symbols of man's immortality and beauty, there is also the desire to possess such treasures, to collect them, to count them and to exchange them, to enhance the value of one's possession.

Piaget observed that at this stage in the evolution of a child's cognitive processes, from one and a half to two and a half years of age, a fundamental transformation takes place in the appearance of symbolic functions. (Jean Piaget: 'The Stages of the Intellectual Development of the Child', *Bulletin of the Menninger Clinic*, 1962) At the earliest level, which he calls the sensory motor level, the child's games and explorations are nothing more than exercises, now they become symbolic play, a play of fiction; these games consist in representing something by means of something else. It is the symbolisation of mental images by objects or imitative behaviour. In this stage, dominated by the acquisition of skills, logical classes and logical relations, numbers and concrete relations in space and time emerge. The simplest operations are concerned with classifying objects according to their similarity and to their differences. This activity includes what is called the operation of serialising, that is, arranging objects according to their size or their progressive weight. These operations can be subsumed under the term 'quantification'.

It would not, however, be possible to collect precious objects and exchange them, to classify and arrange them according to the values ascribed to them without the ability to count and without the development of logical rules. The taboo upon contact and play with anal matter is not only internalised to become a primitive Superego, but it becomes abstracted into a game of rules, by which the child actively re-enacts parental taboos and imposes them upon the objects of his environment. He masters his anxiety by producing his own rules, his own precepts, which determine what is acceptable and what is not and how certain objects compare with others. The game of rules not only becomes highly fascinating to the child, often acquiring the character of obsessiveness in varying degrees, but it produces logical thought processes and the concept of numbers. The child is much preoccupied with defining, separating and categorising objects, and gradually the values ascribed to objects become abstracted into independent value-concepts. In his logical games objects often quite valueless in themselves represent values insofar as they serve as symbols for his logical exercises.

The rule games, of which there are an almost infinite variety among children and among grown-ups, as for instance the playing of cards, chess and dominoes, even sports, which are a constant challenge to man's mental and physical ability to pit himself against the rules he has imposed upon himself, originate out of an emotional need to impose order on a confusing environment; he must define what is acceptable and what is not, what is good or bad, right or wrong. It also forces him to distinguish between what is analogous and what is not, what can be connected with what, and what is separate, and the concept of unification and specification leads to logical operations. The foundation of logic lies in the distinction between A and non-A, and the criteria by which we can judge A to be separate from non-A. Such distinctions relate not only to objects but also to concepts and to logical categories by which we judge objects and actions and ideas of objects and actions. They become rules for cognitive discrimination, and eventually develop into criteria for what we consider to be true or false.

Only if this high degree of projection and abstraction is accomplished are we able to count and conceive of numbers and, by applying the rules of logic to the numbers, evolve mathematical operations. But insofar as we are able to count and employ mathematical operations, we can amass and divide, we can manipulate objects and things on a large scale and eventually achieve both active as well as cognitive domination over the environment.

As soon as a culture establishes a consensus of the meaning of numbers and the worth of material objects, man can collect and evaluate objects, he may buy and sell, invest and make profit. This capability is not an invention of capitalism, but capitalism is an expression and development of this capability, its product and not its cause. Capitalism merely emphasises this capability, provides enhanced motivation for its exercise and gives it dominion over all other considerations. In particular, it transforms the act of production and the significance of the product as an expression of the soul of its producer into a commodity to be accumulated, possessed, bought and sold.

2. GOLD, MONEY AND FAECES

And still the connection between gold, money and faeces continues to operate in the unconscious, in the dreams of individuals and in the folklore of cultures, and their ambiguity is equally manifest. The gold which is clean makes people rich and honoured, and the rich are the clean ones, but, obversely, the gold which the rich possess also symbolises dirt and impurity. Despite the complex displacements of the anal libido, the magic of gold, the primary of all faecal symbols, retains its universal attraction and also its ambiguity. On the conscious level, it remains the foundation of economics and finance as the measure of monetary value, while on the mystical, religious level, or in left-wing politics, it symbolises everything that is dirty and evil.

The various associations of money with faeces are widely reported in psychoanalytic and anthropological studies, and appear in cultural myths, fairy-tales and also in dreams. In 1908 Freud wrote:'We know that the gold which the devil gives to his paramours turns into excrement after his departure, and the devil is certainly nothing else than the personification of the repressed unconscious instinctual life.' The polarisation between the good libido and the bad libido, the good self and the bad self, is apparent in people's reactions to faeces, as well as to its sublimated form as money. In the equation of money with faeces – which is very widespread – we can see this polarisation clearly at work. In popular dream interpretation faeces always means wealth, and the metaphors of all languages contain allusions to the above equations: excrement: money; dirt: treasure. A millionaire wallows in money, a person in financial difficulty is called constipated or, in American colloquialism, 'up shit street'. Officials of the German Federal Bank are called 'Dukaten-Scheisser', that is, ducat-shitters, and someone who no longer knows how to pay his debts is 'up to his neck in shit'. A wealthy miser is called filthy, the rich are said to be filthy rich or stinking rich, and in Germany they are so rich that they stink.

The Emperor Tiberius had an anal obsession which caused him to fear that he was made of faeces and was considered to be faeces by others. He therefore forbade the Romans to enter public toilets with rings or gold coins showing his portrait. Before Romans defaecated they had to rid themselves of all portraits of the emperor. The most convincing proof for the validity of the equation of money and faeces, as well as its polarisation of good and bad, comes from the analysis of neurotics and psychotics. During the manic phase, excreta are often collected and quite seriously offered as means of payment, while during the depressive stage entire sheaves of bills are taken for faeces and thrown into the toilet.
(Ernest Bornemann: The Psychoanalysis of Money, Urizen Books, 1976)

Often anal neurotics react to a disorderly room, a messy drawer or closet as if they were intestines filled with faeces, and take pleasure in allowing such disorder to grow until either they suddenly decide to eliminate it by tidying up, as if finally voiding their long constipated bowels, or they feel overwhelmed by the encroaching mess and become depressed by their inability to clean it up.

The transformations of the anal libido and, in particular, anal projective processes play an important part in the emergence of civilisations and are a key factor in the process of socialisation. Through the anal libido the child makes his private self public, the individual becomes a social being as his products become objects to be shared with others. They provide a focus of interest for himself and for the people of his environment and, inasmuch as they participate in play and work activities, they become a community.

In order to understand the psychological problems which the anal libido encounters, we must first of all consider the close interaction between the process of internalisation and projection. If the breast gave out – projected – satisfying libido sensations, they will be introjected by the child, they become part of the child's self and engender a good self feeling in it. In this case, the anal projective processes represent the good self coming out into the world, and the child will want to present it to the mother and, later, to the world as a gift offering in appreciation of her good libido. Indeed, we could say that by presenting its good faeces to the mother the child acknowledges her good libido which she has projected onto it. It is an offering of gratitude, a kind of sharing between mother and infant. The good libido, which was first embodied in the milk, is now embodied – materialised – in the faeces. The libido, which the infant experiences during the intake process, will be re-enacted in the output process. This we may call the pleasurable self-affirmative form of anal self-projection. Love is returned for love, pleasure for pleasure, self-projection and production will be experienced as a pleasurable, creative act to be shared with others.

3. ANAL RETENTIVE SYNDROMES

The child which has acquired a holding-on, squeezing primacy in his lips and his mouth, and has transferred this disposition to his narcissistic stage of development, will also transfer it to anal production. The tight musculature of the lips and jaws will now extend to the anal sphincter muscles, and tension spasms will dominate its anal activities and spread to the stomach.

The bad libido, which the child has introjected up till now, will emerge in its anal projection. He will want to deprive the mother by withholding the faeces from her when she expects them, and will adopt a variety of anal retentive mechanisms. He will become stubborn, obstinate and even spiteful. He will be withholding with his product just as he felt the mother to be withholding with her product. The mother who did not give the child what it wanted will not receive from the child what she wants. Such children will obstinately spend hours on the pot, and only let go when not expected to. This kind of obstinacy also provides substitute gratification, for, by not letting go of the faeces, the child experiences the satisfactions of the tensing, holding-on libido, and by letting go when not expected to do so, it ensures that the mother cannot spoil them or take them away. And by soiling itself the child will, in fact, retain contact with the faeces.

The agonised pleasure of holding on to oneself, squeezing oneself into inaction, the compulsion of not doing what one has to do, holding on to one's tensions and frustrations as if they were possessions which one cannot relinquish, represent the transformation of the infant's tense lips and jaws which hold on to the mother's breast into the retentive compulsions of the anal libido, dominated by tense sphincter muscles, buttocks and stomach walls. There is the added reassurance that by holding on to oneself one exists, whereas if one were to let go one would get lost and disappear in a dangerous outside world.

Retentive attitudes also appear in relation to the anal product. Having produced the faeces, the child will want to retain them, and he will react to their disappearance with acute anxiety. Such individuals, when they grow up, frequently experience anxiety when flushing the toilet; they feel it as a kind of annihilation, a part of themselves disappearing into a void. This trait leads to marked acquisitiveness, to hoarding, compulsive saving and often a relentless pursuit of material possession and wealth. The personal worth of such individuals is represented by the things they possess, they are a manifestation of their identity – 'I am what I have'. Fromm's concept of 'the having mode' finds here its fundamental representation. Behind such obsession with the acquisition of things there is an anxiety that everything might disappear, that the individual surrounded by an apparently indifferent or even hostile environment feels threatened with loss of identity or even self-extinction. (One must, however, draw attention to the fact that such anxieties with their compulsion for hoarding and accumulation of wealth can arise among people who find themselves in an alien and hostile world, such as pioneers opening up a new continent or immigrants in a country whose culture is alien to them. In such cases we can speak of narcissistic insecurity which needs to be reassured by the accumulation of possessions.)

Anal tensions can lead to anal aggressiveness in the same way as oral tensions frequently lead to oral-aggressive, cannibalistic drives. In this case, the faeces will be felt to be a kind of weapon to attack mother and to punish and upset the environment. Obstinacy and spiteful attitudes can be called passive punishment, by which the child revenges itself on the mother. Active punishment we may call the urge to throw the faeces at the mother, to soil her with them and make her suffer the agonies of being a bad object and as despised as the child has been made to feel by her. Such drives produce defiance and the urge to upset and annoy people by outrageous behaviour. The individual who felt orally and narcissistically rejected will use its anal functions aggressively by soiling the environment and by 'besmirching' people. They will tend to become 'muck-rakers' and develop a sharp eye for people's weaknesses, a talent to humiliate them and make them feel dirty, inadequate or nasty. They will be what Nietzsche has called 'the guilt-makers', as they can gain great satisfaction in besmirching people's characters and making them feel unwanted and despised, as they have been made to feel themselves as infants.

Anal defiant and anal aggressive drives play a large role not only in certain individuals but also in subcultures devoted to rebellious attitudes. People who as a class or as an ethnic group have experienced a narcissistic injury, a sense of deprivation and insult to their dignity, or who are encouraged to think so by political propagandists who have an interest in arousing opposition to the social establishment, will often adopt an anal defiant attitude. They will pollute, degrade the hostile environment by either actually throwing dirt at it and being ostentatiously dirty or by behaving and talking in a dirty, obscene, outrageous manner. We can indeed speak of the proliferation of an anal aggressive subculture in times of political and social crises.

4. THE CLEAN AND THE DIRTY

As we have said, there is a universal taboo among human beings on the playing with faeces and their ingestion, and it is therefore rational that a mother should prohibit such activities; however, the manner in which these prohibitions are imposed by her are subject to certain cultural variants and, in particular, to the mother's own emotional complexes. Parents who have undergone a conditioning of anal anxiety project their anxieties and defences on the child's anal activities, especially in the form of disgust. Now, the child is most sensitive to these reactions, and a show of disgust or annoyance will make it feel that what it has produced is bad and therefore that it is bad and unacceptable. Disgust is one of the most powerful signals communicated from one person to another, and the facial expression accompanying it shows a sense of utter rejection and distaste. If the child experiences parental disgust towards the product he has produced, he is usually made to feel that he is disgusting, dirty and unacceptable. He will split himself off from his product as if it had nothing to do with him. In this case it will appear as Ego-alien and a threatening monster. The product is split off from the producer and appears to have a life independent and separate from the self. This process is responsible for the development of paranoia, phobias and free-floating anxieties.

Besides this splitting of the self from the product, there is also a splitting of the self-image into the dirty self and the pure self. The dirty self, dominated by anal drives, is split off and projected outwards and seen in the dirty people – the lower classes, the impure. Cleanliness becomes synonymous with purity, with good-ness, whereas uncleanliness becomes symbolical of all that is disgusting and 'low'. The dirty people represent the repressed anal fantasies of clean people and are, therefore, not only considered uncivilised, distasteful and belonging to a lower order, but are a constant threat to the pure classes. Dirty people are constantly held before children as the horrid example of what would happen to them if they do not behave and keep themselves clean and pure. Gypsies, Jews, Negroes, foreigners, the lower classes are symbols of anality – examples of all that is dirty and unacceptable.

Cleanliness rituals are an important aspect of all cultures, cleanliness being equated with godliness, with being accepted and with being superior. The opposition of pure and impure, higher and lower, the mundane and the spiritual, plebeian and aristocrat, plays an important part in the structure of societies. A hierarchy develops which reflects the psychic hierarchy between dirty and clean, where the earth-bound, soiled, labouring working class is confronted by the clean aristocracy who are never soiled by labour. The ruling class becomes the representative of purity, of the pure men who wash, who refuse to eat certain foods considered to be unclean, who wear clean garments and do not need to get dirty with unclean labour. 'The hierarchic system', as Nietzsche observed, 'centres round the clean and unclean, the pure man and the dirty man'; it reflects the conflicts of the anal libido and society's attempt to resolve them.

Let us look at clinical examples of the anal conflict and the process of splitting-projection as it occurs in individuals.

In the treatment of a patient who suffered from a paralysis of the lower vertebrae of the spinal column and also had an intense snake phobia, we found that the snake represented the faeces, to which a snake-like motion had been ascribed. The rhythmic, snake-like movement represented his bodily movements in the process of defaecation. The libidinous sensations aroused by the rhythmic movements of defaecation had to be repressed as they suddenly aroused intense anxiety in his mother. She herself had shown great interest in the child's anal sensations and activities, and continued to wipe his bottom regularly until he was about four years old. When her husband severely admonished her for these intimacies towards the child, she stopped them suddenly. The child experienced the cessation of an activity which had become the centre of his libidinous excitement and satisfaction as a rejection. The erotic movements of his anal libido were blocked and split off from the ego and symbolised by a snake, which continued to embody the repressed libido. Thus it became a source of anxiety, even of terror, and caused him to adopt obsessive avoidance activities to repress his anal sensations. One of the defence mechanisms he adopted was the pulling up and tensing up of the lower part of his spine in order to neutralise anal sensations, and over the years this produced a deformity of the spinal column.

When, during treatment, he began to re-experience and act out the rhythmic motions which accompanied his infantile defaecation process, and became aware of the pleasure which they had aroused in him as a child, he gradually overcame his fear of snakes, and his spinal column came alive again, as it were, rectifying its deformity. He accepted this libido as part of himself, and it ceased to be a cause of anxiety.

It is interesting to notice that all sensations which were considered by the patient as being dirty were projected upon the external object, the split-off representation of the self in the form of a snake, and then his conscious self could be clean and admirable. Indeed, this particular patient, while terrified by the alter-ego, the snake, has a very aristocratic bearing and life-style. He is most meticulous in his dress and personal appearance, devoted to refinement and good taste. He dealt with his anal impulses and fantasies by splitting them off from his Ego and projecting them on to a symbolic embodiment, as represented by the snake. As, however, he did not manage to repress or sublimate these impulses, partly because they completely contradicted his Ego ideals and partly because they absorbed a large quantity of his libido, they remained a constant threat.

In the process of splitting the child refuses to acknowledge the product – his projection – as a manifestation of himself; it is cut off from the self and appears as an external and independent object. That part of his libido which is unacceptable to the Ego is repressed, split off from it and projected outwards; it embodies all the sensations and urges which the Ego has denied to itself. Just as repression does not eliminate the emotional processes but pushes them below consciousness, as it were, so in splitting-projection the libidinous drives and sensations do not disappear but are made to take place outside in the split-off objects. However, these objects, representing forbidden impulses, become a threat to the Ego. The split-off self, which will be seen as an external force, as an external being, becomes the perennial dangerous 'other', as if the split-off part of the self were angry with us for not being accepted, and threatens to attack us. Indeed, one can say that as our own Ego hates that part of the self which we split off, that part of ourself which has been split off and rejected hates the Ego that has rejected it. Thus, the world outside becomes populated with dangerous images, the ghosts and monsters, the living and pulsating things which we cannot tolerate as our own and which reappear as a danger to us.

For instance, the child who has repressed the urge to play with faeces and soil material, and the desire to mould it into a manikin figure, may become afraid that it will itself become the object to be moulded and manipulated by the external monsters. Hallucinations of being manipulated, of being subjected to the will of outside powers will emerge frequently in individuals who (a) developed a strong urge to play with faeces or substitute objects and to manipulate them, and (b) had to repress this urge and project it outwards. The repressed urge then makes the Ego into its object.

We can show this process in the following case: A young man, aged 24, had suffered from hallucinations that certain individuals amongst his acquaintances, or sometimes his parents, controlled him from a distance and manipulated him in various ways, as, for instance, by carrying out psychological experiments with him which reduced him to being a laboratory animal, or that they experimented with his sexual responses by presenting him with women who subjected him to sexual stimulation, aroused him, and thus caused him to suffer acute embarrassment. He felt that his mind was not under his own control but controlled by the experimenters, and that he was never left alone by them. These hallucinations evoked in him acute anxiety as well as anger, but he felt powerless against them.

As a child, this patient had developed a high degree of anal libido and an urge to play with his faeces and, later, with faecal substitutes like mud and sand as well as mechanical toys. However, his parents, who strongly repressed their own anal urges and particularly their urges to play with mud and dirty things, but successfully sublimated their desires into the somewhat snobbish pursuit of intellectual-academic careers, responded with anxiety to the child's play interests and adopted a disparaging attitude towards them. Soon the child became afraid to play with things, to touch and hold objects with his hands, and became extra-ordinarily clumsy. Powerful taboos inhibited the development of manipulative skills, and not only did his skill acquisition remain underdeveloped but it became dissociated, disorientated, and he rejected the objects symbolising his anal interests. He constantly dropped things and 'messed them up'. However, in his imagination certain individuals enacted all the manipulative skills which had been denied to him, and he became their manikin. While he acts out the taboo by being clumsy, that is, throwing away the objects he is not allowed to play with, his unfulfilled desire is projected onto others, who then act them out and play with him. But as the denial of his pleasure arouses anger in his Ego, the anger is also projected onto the others, and they manipulate him in an aggressive or destructive manner.

On the individual level these processes can produce a wide range of paranoias in various degrees of intensity, with persecuting images such as devils or deities, or machines, or rays, or voices manipulating and threatening the psychotic individual, while on the cultural level the 'other' is perceived as the enemy intent on destroying or poisoning one's homeland, race or religion.

5. OBSESSION AND RITUAL

There is yet another way which the child's Ego adopts in order to cope with anxieties aroused by the anal libido, namely, obsessive undoing. Instead of splitting the Ego from the unacceptable anal desires and sensations and making them appear as nasty and dangerous phenomena that exist in the outside world, it will attempt to negate them by means of obsessive acts and ceremonials.

We have spoken earlier of the mental processes concerned with order, distinction and separation, all of which naturally emerge during the anal projective period in a child's development. They are sublimated expressions of the manipulative and controlling urges, they facilitate the acquisition of skills in handling materials, of rules that govern games and the relationship between things. They also provide the foundation for exchange and trade as well as for logical concepts which govern the relationship of ideas. All these activities are acceptable outlets for the anal libido, and enhance the development of mind and culture. But if the anal libido is too strictly barred from expression and thereby denied sublimated displacement, it will continue to exercise strong pressure on the Ego, which will be overwhelmed by anxiety and will attempt to deny the impulse. The anal impulse will become a threat, and the Ego will have to counteract the energy aroused by it through active negation. For instance, the urge to handle and play with dirty things has to be counteracted by obsessive cleaning and washing of the hands or any part of the body that may have contact with dirty, things. Such negation takes the form of an active ritual in order to overcome an otherwise unbearable anxiety. Every impulse that appears as an overpowering threat to the Ego or a temptation has to be warded off by means of ceremonials of undoing. However, as the anal libido denied continues to exercise its demands, such ceremonials of negation become an obsessive, i.e., circular activity. They do not provide a discharge of energy but present an attempt to block it, and as the blocked energy remains unfulfilled it will continue to seek discharge, producing recurrent anxiety. Obsessive rituals provide a pattern of defence that is never successful and never ceases.

The child caught in overpowering anal taboos must attempt to cope with his anxieties by means of obsessive rituals, i.e., he has to be his own priest, performing ceremonial acts of denial and cleansing, whereas society employs professionals to carry out the public ceremonials designed to propitiate and counteract the collective anxieties. The ceremonies of the priest are institutionalised obsessions. Freud found a close connection between the protestations of the pious – that they know that they are miserable sinners at heart – with the sense of guilt of the obsessional neurotic, while the pious observances (prayers, invocations, incantations, ritual acts, etc.) of religious people can be shown to be similar to the ceremonials of obsessive individuals.

The analysis of obsessive acts has shown that individuals who suffer from compulsions are dominated by a sense of guilt which has its origins in anal tensions and conflicts. They give rise to a state of anxious expectation or anticipation of some great misfortune. When the compulsion is first formed the patient is conscious that he must carry it out both physically as well as mentally lest a misfortune should occur. Thus a ceremonial act begins as an act of defence, as a protective measure.

We can consider obsessive ceremonials as play devoted to the negation of play or, rather more precisely, play devoted to the demonstrative negation of anal pleasures. By its transformation of pleasure into rituals of duty, people are relieved of their sense of guilt, anxieties are eased by the public denial of temptations. Thus the extraordinary situation arises that a severe pathology, namely obsessional neurosis, becomes a cultural institution, and one which has dominated societies through the ages. We say that culture itself is the stage upon which the obsessive play is enacted, where the priests enact the Ego, which attempts to purify itself from the temptations of the anal impulses by means of ritual negation, and members of a culture are participants in the ritual play, identifying with the ceremonial activities acted out by the priest; they are the chorus as well as the audience; the victory of their Ego over the Id depends upon the successes of the priest, upon the power of his magic to defeat the temptation of the instincts and to carry out the successful acts of cleansing and of mental denials – the collective victory of the taboo. (In secular society, the role of the priest is taken over by the Führer, Chairman or President.)

The hierarchic system of society, as we have remarked, centres around the clean and the dirty, the superior and the lowly, the aristocrat and the plebeian. All rulers or ruling classes claim for themselves the charisma of purity and cleanliness, with their perfumes and shiny clothes and sparkling jewellery, and they take care that the priests and ideologues perpetuate their image of purity in the minds of the population.

In fact, the priest performs the public washing in order to get rid of the dirt which clings to people's bodies and to exorcise the dirty fantasies which defile their minds. He places the vessels containing holy water at the entrance to the church, he conducts the bathing ceremonies in the holy rivers or submerges the converts in lakes or sprinkles them with holy water. Among the Jews of ancient times, every man had to bathe in the 'mikvah', the holy bath, before entering the temple; nowadays, it is only the women who have to be cleansed in this ceremonial bath. (I am told, however, that among the very orthodox, the men also have to take a ceremonial bath.) There is no end to the variety of purification rites among all cultures and religions, and they have been described in detail by anthropologists, while the obsessive syndromes of neurotic individuals have been widely reported in psychoanalytic literature.

The public rituals of cleansing and immersion continue in a large variety of symbolic forms in our own time. In the contemporary theocracies as, for instance, the communist dictatorship of Soviet Russia every citizen had to read Karl Marx, and he was not considered cleansed from the obscenities of bourgeois or Christian prejudices unless he had immersed himself in the Holy Texts of Marxist-Leninism. The ritual incantation of these texts in their educational systems – from primary school to university – was no different from the priest's incantations which the congregation has to repeat after him in church. We all have to mouth various magic sentences or slogans, and have to learn them by heart in order to be considered full members of our culture and be accepted by the priest, the king, the ruler or the party. Ritual incantations represent obsessive undoing, a warding-off of dirty and evil impulses by means of magic words and their endless repetition.

It can be argued that cleanliness rituals encourage people to follow certain rules of hygiene, and promote health, well-being and the raising of aesthetic standards; furthermore, one can point out that the incantation of certain phrases is a well-known aid to the learning process of children as it helps them to acquire a range of knowledge, even of wisdom, which otherwise would remain inaccessible to them. However, while the injunction to uphold certain rules of hygiene can be considered perfectly rational and in accordance with the human taboos against playing with anal products and infectious dirt, the obsessive preoccupation with rules does not necessarily promote cleanliness. There is a fundamental difference between obsessive acts and the rational pursuit of cleanliness, just as there is a difference between obsessive mouthings of magic phrases and the rational exercise of the intellect. The former are circular and self-enclosed, while the latter are open-ended and unfolding. The former, indeed, prevent the exercise of rational thought processes, and even the pursuit of cleanliness is inhibited by obsessive ritualisation of it, as can be seen in the dirty conditions of holy rivers. It is not cleanliness, wisdom or justice which obsessive ceremonials promote, but a sense of reassurance, making the ceremonial into an end in itself. Cleanliness rituals have no more to do with the pursuit of cleanliness than the incantation of slogans has to do with the pursuit of the truth.

However, while projection, splitting and obsessiveness emerge with the anal primacy, they are not confined to it but are subsequently related to other areas of the libido. Once established as a mode of operation in the psychic apparatus, they are applied to other libidinous primacies and, in particular, play a very important role in genital sexuality. For instance, if oral-aggressive fantasies remain strong and have to be repressed, they will be later projected in fantasy upon the mother, and she will appear as an aggressive object. The cannibalistic urges, which were directed towards the breast, will be projected on to the breast, and the child will harbour fantasies of being attacked by the biting breast. The child which as a baby wanted to bite the breast will develop fantasies of the biting nipple in the form of a beak, a dragon doing everything to the child which as a baby it wanted to do to it. In the same way as the child's mouth wanted to bite the breast during the oral stage, so with the emergence of genital drives the aggressive mouth is projected on to the vagina that wants to bite the penis. Fantasies of the *vagina dentata* – the vagina with teeth – the frightening crab, the witch emerge in the boy's imagery of female sexuality, and his genital drives will be dominated by sadistic as well as masochistic fantasies.

In the case of the girl, the situation is not very different; if oral-aggressive urges remain powerful, her genital drives will be dominated by fantasies of her own vaginal teeth that are squeezing, biting and castrating the male. Her unconscious self-image will assume the form of a destructive monster, a crab, a spider, and she will suffer from acute fear of being a danger to men, despicable and frightening. Her own oral-aggressive drives will be transferred to the vagina, and the penis of the male comes to represent the mother's breast as the object of her aggressive-sadistic drives. As her conscious Ego, however, cannot accept those images, she will subsequently project them on men, and see them as destructive and aggressive. While such women frequently resent the 'sadistic nature of men's sexuality', preconscious fantasies of rape and degradation remain their only means of sexual gratification.

Thus the processes of projection produce a wide range of pathologies and fantasies, which extend from anal-erotic to oral-aggressive and genital drives. Such fantasies, still being unacceptable to the conscious Ego, will be split off from it and projected on to the outside world in general, where they exist as Ego-alien and threatening powers, a constant source of anxiety. The sadistic drives projected on to the object world thus turn the Ego into a victim of its own fantasies.

The processes of projection are employed by the Ego to externalise internal sensations, and if they are bad, to get rid of the poison, so to speak, that accumulates in the psyche. The Ego, in order to defend, that is, cleanse the narcissistic self from these painful aggregations, has to project them outwards and to unload them upon the world. The world thus becomes a dung-heap, as it were, of drives and fantasies which the Ego rejects and finds unacceptable.

6. FURTHER ASPECTS OF THE INFANTILE LIBIDO

In our discussion of the main stages in the development of the early pre-genital libido we have paid most attention to the oral, narcissistic and anal primacies. While these may be regarded as the most important – insofar as they lay the foundations for the psychic processes which characterise the human being, namely, introjection, identification, narcissistic self-awareness and projection – we must remember that the libido attaches itself to and energises practically all forms of organic activities which are important for the preservation and development of the individual and produce a large variety of symbolic representations. For instance, urination is not merely a biological or mechanical activity but has considerable amounts of libido excitement attached to it. It plays a large part in the child's compensatory activities, particularly as a defence against narcissistic deprivation and loneliness. Infants often wet themselves as a compensation for oral deprivation, when the flow of urine acts as substitute for the flow of milk, and it also acts as substitute for the warmth of bodily contact and embrace, of which the child may feel deprived. It is in this instance a compensation for sensory deprivation in infants who are left alone for long periods. Later, the pleasure of letting go, of allowing the flow of urine to break down the sense of control and isolation becomes associated with genital letting go, with the passive giving oneself to the pleasures which, with the onset of genital primacy become associated with orgasm.

In women particularly the sexual urge of letting go is frequently associated with the urethral libido, partly no doubt due to anatomical reasons, the urethra being close both to the vagina as well as the clitoris. There is also a close connection between crying and urination as a method of discharge from tension as well as a call for attention. However, the most important aspect of urethral gratification lies in its symbolisation of wetness against the dread of dryness, a dryness which is experienced on the oral level as a major anxiety, and on the narcissistic level as a sense of isolation. The sense of dryness represents deprivation and it also, in turn, signifies anxiety. The symbolisations of dryness as the desert play a major role in the imagery of all cultures. However, the varieties of urethral gratifications and compensations, the pleasures of letting go evoke particular anxiety and parental censorship, and become a source of shame. Indeed, the sense of shame is deeply related to urethral eroticism and connected with the overall desire of being wet, which, in turn, later becomes identified as shameful weakness.

Fenichel and Karl Abraham have described ambition as the struggle against this sense of shame. On the other hand, the urethral libido as a form of projection can be sublimated and symbolised as the sparkle of fountains and the thrill of waterfalls. The child's fascination with flowing water and with boats floating on rivers or rivulets are universal manifestations of the urethral libido. In the playing of music and listening to it the rhythmic sensations and experiences of urethral flow are re-created, forming one of the most basic of all artistic sensations. But here too as in all other libidinous primacies, whether internally experienced or projected, we find different emphases upon affection or aggression, a sense of tension and release from tension in the experience of harmony, an expression of forceful and powerful discharge as against a merging with the universal flow and rhythm of life. The dialectic between aggression and tension on the one hand, and the release from tension to experience the oceanic sensations of unity with all life was most clearly understood and re-created by Beethoven, whereas the sparkle of fountains and of crystal chandeliers is mostly associated with the genius of Mozart.

Your love hath been, not long ago
A fountain at my heart's door,
Whose only business was to flow;
And flow it did; not taking heed
Of its own bounty, or my need.

(Wordsworth)

We have mentioned the importance of muscular eroticism, of the libidinous importance of the skin and of the sense of touch. Psychoanalysts have been able also to observe the process of scopophilia, i.e., the pleasure of looking. Scopophilia is the main component in children's sexual curiosity and can relate to the desire to know about the sexual facts. The desire to observe sexually stimulating occurrences may be a part of the wanting to know, and may be expressed by the continual asking of questions. The pleasure of looking may be sublimated into an interest in research and inquiry, but these may be blocked if visual observation and the desire for looking encounters strong taboos and becomes a source of acute embarrassment.

The pleasure of looking can encounter powerful inhibitions when directed to sexual scenes or the secret parts of the body, particularly the genitals of the other sex. But not only the desire to look but also the desire to be looked at, to exhibit one's genitals can cause visual disturbances, for the libidinous excitement of looking and looked at are interrelated. The origins of visual disturbances, such as short-sightedness can frequently be traced to the first puberty, when with the eruption of sexual urges, at about four or five, scopophilic desires are strongly stimulated and can produce feelings of shame and visual inhibitions. Then the eyes that want to look become a source of anxiety, and they have to hide themselves, so to speak, they can draw back and cause the eyeballs to tense up. The need to pretend 'not looking' can become a physiological reflex that remains fixed.

The counterpart to scopophilia is exhibitionism. Exhibitionism has its roots in the desire to look at oneself or to be looked at, and as such is strongly connected with narcissistic needs. The fixation upon exhibitionism is a compensation against the fear of not being acknowledged or even of the fear of not having the right to be visible. As an over-compensation against narcissistic as well as genital castration anxieties, exhibitionism is employed as a kind of magic that is able to attract other people's attention or to influence their minds. We find such exhibitionistic impulses often amongst manic-depressive persons, who in the manic state exhibit themselves naked in streets and open places in order to convey some special message to the onlookers and to impress them with their own omnipotence.

Conversely, such syndromes often produce hiding compulsions, secretiveness and an inability to pursue any goal to its completion. Exhibitionism can also relate to the anal level when showing the buttocks is a compensation firstly for the non-acceptance of the anal libido, having been made to feel it as dirty and shameful. Showing the bottom can be seen as an insult to those to whom one exposes it by making the onlooker dirty, projecting the dirt upon him and thereby cleansing oneself, so to speak, wiping one's bottom in the face of the onlooker and making him feel dirty; and secondly for a sense of genital castration, particularly among women who as children desired to identify with boys and developed a fantasy of having a penis, and wanted to show it off like boys do. Their penis, however, being only imaginary, is made to feel unreal, unaccepted, not allowed, and is transferred to the more real bottom. The real bottom becomes highly libidinised, and will act as a focus of attention-seeking and pride. For women who adopt this type of compensation for their imaginary castration, showing off the bottom becomes an important sexual fantasy, which usually has to be repressed, and, in turn, makes them feel forever inadequate and socially inferior. A constant battle between pride and shame, superiority and inferiority will dominate their personalities and bedevil their personal relationships. Also, while many such individuals will develop high aesthetic expectations and obsessive perfectionism, they will forever be plagued by doubts about their ability to fulfil these expectations. They will be burdened by indecisiveness and never feel sure of having made the correct choices. A self-defeating compulsion will dominate their lives, often leading to pronounced affect blocks and self-destructive urges.

The Self and the Species

1. THE EMERGENCE OF THE GENITAL LIBIDO (THE FIRST PUBERTY)

It is well known that nature goes to inordinate lengths to secure the perpetuation of a species and to enforce the processes of procreation. Who does not know of the sacrifices which many species endure in the process of reproduction and the complex ways they adopt in order to secure the life of their offspring?

It has been said that the individual is merely an agent which transmits the programming genes of a species from generation to generation. There is no doubt that the sexual instincts are genetically programmed, but in higher mammals and especially in human beings psychological processes such as erotic fantasies and libidinous fixations are superimposed upon instinct.

We have seen that in the development of individuals, in the process of their evolution and growth, in the unfolding of their organic and psychic potential, the libido attaches itself to a succession of activities and at various stages gives them primacy over the others. By means of the libidinous urges the individual is compelled to follow the needs of the organism. It is as if nature had provided a pleasure-seeking energy that attaches itself to the important self-preserving and species-preserving activities, and motivates these activities by an almost irresistible drive which, if fulfilled, rewards the organism with a sensation of pleasure, while frustration or denial arouses sensations of anxiety, aggressiveness and tension.

While the species-preserving functions of the individual are given high emphasis by nature, it is necessary for the individual, as the link in the chain of the life of a species, to protect itself, and for that purpose the self-preserving functions and those directed to the growth and development of the individual organism are cathexed with sufficient quanta of libido to ensure that they are carried out.

In the development of the individual, in the process of its evolution and growth, libidinous energy is channelled to a succession of vitally necessary functions. We can define the development of the pre-genital libido, which we have observed in the previous chapter, as serving the purpose of:

1 Directing the child towards oral activities for the incorporation of food and communion with the mother.

2 Establishing the child's awareness of itself as a separate and distinct individual by making the self an object of libidinous gratification.

3 Establishing the process of self-projection, thus assuring the child of its sense of identity in the world and its capacity of producing and manipulating objects.

We might say that the early transformations of the libido serve the preservation and development of the individual, and at the conclusion of the development devoted to individual self-preservation there occurs a concentration of the libido upon the genitals.

Of course the pre-genital or infantile primacies of the libido do not cease to operate with the advent of sexual maturity. While the self-preserving activities must continue, the emphasis of the genital sexuality lies in giving oneself to another person, in protecting the person one loves. Once the skills and the habits of the infantile pre-genital libido are established, their patterns structured and a person's basic character formed, the libido goes beyond the needs of self-preservation and develops as a self-giving, object-directed energy. By it the individual transcends its self-preserving functions and becomes devoted to the service of ensuring the life of his species, and by giving himself up in orgasm he enters a moment of eternity. He participates in life beyond the confines of individuality, and by merging with another person he loses himself, so to speak, and partakes in the universal life of his species – he becomes one with the life that vibrates in the universe. This is not merely a poetic notion (although it is the perennial theme of poetry) but the description of an experience which characterises the life functions and a person's achievement of maturity. He no longer merely belongs to himself alone but to another, he communes with the life of the species, with life itself. He serves the perpetuation of life. He not only experiences a moment of eternity but he creates eternity, on both the biological as well as the psychological level.

And the woman becomes the agent of eternity and the symbol of everlasting life, the being who ensures that life continues by drawing the male out of his confines. By representing the claims of the species she ensures his capacity for self-transcendence.

The sexual drives are no longer merely concerned with the preservation and affirmation of the self but the giving of the self to another, to fuse with another human being in the orgastic act. The pre-genital and auto-erotic drives do not disappear but they lose their primacies, that is, their energies are subordinated to the genital impulses; they frequently stimulate and enhance them but gain their fulfilment through genital excitement and orgasm. For instance, oral, narcissistic or anal sensations no longer gain fulfilment simply for their own satisfactions, so to speak, but they are an adjunct to the gratification of the genital system. In the love-making of adults the pre-genital, infantile urges re-emerge as 'foreplay' and obtain renewed gratification and, at the same time, stimulate genital arousal. That the infantile areas of the libido do not disappear during genital primacy is shown by the fact that in adult love making erotic, activities such as sucking, kissing, looking, smelling, touching and exploring play an important part, even while genital orgasm provides the ultimate fulfilment. Every fulfilling sex act of a mature individual is, as it were, a recapitulation of his sexual development.

However, while with the onset of the first puberty large amounts of the libido are directed to the genitals, in human beings the process of maturation is delayed ('maturation delay') and the individual has to wait until twelve or thirteen when reproduction ability is actually established. While little girls frequently harbour fantasies of having father's baby and of being his wife and boys imagine that they can displace father, neither boy nor girl is physically capable of procreation during the first puberty. Despite his psychological urges to be rid of his father and take his place, the boy continues to need his protection and guidance and the girl continues to depend on her mother; indeed, they are still children, immature and in need of parental protection. As the maturation process is delayed in human beings till a later stage of development, the sexual urge soon becomes repressed and is overtaken by the latency period which lasts from about seven years to twelve years when the genital primacy once again erupts with greater force, this time accompanied by physical, procreative maturity. (The causes of this delay in maturation of human beings have been the source of much puzzlement, and I shall in a later chapter enquire into the processes which can be held responsible for this phenomenon, but shall mention here some of the factors involved.)

As cultures accumulate an ever greater store of knowledge and of skills, children have to be taught and trained to master them, and can only be considered mature and able to take their place as full members of their society after they have achieved a measure of proficiency in the skills of their culture and become capable of handing them on to their offspring. Thus the higher a civilisation and the more complex and varied its skills, the more prolonged the learning period and the duration of childhood. Even at the age of twelve or thirteen, when the human being is sexually, that is, reproductively mature, he is still a child and continues to need the protection and love of his father and mother. While the libido sends a massive flow of energy to the genitals at about twelve years of age, making its urges well-nigh irresistible, the boy or girl will not consider sexuality as being directed towards procreation but as an end in itself. Indeed, the act of procreation appears as a danger to be avoided at all costs, a source of very considerable anxiety to young people.

While there is no doubt whatsoever that the drives of genital sexuality serve the processes of reproduction, the libido energy and the instinctual processes connected with them demand gratification and discharge whether they are connected with procreation or not. We have seen that the first object, the first person to whom the genital drives are directed is, in the case of the boy, his mother, and in the case of the girl her father. With the strong stimulations which the child begins to experience in its genitals, it will feel drawn towards the person of the opposite sex. Sexual exploration gains a new and powerful impetus when the boy wants to explore and feel his mother's body, to cuddle up to her while experiencing sensations of sexual yearning that are accompanied by a new feeling of tenderness and love.

The boy's desire to have mother for himself and join his genitals with hers is kept secret; a sweet and mysterious longing possesses him, but equally a sense of fear and puzzlement, for he knows that he is only a small boy and cannot in actuality do with his mother what his father does, and he knows also that he cannot possess her or displace his father whom he needs and loves and depends upon. Nevertheless, he cannot avoid the wish that father should disappear and leave him alone with his mother; and the wish for father's disappearance runs close to the wish for his death, so that the boy can be the man and the mother's husband. It is true that his mother has been his love-object since earliest infancy insofar as the child needed her for the gratification of his needs. But he loved his mother as a way of loving himself, now he wants to protect her and wants her as his love-object. He wants to supplant the father as mother's favourite, as the man upon whom she can depend and lavish love.

It is difficult for grown-ups to comprehend these desires in the little boy, and few mothers can be consciously aware of them. He cannot gratify those desires but nevertheless they dominate his sensations and his fantasies. He experiences in himself the impulses of the male while he is still a child. Indeed, he knows himself to be a child while he is driven by the urges of manhood.

2. THE INTERACTION BETWEEN GENITAL AND PRE-GENITAL LIBIDO

The fact that the first puberty occurs at the fourth or fifth year does not mean that the genitals did not previously function as an erotogenic zone. As an organ of erotogenous activity the genitals are highly effective from birth onwards, and genital masturbation can be observed in infants. One must always remember that the development of the individual does not take place in a mechanical manner, that is, with one stage neatly following another stage, but in a biological form, that is, all libidinous drives are present at the same time but one acquires primacy over others during certain stages of his evolution.

However, the progression to higher stages of development rarely proceeds smoothly. We have seen that fixations upon early libidinous primacies can cause them to persist alongside newer primacies; if the libido encounters difficulties at a certain stage it tends to regress to earlier stages of development. Freud used the analogy of an advancing army in enemy territory leaving occupation troops at all important points: 'The stronger the occupation troops left behind, the weaker is the army that marches on. If the latter meets a too powerful enemy force, it may retreat to those points where it had previously left the strongest occupation troops. The stronger a fixation, the more easily will a regression take place if difficulties arise.' (Sigmund Freud: *Introductory Lectures in Psychoanalysis*)

Disturbances in the transition from one primacy to another occur in all individuals as newly emerging primacies are influenced by the older established patterns; for instance, the genital libido will always be influenced by the characteristics which pre-genital primacies have adopted. This is not merely a question of neuroticism or psychotic disturbances, it is a process which operates in the development of every person's character.

Many psychoanalysts have described the early genital period as the phallic stage, characterised by aggressive impulses due to the penetrative urges of the penis. The genital organ can at this stage absorb aggressive-sadistic dispositions of the pre-genital period, and give them a new dimension and a new power for self-expression. While this process of displacement of oral-aggressive upon genital-aggressive drives frequently occurs during this stage, it is not necessarily so. I consider the phallic stage a manifestation of narcissism, and call it phallic-narcissistic, as the early manifestations of genitality are an expression and reinforcement of the narcissistic libido. What mostly distinguishes phallic sexuality from genital sexuality is that it relates itself to the self rather than to another person. Its goal is the assertion of masculine identity rather than an urge to merge with another person.

Freud often declared that a measure of aggressiveness is inevitable, even necessary in the constitution of male sexuality, insofar as the active agent of procreation, the male, must initiate sex and ensure that it is successfully carried out. What Freud no doubt had in mind was that the sex-repressive civilisation, the resistances which the world sets up against sexual pleasure and the resistances of the woman who reflects in her person the sex-denying attitudes of her culture, has to be overcome by a measure of aggressiveness. A certain amount of aggressiveness is even required of the male if he is to convince the woman that his sexual desire and love for her is genuine and reassuring enough for her to yield to him. No doubt when taboos of sexuality are prevalent in a culture and people armour themselves against its sensations, the man must break down his own armour and that of the woman. He has, so to speak, to penetrate through her armour, which blocks the gratification of genital urges. In this way genital fusion, the affectionate embrace between the sexes is transformed into an act of aggressiveness, a kind of battle.

The phallic urge to destroy the barriers to gratification will frequently be repressed from consciousness and projected on to the vagina, transforming it into a spider, a pincer, a mouth with teeth threatening to castrate the boy. He will be aroused by these fantasies and at the same time frightened by them, producing a combination of desire and fear which later will manifest itself frequently in *ejaculatio praecox*.

So both the threats of a sex-denying culture in general, as well as the castration threats of the destructive female will make the boy phallic assertive, and he will enter into a phallic competition with the world and with other boys or with girls to prove that he can defy the danger which they present to him. At such times he needs the constant reassurance of a father-figure with whom he can identify, to draw strength from him, from his big and powerful penis, from his ability to cope with women and be master over them. For it is not sufficiently realised how much the boy feels exposed and threatened in his need to prove his masculinity. It is at these stages that the reassurance of a male whom he can take as his model becomes very important.

Many boys who as infants have experienced profound oral-aggressive urges will suffer from the fear of having their penis attacked by the cannibalistic female. Not having experienced the reassurance of a libido-yielding breast, but being driven to attack the primary object in order to gain response from it, they will be frightened that their penis is going to be attacked by the woman. They will be dominated by fantasies of sexual union as a form of castration or mutilation, and will come to associate the experience of letting go and of loss of control with the threat of losing the penis. There is another narcissistic threat which the boy encounters during the phallic phase. According to Freud, children at this age do not yet take possession of a penis as a sexual characteristic of being male. They react to another child not as a boy or as a girl but in terms of 'with penis or without penis'. When the boy is forced to accept the existence of persons without a penis he assumes that they did once have one but lost it. Although I am not sure that the boy is unaware of the different quality and characteristic of the girl compared with himself, or *vice versa*, there is, however, little doubt that the boy experiences a shock upon seeing another child without that organ that he has come to prize so highly. The idea that the girl has lost hers or had it cut off does in fact arise frequently at that age, but this reaction will be over-determined in its degree of emotional disturbance by his already existing fear of castration, due largely, as I have said, to earlier oral-sadistic dangers. The sight of a girl's empty space, where the penis should be, evokes in such boys castration anxieties, whereas, as I have witnessed, boys who have not experienced oral-sadistic anxieties will take immense interest in the phenomenon of the absent penis and, while somewhat anxious or guilty about this 'injury' to the girl, will try to find out what happened to her penis and what she has instead. Somewhat guilty and protective attitudes towards women will have their origins in this discovery. On the other hand the large number of boys who are predisposed to the anxiety of having their genitals injured or attacked assume that the girl's penis has been mutilated or cut off and taken from her. In this case they will experience a trauma when seeing a girl naked, and frequently experience a screen image of a gaping wound between the girl's legs. Their by now unconscious cannibalistic fantasies will re-emerge in the image of the 'mouth of hell', with the 'Queen of the Night' and other witch-like females seeking revenge by attacking the penis and taking it away from the boy.

One form of defence reaction against this fear is to adopt the attitude that he is not really different from the girl and that he does not want his penis. This has been exemplified by a little boy of eighteen months who suffered from an early phallic castration anxiety, who, when his mother once again scolded him rather vehemently, cried out: 'I don't want my penis, I want to wee-wee like mummy does.' Such a boy will acquire sado-masochistic conflicts. On the one hand, he will want to offer his penis to the sisters or mother, while, on the other hand, he will be frightened of them for wanting to take it away from him. While being sexually excited by such fantasies, he will bitterly resent women for threatening him.

These fears and fantasies continue to play a large part in the underworld of man's psyche, and they are reflected in numberless myths that populate the underworld of patriarchal cultures. The myths of Bacchus and Osiris, of Attis, Adonis, Cronos and Uranus are redolent with stories of castration of the male gods by the female goddesses. The rituals of Dionysus-worship centre around a springtime celebration of wine drinking and sexual orgies, followed by the tearing of a male by female maenads and the scattering of his genitals over land and sea to ensure the fertility of the earth. In the myth of Osiris, the body of the god is similarly dismembered, while special attention is given to his castration and the disposal of his genitals. Osiris' wife Isis is represented as both the chief mourner and avenger, and, as we can see from other myths but above all from the psychoanalysis of individuals, the mourner is in reality the perpetrator of the deed.

Other versions of the same myth complex are that of Attis (whose devotees or priests castrated themselves as an act of devotion to the goddess), of Adonis castrated by a male rival in the shape of a boar (who is really a servant of the female goddess) and mourned annually by the women, of Pentheus torn to pieces by the wild women or maenads, of Orpheus, Uranus and so on. These myths derive from late matriarchal cultures in which the gods were acolytes of the goddesses whom they served sexually, the sexual act becoming increasingly sadistic and violent. Thus the sexual act was associated with the mutilation of the male genitals, the goddesses finding satisfaction only by the dismemberment of the male and the cannibalistic devouring of his genitals.

I should like to illustrate this situation, which must appear rather bizarre to many readers, by the case of a young man who was twenty-two when I first saw him, the youngest of three children, with two sisters who were eight and eleven years older than himself. His father was a prominent physician, much admired by his colleagues and by the patient's mother and worshipped by his sisters. He was about forty-five when the patient was born, and far too busy to show much interest in his young son. His mother was forty-three when he was born. As a baby he felt his mother's breast to be weak, collapsed and lifeless, and developed strong, aggressive urges of attacking the breast, which made him afraid of injuring his mother, in view of her frail condition. Indeed, the mother felt extremely insecure in her relationship to the baby due to her age, which she felt to be too advanced for motherhood, making her afraid that she no longer had the strength to satisfy the needs of her late offspring. She projected her own sense of inadequacy and weakness upon the boy, feeling him to be weak and frail, and adopted overprotective, anxious attitudes towards him, with the result that from the earliest age he felt unsure of himself and introjected the mother's image of him as a weak and inadequate child. He did not dare to do things spontaneously, and in his play he constantly depended upon his mother's and his nanny's support and protection while at the same time intensely resenting his dependency upon them.

His sisters did not welcome their young brother, they teased him and, as he felt, constantly impressed upon him his inadequacy and weakness. In reaction, he began to be over-assertive but without any confidence, which in turn led his sisters to ridicule and denigrate him or to protect him in a patronising manner. During his first puberty, strong, phallic-aggressive urges began to make their appearance, and he had many dreams and fantasies that his sisters attacked his erect penis. These fantasies aroused strong sexual feelings, and on the one hand he was excited by the danger of having his penis attacked, and on the other hand this presented a challenge to survive his sisters' attack, thereby defeating them and making his phallus supreme. While he offered his phallus to his sisters in order to placate them, he at the same time would retain it and emerge victorious over his attackers. Sado-masochistic urges became a dominant feature in his life, making him both submissive as well as aggressive and domineering. Later in life he was obsessed by fantasies of being very special, and constantly asserted his superiority, often quite aggressively, while suffering from paranoid fears of being attacked. His aggressive, domineering urges were constantly defeated by a sense of his own vulnerability, imagining that his family as well as the world were determined to attack and denigrate him. On the anal level a similar conflict occurred. His faecal product became a weapon by which he asserted his sense of importance, but at the same time he was afraid that it would be attacked or taken away from him, thus once more causing him to be afraid of being emasculated. He developed an acute conflict between anal-assertive and retentive drives, which produced a profound stammer when he could not for many seconds or even minutes pronounce his words. But when he did manage to speak it was in a very assertive and very loud manner. In his images, a free-floating rage produced fantasies of tearing people limb from limb, which in turn caused intense muscular blocks and inhibitions, so that he could barely step off a pavement without falling over. When I saw him he had entered into a solicitor's office, only to be told after a few weeks that he was too incompetent to continue his employment. The long periods of acute feelings of inadequacy and inferiority thus found their confirmation, and he entered an acute depressive state. Phallic-aggressive drives are fairly common among boys during the early stages of the first puberty when their genital sensations make them desire their mother sexually, evoking masculine urges to possess and to dominate the giant lady. The boy wants to be a man but he is a child, and he knows it. His fantasies of dominating the mother and of possessing her are contradicted by his smallness and his dependency upon her. He is both excited and frightened by his perception of the giant lady's sexual needs which he knows he cannot satisfy. He wants to be masterful but feels inadequate as his masculinity is trapped inside his childish body, his physical and mental development has not kept pace with his biological sexual urges. An aggressive rage will often overwhelm him, and his little penis will in fantasy acquire the image of a powerful weapon to overcome his own limitations and to attack the inaccessible mother. The urge to satisfy her and to dominate her will occupy his imagination, and often continues to play a major role in his sexual fantasies.

Phallic-aggressive urges thus act as a compensation for the boy's and a man's sense of genital inadequacy if he fails to achieve a satisfactory transformation from being a man-child to being a man. (This explains why so many men often see women in their pre-conscious imagery as large and quite overwhelming, and despite being married or having had fairly normal sex relationships for years still have the rather frightening and intimidating image of women being much larger than themselves. It can often be a source of amazement to themselves and to the analyst when men well over six foot tall still imagine themselves quite small in relationship to women who in actuality are much smaller than they are.)

There are many reasons why a man remains fixated upon the phallic level and fails to achieve a satisfactory transformation from child to man and what we call 'mature genitality'. One reason is that he is arrested in his development by the fixation of his libido to his childhood relationship to his mother and wants to remain a child and does not want and cannot sever his ties to her in order to grow up. These traits will be specially pronounced in boys who have a particularly close relationship to mother and whose fathers are either absent for long periods or weak and subservient to the mother. Such boys suffer from the lack of a convincing masculine model to guide and encourage their development and facilitate a successful male identity. Another reason for the difficulty of achieving satisfactory transformation to manhood is the boy's encounter with the vicissitudes of the Oedipus complex which characterise our patriarchal culture.

But before we look at the Oedipus complex in the male, let us consider the sexual development of the girl.

3. THE SEXUAL DEVELOPMENT OF THE GIRL

According to Freud, nothing is yet known of maleness and femaleness during the pre-genital, oral and anal primacies of children. It is only during the 'phallic stage' that maleness comes to life, but not femaleness. The antithesis runs: the male genital organ or a castrated condition. Not until completion of the genital development at the time of puberty does the polarity of sexuality emerge as male and female.

It was one of the achievements of Melanie Klein and her co-workers to have found ample evidence that vaginal sensations and impulses occur in the girl long before the onset of the 'phallic period', and that vaginal responses of varied intensity can already be observed at the breast-feeding stage in girls, just as there is ample evidence that the male infant experiences genital arousal during breast-feeding. Infant boys have been observed to have erections and to masturbate during breast-feeding, and girl babies show unmistakable signs of genital arousal often accompanied by masturbatory movements at this very early stage.

I have frequently found during the analysis of women that they have experienced strong vaginal sensations accompanied by orgastic spasms from the age of one and a half years, and that little boys experience a genital arousal during breast-feeding if that has been prolonged to nine months or more.

If we consider the similarity between mouth and vagina, the similarity of their physiological function of intake and swallowing and, above all, their high degree of libidinous investment, then it will not surprise us that there is a strong relationship in the sexual nature of the two organs. Following the lead of Karl Abraham, Melanie Klein has not only recognised the similarity and complementariness of these organs but has described their interaction in the observation of the vaginal arousal of infant girls during breastfeeding. Furthermore, she has drawn our attention to the fact that as soon as girls are weaned from the breast they turn towards their father, replacing the breast with the penis as an object of oral desire. Melanie Klein and many other child analysts since then have also observed that these oral desires are accompanied by genital impulses. Under the dominance of oral primacy the father's penis is an object which the girl wants to suck and incorporate via the mouth, and these urges and fantasies are already accompanied by vaginal sensations and spasms. Helene Deutsch has pointed out: 'Already very early on in her life the small girl in taking her father as the object of her affection next in order to her mother, directs towards him a great part of that true sexual libido attached to the oral zone with which she has cathexed her mother's breast, since in that phase of her development her unconscious equates her father's penis with her mother's breast for giving suck.' (Helene Deutsch: *The Psychology of Female Sexuality*, 1925)

When the little girl turns to her father's penis as the wished for object, several factors make her desire for it very intense. The demands of her sucking impulses, heightened by the frustration she has suffered at her mother's breast, create in her an imaginary picture of her father's penis as an organ which, unlike the breast, can provide her with a tremendous and never-ending gratification. In her imagination it becomes an object which possesses magical powers for providing gratification. Melanie Klein also observes that since the oral frustration she has suffered has stimulated all her other erotogenic zones as well, and has aroused her genital tendencies and desires in regard to her father's penis, the latter becomes the object of her oral, urethral, anal and genital impulses at the same time.

I do not believe, however, that it is merely the frustrations which the girl experiences at her mother's breast that stimulate her vaginal libido. The stimulations of the oral sphere in the act of sucking arouse vaginal sensations automatically and do not depend for their arousal on oral frustration. There is no doubt about the similarity of the oral and vaginal activities and the interacting stimulation which occurs between the two. The lips which reach forward when they become aware of the breast, the desire to open the mouth to receive the nipple in response to the libidinous sensations emitted from it, exercise a stimulus on the vagina, and it will make equivalent involuntary movements. If we bear this fundamental correlation between the two organs in mind it will explain many problems in the psychology of women which have previously remained shrouded in obscurity. If what I have called the embracing and sucking aspect of the oral libido finds responses and satisfactions at the breast, the latter will appear as a loving and responsive object. The memories of the good sensations and good image of it will produce the image of the good penis and good father, and the girl will turn to him with trust as a new object of her oral needs, which had been disrupted by the shock of weaning.

If a large part of her oral libido has been transformed into aggressive-cannibalistic drives, these will most likely be directed towards the penis. In the same manner as the infant projects its own aggressive instincts on to the breast and sees it as bad and dangerous, so the girl will think of the penis as having extremely dangerous attributes. She will be tied to this dangerous object by the bonds of a sado-masochistic cathexis which arouses both her excitement as well as her fears. Moreover, the structure of her oral libido and its impact upon the musculature of the mouth will, generally speaking, affect the libido and muscular structuring of her vagina. (I describe the interactions of the hormonal and muscular systems between the mouth and the vagina region in some detail in my book *Exploring the Unconscious*.) This early structuring of the vagina, while already important, is nevertheless a mere intimation of future developments, subject to numerous modifications.

However, the oral-vaginal desires of the little girl towards her father, whichever way they are over-determined by her experiences at the breast, will encounter his actual responses. It is not sufficiently realised how important it is for the little girl to know of her father's penis, that her avid interest in it is met with a positive response, that is, that she can see it, know that her father has a penis and that she can be proud of it. Her whole feminine self-confidence will, in many respects, depend on her awareness of its existence, her feeling that it is there and, as it were, belongs to her, as her father's daughter. Many girls experience considerable anxiety due to the impression that their father does not have a penis, or that it is deliberately hidden from her.

There has been much argument about what happens if the girl has no father. Are we to consider what we have described here as an instinctual drive or regard the girl's desire for the father as a response to her experience of his proximity? If the latter is the case, then the girl would have no innate desire to turn to the male as an oral and also vaginal object if the father is absent.

The argument about the absent father has been answered by many psychoanalysts by maintaining that we are dealing here with an instinctual-innate drive which, in the case of an absent father, causes her to imagine herself having a father to whom she turns in her fantasies. There is evidence that girls without a father develop such fantasies about a father-figure and are constantly in search of a substitute upon whom they can project their fantasies. In my own experience with patients who did not have a father, due to his death when the patient was still young, divorce of parents or one-parent family, I have found that a split emerges between an idealised male object and a sense of mistrust towards men, who are constantly being compared with the idealised image and found wanting. The search in such women for the ideal male tends to make them reluctant to fall in love and to commit themselves fully to an actual man. They will want to retain the image of the ideal man, feel vulnerable to the approaches of men, whom they consider strangers, and the frustration which they have felt as children will constantly re-emerge and impede their capacity for vaginal gratification. An urge for self-reliance and independence will frequently promote predominance of a clitoral-phallic libido, and the girl will tend to identify with the man of her imagination and adopt masculine attitudes.

These are just some of the possible developments in women without a father, and this also applies in cases where the father was absent for long periods or was aloof and indifferent to the girl, sexually inhibited and unable to communicate his emotions.

Infants are sensitive to the libidinous emissions of their parents' chief erotic zones, their breasts, their genitals, their body surface as well as their mental attitudes, particularly their unconscious attitudes. (Indeed, the double bind which arises from parents who are unconsciously blocked, inhibited or hostile, while consciously professing to be affectionate and loving, is one of the chief factors that produces neurotic disturbances and psychotic syndromes). (R. D. Laing: *The Divided Self*) Should the father respond with rejection or indifference towards his little daughter's erotic needs, then her frustration, her sense of being rejected will transform her desire into anger and guilt. If the girl has developed sadistic fixations upon the breast and projected upon the mother images of the frightening witch, she will in the first place hope to find release from these painful images through the haven of her father's love and reassurance. If the father, however, also responds to her advances with rejection, her sadistic drives will be reinforced. Her vagina, like her mouth, will tense up, become angry and aggressive, and the vaginal embrace will acquire the aspect of teeth biting at the penis. She will develop the image of a vagina dentata and will not be able to be vaginally responsive. I should make it clear here that it is of course neither necessary nor desirable for the father to respond 'sexually' to his daughter, that he should want her sexually. It is her father's unconscious as well as conscious acknowledgement of her erotic needs and his pride in his own sexuality, their sexual side-by-sideness, which is what the girl wants – to be proud of her father and the feeling that he is proud of her. For if he is ashamed of his sexuality then she feels ashamed of hers.

Men who are insecure about their own sexuality will respond with guilt and anxiety towards their daughter's sexual advances. Such defensive and anxious attitudes on the father's part will appear to the daughter as a rejection of her sexuality. In the same way as her sexual urges appear to be rejected by her father, she will, in turn, reject and consider them as Ego-alien, dangerous and unwanted. She may adopt various forms of repression, such as muscular tensions, in order to block her erotic sensations, and mental dissociation, by which her erotic fantasies are split off from her Ego and experienced as Ego-alien external forces. If the latter process becomes dominant, it will lead to psychotic dispositions. More frequently, she will either feel men to be hostile to her or she herself will adopt hostile attitudes towards men.

However, the development of the girl's sexuality does not run in a straight line, in the form of gradual intensification of vaginal sexuality culminating in the genital primacy when the vaginal urges gain predominance over all other erotic drives. A complication sets in, a kind of disruption of this development with the emergence of the phallic libido based on the erotic primacy of the clitoris. While this stage in the girl's development becomes easily observable in her behaviour, such as tomboyish assertiveness and competitiveness as well as increased masturbation, the earlier vaginal eroticism has remained largely unrecognised. This apparent ignorance of the woman's early sexual urge, an urge repressed and forgotten by the woman herself, is particularly characteristic of patriarchal culture, which prompts men to deny women an active and self-affirming sexuality.

It is in this respect interesting to note that even Freud, the fearless analyst of patriarchal taboos, was also their victim and their representative insofar as he failed to acknowledge the vaginal libido in the girl before the onset of her first puberty. In ascribing to her a masculine phallic characteristic in her first genital experience, he manifested the patriarchal reluctance to acknowledge the primary nature of the woman's vaginal urges. He fell victim to taboos of patriarchy and its compulsion of seeing a woman as an incomplete or castrated edition of the male. In other words, he carried forward into his rational thought the phallic castration fantasy which the boy harbours about the girl.

The model of the phallus is, according to Freud, 'a male organ', and therefore, 'we can describe the phallic primacy only as it concerns the male child. The corresponding process of the girl is not sufficiently known to us.' By this definition it was assumed that the girl goes through a phallic stage but that we cannot say much about it as the phallus is a male organ. It is a fact that this stage of a child's development was seen by the early psychoanalysts chiefly from the male point of view, as a period in which the boy experiences the first major traumas of castration through his discovery that the organ which he assumes to be a common property of all people is absent in certain individuals, that it must therefore have disappeared or been cut off and that the same thing could also happen to him. It was equally assumed that the phallic period is also responsible for the girl's own castration anxiety, triggered off by her discovery that she lacks this important organ and, subsequently, develops penis envy. In this respect the girl's idea of being at a disadvantage or of having been deprived of the penis, or of having lost it, is completely analogous to the boy's anxiety that he may suffer the same fate as the girl, namely, lose his penis or have it taken away.

There is no doubt that the girl's vulnerability to castration anxiety and penis envy occurs during the phallic primacy – the high degree of libidinisation of her clitoris and its emergence as a primary erotic centre. It would be worth while to ask how it is that phallic-clitoral sexuality occurs at all in girls and can even become a primary characteristic of women. Much work has been done on this subject by the later psychoanalytic researchers such as Melanie Klein, Helene Deutsch, Jeanne Lampl-de Groot, Anna Freud, Rupert Back, Lisbeth Sachs and many others. How are we to explain the transformation of her vaginal sexuality to phallic sexuality centred upon the clitoris? Whereas the boy's genital libido remains centred upon the penis, with girls the genital libido undergoes a transformation from the vagina to the clitoris, to be replaced once more by the vaginal primacy during the first puberty.

If, as we have observed, the boy's phallic stage of development represents an extension of his narcissism, then we are justified in thinking that the girl's phallic stage is equally part of her narcissistic development and a consolidation of her self-image as a sexually active person. It is as if nature intends to make sure that women are endowed not only with a receptive, object-dependent sexuality but also with an active, self-assertive sexual drive.

The argument about the relationship between vaginal and clitoral sexuality was first raised by Freud and then brought to a head by the investigations of Masters and Johnson; it emboldened radical feminists to claim that Freud was the chief protagonist of the castration of women. I have discussed these matters in my book, *The Failure of the Sexual Revolution*. But let me here add to the clarification of these matters, as the interaction between the two organs of sexuality in women is germane to an understanding of the development of female sexuality.

I have mentioned that Freud all but ignored the early manifestations of vaginal libido in girls, and considered the phallic-clitoral primacy as the earliest form of a woman's sexual drives. In his *Three Essays on the Theory of Sexuality*, he wrote: 'When at last the sex act is permitted and the clitoris itself becomes excited, it retains a function, namely, the task of transmitting the excitation to the adjacent female sexual parts, just as – to use a simile – pine shavings can be kindled in order to set a log of harder wood on fire.' Freud maintained that the transfer of excitement from clitoris to vagina implied a development process in which the clitoris should normally give up its excitability in favour of the vagina, and that its failure to do so in less normal cases is associated with anaesthesia of the vaginal orifice.

As we have seen, Freud was wrong in his ignorance of early, pre-phallic vaginal sexuality, but he was right in his conception of the 'non-normal' phenomenon of vaginal anaesthesia.

On the other hand, Masters and Johnson and Mary Jane Sherfey were right to point to the continued excitability of the clitoris in normal sexual intercourse. As Sherfey remarks: 'One of the most significant findings of Masters and Johnson is the fact that the clitoral glans is kept in a state of continuous stimulation throughout intra-vaginal coition, even though it is not being touched and appears to have vanished'. She continues: 'Furthermore, it is also obvious why the thrusting movements of the penis will necessarily create simultaneous stimulation of the lower third of the vagina, labia minora, and clitoral shaft and glans as an integrated, inseparable functioning unit, with the glans being the most important and, in by far the majority of instances, the indispensable initiator of the orgasmic reaction. With these observations, the evidence seems overwhelming: it is a physical impossibility to separate the clitoral from the vaginal orgasm, as demanded by psychoanalytic theory.' However, Masters and Johnson as well as Sherfey were wrong in maintaining that clitoral orgasm takes place equally in local stimulation of the clitoris as well as in vaginal penetration. It is a fact that the woman's experience of clitoral orgasm is vastly different from the experience of vaginal orgasm, and that the anaesthesia or non-involvement of the vagina in orgasm leaves women unsatisfied, restless, angry and frustrated. In *The Failure of the Sexual Revolution*, I speak of clitoral orgasm as an orgastic spasm, as distinguished from full orgastic release. In upholding the primacy of clitoral orgasm, and even denying the powerful experience of vaginal orgasm, Masters and Johnson as well as Sherfey and many other advocates of the female liberation movement attempted to deny the fundamental function of woman's sexuality, a position which is no longer seriously upheld.

However, the question still remains to be asked why many women suffer from anaesthesia of the vaginal orifice and have to rely on clitoral excitement. Freud's concept of penis envy, masculine identification, fear of penetration, is not a universal phenomenon or an inevitable state through which women have to pass, they are pathological phenomena which need to be explained. We are dealing here not merely with biological but above all with psychological processes, i.e., the investment of the libido or its blocking in the relevant organs of sexuality.

The girl infant has usually a well-developed clitoral organ, but her early sensations are centred upon the vagina, as I have observed above. The vaginal sensations can be blocked or inhibited at an early age, however. From birth, we are equipped with all our organs, but it is psychic processes which control the flow of the libido to the various organs and determine their activation. As we have observed, in an embracing, rhythmic sucking of the mother's breast, the vaginal rhythms are also stimulated, the vaginal orifice will enact the oral rhythms and feel sensations similar to those of the lips and mouth. This, let me repeat, is not a mechanical or merely physiological process but one which is invested with very strong libidinous sensations. From the observation of many patients during their analysis of infantile processes, I have found that if an aggressive, clutching, biting, pulling response occurs, pushing the libido forward, so to speak, to a tensing of the lips and towards biting or tearing movements, then stimulation of the clitoris occurs as the representative of the active, aggressive area of the female genitals. This process, moreover, leads very often to the tensing of the throat and trachea, where the process of swallowing and incorporating the primary object is impeded, and then we can observe a similar situation in the vaginal shaft: it becomes tense and tight, and doesn't let go, so to speak. This process is accompanied by a tightening of the solar plexus and the stomach muscles. A tightening of the stomach and the solar plexus evokes a pulling back of the vagina, the vagina rejects the object and withdraws the libido from it: that is, it becomes desensitised. If associated with oral, biting libido it may in girls evoke sensations and images of the vagina dentata, the aggressive, angry reaction against its lack of sensations: it attacks the void, where nothing alive and warm and fulfilling is felt to be.

We have mentioned earlier how our self-feeling depends upon what we take in and incorporate; our narcissistic self-experience depends upon the libidinous attitudes of the primary objects we have incorporated. In order to reach out with pleasure and confidence we must feel that we are accepted and received with love and good libido. If we feel we are bad and our stomachs are tight and the solar plexus anxious, we dare not reach out to the desired object, we anticipate rejection or responses of anger, our mouth, our throat, the penis and the vagina will be apprehensive and frequently desensitised with fear. We have seen this in the case of Mr T. E., whose penis was completely anaesthetised, and there are many graduations of genital desensitisation, both in men and women. But then, the teeth and the claws will be libidinised towards aggressive urges, the penis will appear as a phallic weapon, and equally the clitoris as a phallus, assertive and angry. Many women suffer from irritations, often amounting to pain in the clitoris, and as children they want to tear at it, or have fantasies of having it attacked or cut off. Forceful, angry masturbation frequently occurs with a wide range of masochistic fantasies, and they frequently see the penis as a weapon, a sharp tool that attacks their genitals. Such women feel intense fear of the penis or resent the male as an attacker, and besides suffering from vaginal anaesthesia can develop vaginismus, an acute tightening of the vaginal walls when penetration is either impossible or very painful. It is worthwhile to remember that even perfectly normal women with usually well-functioning vaginal sensations can at times of stress, i.e., anger at being neglected, emotionally hurt or rejected by her man, develop symptoms of vaginismus, often with subsequent depression. We are justified in calling this reactive desensitisation of the vagina, a rejection of the object that is felt to reject them. This is different from chronic desensitisation, when infantile experiences become fixated and determine a person's character and retain their influence upon the personality of the woman.

We must also mention that a girl's transformation from clitoral to vaginal primacies may be inhibited by a mother who feels neglected and denigrated by her husband, and whom the girl perceives to be suffering or ill. In this case the girl will develop ambiguities towards the male, on the one hand wanting to be loved by him and on the other hand rejecting him as he has rejected her mother. The mother who because of her insecurity cannot accept her own femininity, and being frustrated or hurt cannot enjoy her feminine libido, will act as a negative model for the girl's feminine identity. If, on the other hand, the girl's mother on the other hand is satisfied in her feminine needs and self-accepting, she provides a successful model for the appropriate sex role of her daughter. This also applies to the boy: that is, a self-accepting and confident father provides a satisfying male model for the boy.

I have found in women who suffer from psychopathic schizophrenia childhood experiences of a cruel and rejecting father who, moreover, is absent much of the time. On the one hand they want his penis but they cannot tolerate the man behind it. So they dissociate the penis from the man, take it away from him, so to speak, and make it their own in order to have complete power over it. They want to castrate the man in order to seek revenge for his cruelty. The vagina that cannot anticipate being loved will reject and hate. However, quite apart from such extreme experiences, the libidinous inhibitions common in our culture cause a very high proportion of women to suffer from a tense and pulled back vagina, a sense of alienation from their genital sensations; they seem unable to communicate with their vagina, they don't know it, it does not seem part of themselves.

Many girls produce pronounced exhibitionistic urges, partly as a compensation for not having their genital sensations recognised and for the very natural reason that unlike boys their genitals are not visible. Female exhibitionism is actually a healthy and natural urge and finds its cultural sublimation in adornments of all kinds, dancing, make-up, clothing and jewellery – secondary sexual characteristics, as Darwin calls them. But again, if these urges meet with too severe prohibition or embarrassment, then girls gain the impression that they must hide themselves or that there is something wrong with their sensations, and their female characteristics feel not acceptable.

In a psychological assessment of these processes, it is important that we do not become ourselves fixated upon simplified definitions which mistake phenomena for rules, but always enquire into the processes by which pathological phenomena develop.

Varieties of Oedipus Complex

1. RIVALRY AND IDENTIFICATION

It is just at the time when the boy feels the urges of masculine desires welling up in him that he needs his father as an ally and as a model. At the same time as he wants to be rid of his father to take his place, he most depends on him in order to identify with him and acquire his masculine attributes. As we have said, the mother, whom he desires, appears very large and powerful and fills him with feelings of inadequacy, both sexually as well as personally. The smallness of his penis makes him anxious as he knows that it could not satisfy the large organ and the powerful needs of the mother, who only recently considered him her baby. Indeed, fears of their smallness and inadequacy permeate the unconscious of many males, and fantasies of the woman's enormous vagina and of her insatiable needs are the sources of endless jokes and tales. These jokes and stories reflect a real anxiety, which men carry forward from this early period of their sexual development. Also the fear of the mother's sexual desire for the boy – a fear partly engendered by his awareness of her libidinous sensations for him but more usually the product of his own wish fantasies and projections – makes him afraid that her powers would be overwhelming and that he would be unable to cope with them. It is in this situation that he looks to his father for guidance and, above all, for identification. He needs to introject the powers of his father in order to cope with the giant lady whom he desires. He will look with keen interest at his father's penis and will be proud of his big father even while, on the other hand, he will be jealous of him. Jealousy and admiration will be in constant conflict with each other.

If the boy's jealousy and the desire that his rival should disappear are dominant (disappearance is often analogous to death in the pre-conscious imagery of the child), then he could become terrified of losing his father and guilty about having caused this loss. (Wanting the father to disappear is associated in the child's mind with wanting him to be dead – that is, with wanting to kill him.) The wish for father's disappearance is strenuously repressed by the Ego, which needs him and feels the hostile impulses as a danger to his male identification, a danger to himself as well as to the father. Thus the desire to kill the father in order to make him disappear will be repressed from consciousness; being repressed, it will not cease to be active as an emotional force but will undergo projection upon the father, who will then be seen as imbued with hostile-aggressive attitudes which the boy preconsciously feels towards him. The splitting and projection processes, which we have observed at the earlier stages of a child's development, will re-occur here on the genital level and produce the fateful conflicts of the Oedipus complex.

It is well known that Freud thought he had found the origins of the Oedipus complex in a traumatic event in prehistoric times which continues to influence the psyche of mankind and is responsible for the emergence of civilisations. Taking a suggestion from Darwin, he proposed that man originally existed in a condition which he called the 'primal horde' – a single tyrannical father dominating the family group, enjoying the favours of a number of females and excluding the sons as they achieved sexual maturity.

He conceived the 'primal horde' as the original human family, made up of an all-powerful, jealous and aggressive father who maintained a harem and drove his sons out of the household when they became sexual rivals. However, 'one day the expelled brothers joined forces, slew and ate the father, and thus put an end to the father's horde. Thus together they dared and accomplished what would have remained impossible for them singly. Perhaps some advance in culture, like the use of a new weapon, had given them the feeling of superiority. Of course, these cannibalistic savages ate their victim. This violent, primal father had surely been the envied and feared model for each of the brothers. Now they accomplished their identification with him by devouring him, and each acquired a part of his strength. The totem feast, which is perhaps mankind's first celebration, will be a repetition and commemoration of this memorable, criminal act with which so many things began – social organisation, moral restrictions and religion. In order to find these results acceptable, quite aside from our supposition, we need only assume that a group of brothers, banded together, were dominated by the same contradictory feelings towards the father, which we can demonstrate as the content of ambivalence of the father complex in all our children and in neurotics. They hated the father who stood so powerfully in the way of their sexual demands and their desire for power, but they also loved and admired him. After they had satisfied their hate by his removal and had carried out their wish for identification with him, the suppressed tender impulses had to assert themselves. This took place in the form of remorse, a sense of guilt was formed which coincided here with the remorse generally felt. The dead now became stronger than the living had been, even as we observe it today in the destinies of man. What the father's presence had formerly prevented, they themselves now prohibited in the psychic situation of subsequent obedience, which we know so well from psychoanalysis. They undid their deed by declaring that the killing of the father substitute, the totem, was not allowed, and renounced the fruits of their deed by denying themselves the liberated women. Thus they created two fundamental taboos of totemism out of the sense of guilt of the son, and for this very reason these had to correspond with the two repressed wishes of the Oedipus complex (incest and father murder). Whoever disobeyed became guilty of the only two crimes which troubled primitive society.' (Sigmund Freud: *Totem and Taboo*)

It can be assumed with a considerable degree of certainty now that these dramatic events never occurred. Freud's theory of the primal horde was based upon highly coloured, second and third hand tales about gorillas which he obtained in the late nineteenth century, whereas current observations of gorilla troops do not in any way support those stories. But even if there is no evidence that the collective father murder ever took place, and while he was wrong in assuming that mankind's original social and family structure was of a patriarchal kind and the Oedipus complex the universal and necessary condition of mankind, Freud was surely right in trying to trace the origins of human behaviour to its earliest sources in prehistory. We must also remember that he resolved to enquire into the origins of the Oedipus complex in primitive society after he discovered the Oedipus complex in his self-analysis and in the analysis of patients. Whether the actual father murder ever took place or not, there is no doubt that the wish for it, and the subsequent conflicts, play an important role in the psychic make-up of patriarchal cultures which have existed for some ten thousand years.

While in my previous book I have investigated the impact of the Oedipus complex upon the evolution of human societies, we are here concerned with its impact upon the psyche of individuals. For the psychological conflicts which operate in societies are reproduced in its members and the psychological conflicts of individuals are in turn reproduced in society. However, we have to recognise that there are significant variables, many different forms in which the Oedipus complex makes its appearance in the psyche of individuals, just as there are a great many variations in the cultures of patriarchy.

Whereas Freud postulates the boy's urge to castrate or kill the father as a fundamental attribute of narcissistic as well as genital rivalry – that is, competition for power as well as sexual supremacy, I have found that the intensity of this urge varies considerably. While identification with the father's masculine powers is a universal need for the boy at his early genital primacy, it must be remembered that identification is based on introjection, and introjection means taking in, incorporating. However, there are many different ways in which incorporation can take place, and the specific form in which it occurs largely determines the boy's relationship to his father, the character of his Oedipus complex and his identity.

The form of incorporation is largely influenced by the boy's infantile experiences. The predominance of sucking-expansive or aggressive-sadistic urges during the oral stages will influence the nature of incorporation of his father's masculinity and his identification with him. As one important aspect of identification with the father is the fantasy of introjecting, incorporating father's penis, it can take the form of aggressive destruction involving father's castration, with the aim of acquiring its magic for himself and, at the same time, depriving father of his powers over mother. If the boy at the oral stage did not feel that his mother wanted to share her libido with him, and he had to resort to biting in order to experience it beneath the armour of her defences, then the boy will not be able to conceive the possibility of sharing the father's penis and his powers but will have to rob him of it, and by castrating him acquire his powers for himself. This disposition towards sadistic introjection will be further enhanced by a sense of father's rejection of the boy's libidinous needs. On the other hand, if the father shows love and affection for the boy, introjection will be facilitated as loving and sharing. The boy will feel love for his maleness and can share it with his father, he will be proud of his new identity, and phallic castration fantasies will be at a minimum. He may, however, continue to feel his sado-masochistic urges and fantasies towards the woman, consider her as a threat, and turn to his father as an ally against her. Identification with his father will produce a satisfying sense of masculinity, of power and reassurance against the threat of the mother. At this stage, boys will be disposed to show off their penis, handle it and constantly reassure themselves of its presence. In primitive and, indeed, not so primitive mythologies, the phallus is worshipped as a magic symbol to ward off evil forces and the threat of oral-aggressive powers. (The symbol of the cross as the omnipotent defence against the bloodthirsty teeth of Dracula and his women is a perfect representation of this syndrome which has continued to obsess the unconscious mind through the ages.)

A father's love can free the boy from his own aggressive-sadistic complexes and from his resulting anxiety states. This would transform the Oedipus complex into a positive, encouraging

Superego, which, however, repeatedly needs to be reassured by male identifications, as, for instance, with male gangs, with leaders and powerful authority figures.

But of course it is rarely as simple as that, because the mother is not only the object of the boy's fears but also the object of his love, upon whom he remains dependent, and the father is not always the loving and accepting father. If a boy has early experienced powerful genital stimulation from his mother, and I am speaking here of what we call the pre-genital period, he will have difficulty in relinquishing these genital urges and his desires for her. He will remain possessive of her and powerfully resist the father's and any other male's right of access to her. Such boys will go through an hysteric phase of over-excitability during the first genital primacy at five and six, develop manic dispositions, claim constant attention, their socialisation processes will be impeded, they will be egocentric and intolerant of gratification delay; and a free-floating anxiety as well as aggressiveness will dominate their behaviour. The erotic drives towards the mother will outweigh the boy's fear of her, or both fear as well as desire will exist together, and the split between the good, loving mother and the angry and rejective mother will frequently occur and become reinforced by the mother's own anxiety about how to deal with the boy and his clinging attention-seeking and her awareness of a need to free herself from him and him from her. The boy's ambivalence towards the mother will also be projected upon the father, and in the process of identification he will, on the one hand, develop a homosexual bond with his father and on the other hand rebel against it, for it would mean having to relinquish the mother. He will thus be torn between an urge to clutch onto his father, admiring him, and on the other hand hating him. An hysteric, schizophrenic type of splitting, with manic-depressive complexes will make its appearance.

There are, needless to say, many computations and varieties of attitudes possible among individuals during the Oedipal situation according to their pre-genital experiences and the father's own complexes and characteristics, and his relationship to his own mother and to his wife.

It is, no doubt, true that the severity of the internalised father-figure, which operates as the Superego, is determined by the aggressive impulses of the child. As I have mentioned, aggressive, devouring introjection produces an aggressive internal presence of the object which will be felt to be angry and hostile towards the self, always ready to criticise and to attack and to threaten the Ego, punishing and frightening it, making it feel guilty and anxious and producing self-punishing tendencies. The aggressively introjected father, as the previously aggressively introjected breast, can be said to live in the stomach of the child, and there the anger, which the internalised father feels, produces not only psychological fears but also somatic sensations of fear which often originate in the anxious stomach. It is not merely the external nature of the father or the mother but the attitudes projected upon them which determine the nature of the Oedipus complex and subsequently of the Superego.

While Freud at first thought that the Superego is derived from parental authority, being a more or less realistic representation of the father, he later came to recognise (in agreement with Melanie Klein) that the severity which a child's Superego develops does not necessarily correspond to the severity of the treatment it has itself experienced: 'The original severity of the Superego does not – or not so much – represent the severity which has been experienced or incorporated from the object but expresses the child's own aggressiveness towards the latter.' (Sigmund Freud: *Civilization and its Discontents*)

We have seen that what Freud called Oedipus complex, castration anxiety and Superego are actual psychic phenomena, and their meanings are obvious, but their causations, the processes under which they occur are much more complex than he realised. The complexities can be more readily comprehended if we bear in mind that the Oedipus complex is bound to occur in patriarchal cultures with a sex-repressive tradition and that sexual repression arouses aggressive urges towards the repressor – the father and father representatives. However, the boy's aggression towards his father and his fears of him do not merely reflect the father's actual attitudes but contain the aggressive drives experienced during infancy and projected upon the father. They provide the deeper, unconscious layer which determines the character and form of the Oedipus complex in each particular individual, producing a wide range of variations. Infantile fantasies of killing and being killed, which re-emerge during the first puberty and are repeated in the second major puberty, have in turn to be repressed, and the agent of repression, the psychic factor by which the Oedipus complex attempts to resolve itself, is the Superego. It is the internal presence of parental taboos and prohibitions as well as of guidance, ideals and aspirations, and plays a decisive role in the formation of an individual's personality. It is the prime factor which gives rise to the moral sentiment, and governs the internal life of man to a large extent; it transmits respect for custom and tradition as well as social ideals. It influences a person's self-image and his ideas about his role in society. It is the internal transmitter of social norms, and as such provides a sense of cultural cohesion.

2. THE DEVELOPMENT OF THE SUPEREGO

Freud's argument that the Superego is a consequence of the Oedipus complex is very persuasive: 'Once the child becomes convinced of the possibility of castration – due to the warnings of his parents and other grown-ups about playing with his genitals and in particular in consequence of seeing girls without a penis – it becomes impossible for him to satisfy his genital needs, for such satisfaction would be accompanied by the loss of his penis. If the gratification desired in consequence of the love is to cost the child his penis, a conflict must arise between the narcissistic interest in this part of the body and the libidinal cathexis of the parental objects. Normally in this conflict the first of these forces triumphs; the child's Ego turns away from the Oedipus complex.' In other words, the child has to give up the desire for his mother, as otherwise he would lose his penis. Freud continues: 'The object cathexes are given up and replaced by identification. The authority of the father or the parents is introjected into the Ego and there forms the kernel of the Superego, which takes its severity from the father, perpetuates his prohibition against incest, and so ensures the Ego against a recurrence of the libidinal object-cathexis.

The libidinal trends belonging to the Oedipus complex are in part de-sexualised and sublimated, which probably happens with every transformation into identification; in part they are inhibited in their aim and change into affectionate feelings. The whole process, on the one hand, preserves the genital organ, wards off the danger of losing it, and, on the other hand, inhibits its functions. This process introduces the latency period which interrupts the child's sexual development.'

It is, however, not the image of the real father which is incorporated into his Ego to become the Superego but a fantasy image that derives its character from early infantile forms of incorporation. Enough evidence has been collected over the years of therapeutic work to convince us that behind fears of father's hostility is a deeper level of anxiety far more terrifying and bizarre in its imagery. For it is not the worried, somewhat jealous and sometimes angry father whom the boy harbours in his fantasies but a monster out to castrate and devour him. It is such fantasies which populate the boy's mind during the Oedipus complex, converting his love for his mother and his need for the father's protection into the nightmares which continue to permeate man's unconscious imagery right through his life.

While Freud considered castration anxiety to be induced primarily by parents and other grown-ups who in their own sexual prudery experienced anxiety in the child's sexual interest, his masturbation, sexual investigation and curiosity, nearly a century later there is a much more enlightened milieu, which he himself largely helped to create, and parents no longer impose the same restrictions and do not threaten to punish the child for its sexual activities. There is no doubt that the parental responses which Freud considered to be such decisive factors in the causation of castration anxiety were typical of nineteenth century puritanism and, more precisely, Victorian middle-class prudery, which no longer predominate in our time. However, we nevertheless find in many children of even the most enlightened parents, who are particularly concerned not to traumatise their offspring and to give them every possible freedom for sexual self-expression, a high degree of castration anxiety and a no less powerful Oedipus complex.

The far greater opportunity to observe children of the other sex, the cultivation of nudity among children and even parents should largely have eliminated the two main causes postulated by Freud of castration anxiety and the Oedipus complex. But the complex remains almost undiminished. How is one to understand this? It is my opinion that despite the genuine improvement in sexual attitudes and greater tolerance, unconscious anxieties remain with parents, and not merely on the genital level but especially at the pre-genital level, and that these anxieties are common in patriarchal cultures.

Below the public attitudes of permissiveness in sexual matters, there are many layers of usually unconscious fears and inhibitions which communicate themselves to the child. We face an odd paradox which Freud recognised, namely, that it is often among children of the mildest and least threatening fathers that the Oedipus complex is most strongly pronounced. How is it then that such fathers, who rarely punish the child and show it no hostility, produce often quite terrifying Superego images?

It is indeed a contemporary conundrum that the permissive environment, where parental authorities have become almost redundant and hardly dare to impose restrictions on the child's impulses, nevertheless produces profound Oedipal anxieties and Superego terrors in modern children. The hate against authority is undiminished, indeed it has emerged from its restraints among adolescents and manifests itself more violently than before, and the fantasies of a hostile Superego, represented by parents, school, the police, the state or any kind of authority, threaten to cause civic standards to break down.

It is, however, precisely the diminished power of the Superego and its representatives in society which removes the constraints upon the aggressive drives of infancy: the sadistic-destructive urges of the oral primacy, the attitudes of defiance and of aggressive spreading of filth on the anal level, and, on the narcissistic level, the manic types of self-assertion which lack any consideration for others or empathy with their feelings and sufferings. The very weakness of the father and his apparent indifference to the boy's need for male identification, his inability to help him to transform the pre-genital anxieties and aggressiveness into a mature mode of self-expression forces the boy to regress to the realm of infantilism. The pre-genital fixations are not overcome by the introjection of the mature male, and the boy remains, so to speak, a child dominated by his pre-genital conflicts. We can see that the projections which emerge in the Oedipus situations of patriarchy retain many aspects of earlier phases, many characteristics of the childhood of mankind and of the individual. (G. Frankl: *The Social History of the Unconscious*, Open Gate Press, 1989) Thus, the rivalry with the father during the Oedipal period retains aspects of oral-aggression and anal defiance, imposing upon him images of a devouring, cannibalistic monster (Baal, Gog and Magog), who wants to devour the boy, or the sinister figure with the knife (the surgeon, the scientist or the Jew), who threatens to castrate him, or the image of a father determined to make the boy feel dirty and degraded, and many other images according to the prevalent fixations retained by the boy since infancy.

Indeed, we can speak of a psychotic component of the Oedipal conflict which threatens to overwhelm the Ego, and can appreciate the inordinate efforts and complex ways which the human mind has to adopt in order to defend itself from the dangers of its infantile fantasies. We attempt to manipulate these images, trying to make their aggressive and threatening aspects more loving and kindly in order to transform our own aggressive and hostile urges into loving and sympathetic sentiments. We do this by adopting attitudes of submissiveness, gratitude and glorification of the father-figure, assuring him of his omnipotence and begging his forgiveness in prayer. To some extent we can say that these processes are a kind of biofeedback by which we can control our own emotions and sensations. In this respect the mastery of the Superego images is an attempt to master our own drives.

As we have seen, the formation of the Superego takes place by means of introjection-incorporation. The authority of the father is introjected into the Ego and there forms the kernel of the Superego. We no longer then have to confront the father as an external threat but allow him to exercise his will within our own mind, where he acts as the internal watchman, the guide or the punisher, as our conscience, the all-seeing eye, as if the boy were to say to the father: 'You see, I do not oppose you but accept you, and you can dominate my mind by being part of myself. I actually grant you power over me by making you part of myself, and you will be inside me as my conscience, as my guide and my strength, and therefore I will not set myself against you and you do not need to be angry with me.'

How then are the phantasmagoric and pathological Superego images produced in our minds, and how are these images, once produced in the mind, transferred to society?

We have observed the processes of introjection, splitting, projection and re-introjection as they occur from earliest childhood. The child incorporates the mother's libido, reacts to it with pleasure or anger, projects its own sensations and the images of those sensations upon her as the good or bad mother, and then introjects these images so that they become an internal presence of the mother in the shape of the maternal Superego. Superego formations thus occur from the earliest time in the development of an individual, and indeed every libidinal primacy develops its own Superego. The child who experiences oral-sadistic drives towards its mother's breast will project them onto the breast, and the breast will then appear as a dangerous object threatening to bite the child's mouth (sometimes in the form of fantasies of birds or birds' wings attacking the lips – *vide* Freud's study of Leonardo da Vinci – frequently leading to speech impediment), or, later, she will appear as a witch threatening to attack or devour the child.

All kinds of oral-cannibalistic urges and fantasies are projected upon the mother, and her image will exist inside the child as an aggressive and dangerous being, which the Ego tends to abreact, often in the form of hysteric spookery, temper tantrums, screaming attacks or – on the cultural level – in a great variety of fairy-tales representing the battle between the good fairy and the witch.

The unfulfilled and denied narcissistic urges produce not only a sense of isolation and separation anxiety but also aggression and anger towards the neglecting mother; we can call this the anger of the periphery. This anger is projected on to the mother, and the desire to be embraced and enveloped by her is transformed into images of an aggressive and dangerous embrace, very often in the form of spiders whose tentacles threaten to envelop the child and squash it, or jelly-like monsters about to swamp the child in a terrifying embrace, or a giant figure that is about to engulf the child.

On the positive side of the narcissistic Superego we find the so-called oceanic feeling symbolising the yearning for the eternal and unlimited embrace of the mother. The sensation of being enveloped and enfolded by her libido and the feeling of her security is symbolised by the limitless ocean, the mother of all life: 'Our souls have sight of that immortal sea that brought us hither' (Wordsworth, 'Intimations of Immortality'). This oceanic feeling, which Freud recognised as the source of all religions without being able to notice it in himself, is experienced differently on the Oedipal level in relation to the patriarchal father.

The anal primacies produce fantasies of playing with faeces and moulding them, and these fantasies become transformed under the impact of taboos into frightening images of filthy lavatories, dirty rooms full of rubbish, swamps and the fear of falling into them, the dirt sticking to our hands and the whole body, infecting the skin and poisoning it with its nasty substances and odours. It is easy to see that such dangers produce compulsive urges to cleanse and purify oneself, to avert these threats to one's narcissistic desire for a clean and attractive self-image. Above all, there will be frightening images of mother figures showing disgust towards the child and making it feel disgusting, dirty and ugly.

The frequent pre-conscious fantasies of over-full and dirty lavatories often cause great anxiety in children and panic upon having to visit the lavatory, and disturbances of bowel movement among grown-ups. The fear of being dirty can cause a variety of inferiority feelings, phobias about ugliness and unacceptability, whereas fantasies about filth and dirty substances clinging to one's skin can produce actual skin anxieties resulting in diseases such as psoriasis. The obsessive activities of cleansing and purification rituals are of course the most common defences against the threat of anal urges, and can acquire psychotic dimensions in individuals as well as in societies.

The Social Superego

1. THE TRANSFER FROM PSYCHE TO CULTURE

Let no one think that I am exaggerating the fantasies which accompany the Oedipus complex unless he has had occasion to listen to the outpourings of psychotics, the fantasies of neurotic people expressed during psychoanalysis or, indeed, he has paid attention to his own internal thought processes undiluted by the repressions imposed by the demands of civilisation. While such images of the Superego play a large role in the pre-conscious and unconscious mind of individuals, they are usually repressed and invisible, so to speak. However, they are amply manifest in the rituals, symbols and imagery of religions and mythologies. Who can fail to recognise some of these fantasies in the imagery of our own major religions or in the institutions of state, the army or 'the Party' with their absolute claims upon our lives and our thoughts, or in the Church as the body of Christ in which we dwell and find security and salvation, redemption from our sins and assurance of eternal life, or in the declamations of the true believer that by trusting in God he need not worry about where his next meal will come from, for 'God will provide'? Or we can look at the story of Jonah, who constantly argued with God, at his disobedience and his education: 'So they took up Jonah and

threw him into the sea; and the sea ceased from its raging ...
And the Lord appointed a great fish to swallow up Jonah; and
Jonah was in the belly of the fish three days and three nights.
Then Jonah prayed to the Lord his God from the belly of the fish,
saying: "I called to the Lord out of my distress, and he answered
me; out of the belly of the Sheol I cried, and thou didst hear my
voice. For thou didst cast me into the deep, into the heart of the
seas, and the flood was round about me; all thy waves and thy
billows passed over me ... When my soul fainted within me, I
remembered the Lord; and my prayer came to thee, into thy holy
temple. Those who pay regard to vain idols forsake their true
loyalty. But I with the voice of thanksgiving will sacrifice to thee;
what I have vowed I will pay. Deliverance belongs to the Lord!" '

And the soldier who goes to war for his king and country
forsakes his identity, his reason and his judgments, and gives
himself up to the order of the authorities appointed above him,
the generals and sergeants; he acts according to their will and
gives his life for the glory of the nation to whom he belongs. And
by his sacrifice, and by giving up his mind and his life he will
assure the perpetuation of his nation and the eternity of his God.
Who does not know of the claims of 'the Party' (Communist,
Trotskyist, terrorist), which demand the absorption of the individual's will and his reasoning into the received certainty of its
truth, and by transforming the individual into a means for its final
success allow him to partake in its glory? Or the rites of circum-
cision prevalent among primitive and advanced religions as a
symbol of man's covenant with his God, by which God assures
his salvation and promises never to forsake him? These are projections from the psychological processes which occur in the unconscious of the individual, particularly during the Oedipal
conflict, and become fixed, so to speak, in the public images of
cultures.

Another way of mastering the Oedipal conflicts is to divide
the paternal image into a loving and a destructive figure. As the
boy both loves and hates the father, wants him to disappear as
well as to be there in order to protect and guide him during his
maturation process, he projects these opposing feelings upon him
and, at the same time, separates these feelings into separate Super-

ego images. They will acquire the characteristics of the loving, protecting, omnipotent father, the creator of the world and the omniscient judge protecting the boy from destructive images, from the monsters, vampires, devils and gnomes which threaten to take possession of the boy's soul. Indeed, the Superego is split into a great number of different images, each symbolising emotions and fixations and their conflicts. The drama of the battle between them represents the conflicts of our emotions, of love and hate, submission and domination, of revenge and forgiveness, of purity and filth, and many others. The good demons, fairies and deities will know of our love and our good intentions and take our side against the evil in us and in the world around us.

We can clearly recognise four aspects of the Oedipal Superego:

1) there is the good God who loves and cherishes us, who makes us feel good and takes pleasure in our happiness;

2) there is the good God who gets angry when we do not act in a loving and generous manner but give way to our destructive impulses and generally deviate from our own innate goodness;

3) there is the permanently angry God who considers us to be innately sinful and unable to improve by our own effort. In this case we can only please him by our confessions of guilt, and by being prepared to sacrifice ourselves and the evil that is in us. In the second case both our bodies and our souls are considered basically sound but we have to perfect ourselves and our minds in order to please Him and avoid the temptations of evil. This can be considered the fundamental concept of Judaism. In the third case our bodies and souls are considered basically sinful, and we can only find salvation by identifying with the sacrifice of Christ and the mediation of the God-Mother who by her love transforms God into the all-loving being, as under 1);

4) there is the devil, the symbol of the sexual and anal urges, the evil-scheming Mephisto, the dirty devil who threatens the boy and tempts him away from his love for God. But there is also the good devil who shows us how to enjoy ourselves, who can dance and sing, make music and recite poetry – the perennial Rabelais and Picasso, the *élan vital*, Pan. He is the innocent devil who laughs and is curious, the begetter of the arts and sciences, the cheerful philosopher whom Nietzsche tried to emulate and

whom Russell admired. (G. Frankl: *The Failure of the Sexual Revolution*, Kahn & Averill, 1974) He is the impish spirit of Einstein which bursts forth in his music and in his funny poems.

These manifold representations of man's Oedipal and Superego symbols, their battles for supremacy in the pantheon of our souls are repeated in an almost endless variety of human myths and religious systems. We can also consider the manifold symbolic projections of human cultures as the transfer from personal-internal experiences to public experiences, which make a culture into an organism of collectively shared and understood images and provide common identity and catharsis for its members. Understood in this way we can say that man's cultural reality, his civilisation, represents a transfer of internally experienced complexes and fixations onto the outside world. The foundations for these collective projections are laid during the first puberty and are elaborated in the fantasy world of the latency period, the long period of sexual renunciation before the boy or girl is considered mature enough to procreate and take his or her place as a full member of the community.

2. CULTURE AND GRATIFICATION DELAY

In patriarchal cultures children have to repress their genital cravings (which are essentially incestuous), and their sexual development is interrupted by the onset of the latency period. It is interesting to notice that at this time, at about the age of six years, children start school and so begin the long task of acquiring the accumulated skills and customs of their culture. One can say that the latency period is a drawn-out period of gratification delay and enables the undischarged sexual urges to be converted into learning, skill acquisition and all kinds of disciplined activities. Discipline means the ability to restrain instinctual drives and make their gratification conditional on the performance of certain tasks. The execution of these tasks has to be examined and tested according to certain rules set up by the Superego representatives in society, the teachers, masters and judges. The great majority of communal activities, from work to sports, from study to the playing of games, are based upon rules which have to be accepted, for otherwise these activities would be meaningless. It is within the framework of rules that individual initiative can be exercised. The exercise of discipline, therefore, means that the individual is prepared to control the direct expression of instinctual drives and to transform them to satisfy the norms and rules demanded by the Superego and its social representatives.

One can say that a large quantum of genital libido which is blocked from expression regresses to pre-genital levels and re-activates them. For instance, learning to manipulate material things and transform them into recognisable images evokes the motivations of the anal libido with its pleasures of handling and manipulating material. The genital libido, subjected to a prolonged period of repression, flows into the reactivated pre-genital activities which are now methodically developed by the representatives of a culture, the father and father substitutes, teachers and all kinds of educationalists, in order to serve its interests and goals. In this way the development of the individual is brought to a higher level; he is enabled to acquire some of the skills and knowledge of his civilisation before he is ready to reproduce. But even then, at the onset of the second puberty, when after a delay of some seven or eight years he is physically capable of reproduction, he is still immature, culturally speaking, and has to delay further the full expression of his reproductive sexuality; he has to accumulate many more skills before he is considered mature by his culture.

Besides the evocation of the anal libido for the purpose of learning to handle things in preparation for productive work, we find many other forms of regression to the pre-genital libido in the service of maturation. The processes of learning and study reactivate the child's curiosity about life and the mysteries of birth and sex.

The urge to know things, how things relate to each other, what causes things to be the way they are, and to ask why and how things happen is basically motivated by sexual curiosity now directed to disciplined and planned enquiry. The urge to penetrate behind the surface of things and to find the deeper reality which underlines them represents also a reactivation of the oral-aggressive drives determined to penetrate through the barriers that surround the maternal libido. The drive to know, therefore, also

137

means to penetrate the secrets of nature and to remove her veils. There is no doubt that both curiosity as well as the penetrative urge play a large part in the drive for knowledge which re-emerges after the first puberty, and provide a powerful incentive for learning.

We devour books, we take in knowledge and make it our own, we not only want to penetrate to the hidden secrets which make things happen the way they do, we also want to incorporate the thoughts of our father and devour his knowledge. We not only want to open the veils which hide the secret of Mother Nature but also to make God, the Father, open one fold of his mantle after another to reveal to us the secret of his power and let us share some of his knowledge.

So we begin to ask all kinds of questions about God, of Heaven and Hell, where the world is going, where it comes from; we are ready to imitate the rituals and ceremonials which concern the higher existence beyond the confines of reality. We are ready to learn about magic and be awed by an Almighty Power who makes it all happen and upon whom our lives depend. The image of the universal father arouses immense fascination, for we suspect that he is a greater Father than our own and governs the big world which we are just beginning to discover.

However, in the reactivation of the pre-genital libido during the latency period, its characteristics and its conflicts will also re-emerge and will influence the progress of learning. For instance, if the anal retentive syndromes were pronounced during infancy the child will usually develop a talent for craftsmanship but may find it difficult to finish a product or endlessly delay its completion in case he is made to part with it. On the highest level of artistic perfection we find this syndrome in Leonardo da Vinci who failed to complete many of his greatest works and could not bear parting from them.

If fixation upon anal gratifications and the desire to handle faeces has not been sublimated and transferred to substitute materials, then the fear of being unclean and dirty will create anxiety, and guilt feelings will inhibit the child's ability to manipulate objects, and the acquisition of skills will be impaired. The child will become extremely awkward, drop objects or handle them wrongly as if afraid to touch them, and generally develop all kinds of work impediments. Anal fixations also tend to inhibit spontaneous responses and create an over-dependency on authoritative rules and on being told what to do. Persons dominated by such characteristics will demand permission from the Superego for any kind of action, will rely on exact instructions and need the reassurance of being given orders.

Pronounced oral-aggressive dispositions in childhood can, on the other hand, produce an intensified urge for study and acquisition of knowledge. Freud has spoken of the disposition to analyse things as an expression of the oral-aggressive urge to attack objects and take them to pieces. The satisfaction which this activity provides is re-enacted in the satisfaction of analysing whole chunks of knowledge into its component parts; it also gives the satisfaction of crushing dogmas or established prejudices. As an infant enjoys investigating little pieces by putting them in his mouth, biting or chewing them or rolling them around, or, later, taking things to pieces to see what is inside them, so the analytic mind gets immense satisfaction in observing the parts of the whole and the way they interact.

However, the exercise of discipline and submission to rules is a precondition for all types of learning. The modification of instinctual gratification into rule-governed activities and the acceptance of gratification delay is a dominant characteristic of the latency period, governed as it is by the repression of sexuality. The latency period can therefore be regarded as the civilising period *par excellence*. It enables the child to submit to the demands of the Superego, and its social representatives, and to the requirements of the maturation process in preparation for civilised adulthood. In his 'Essay on Criticism', Alexander Pope wrote: 'True ease in writing comes from art, not chance, as those move easiest who have learnt to dance.' When an admirer of the twelve-year-old Mozart expressed amazement about the natural ease of his piano playing, young Mozart very angrily retorted that it took him many years of hard practice to obtain his mastery.

However, there occur situations when the power of the Superego, in both its individual manifestations as well as its social representation, is significantly weakened and ceases to be convincing. Then the regressive processes, which occur during the latency period, are deprived of their direction and of the rules by which they become sublimated into learning and skill acquisition. Regression then remains regression, and infantile primacies once more acquire domination over the child. His ability to concentrate will be profoundly impaired; he will be unable to accept discipline; he will turn against study, school and the authorities which make demands upon him. A restless search for immediate gratification and dissociated behaviour will dominate his personality. He will defy the rules and his teachers, he will be unable to study, he will be bored, aggressive or withdrawn. And even the rules of sports and games will be unacceptable, making it frequently impossible for him to participate in games. Such traits can emerge more powerfully after the second puberty during adolescence in the form of hooliganism or delinquency and other patterns of defiance, and present a major problem in a culture which has lost the conviction and power to convince young people and guide them towards standards of civilised modes of behaviour. We shall return to this problem later.

3. SYMBOLS OF THE SUPEREGO

While, therefore, the transformation, i.e., sublimation of pregenital primacies into disciplined learning activities can be regarded as one of the important aspects of the maturation processes which occur during the latency period, these transformations are made possible by the goals and controls imposed by the Superego. While it is the fashion amongst libertarian and revolutionary philosophers to preach the abolition of the Superego, the abolition of authority and the breaking up of the shackles which men have forged around themselves, we have seen that human beings need a guide and a judge to evaluate their behaviour and to direct their thoughts.

It is true that the symbols of the Superego are practically all-encompassing, and there is no personality and no culture which is not controlled or directed by them. As Lacan has put it: 'Symbols, in fact, envelop the life of man in a network so total that they join together, before he comes into the world, those who are going to engender him "by flesh and blood"; so total that they bring to his birth, along with the gifts of the stars if not the gifts of the fairies, the shape of his destiny; so total that they give the words that will make him faithful or renegade, the law of the acts that will follow him right to the very place where he is not yet and even beyond his death.' (Jacques Lacan: 'The Function and Field of Speech and Language in Psychoanalysis', *Ecrits*)

Lacan the structuralist, however, takes the symbolic entities as given, as a structure of significations which operate in cultures and determine its human relationships and its patterns of behaviour. While it is true that men's cultural horizons are inhabited by symbols, the structuralists externalise those symbols and fail to emphasise the mental processes by which they are produced. According to Lacan, it has been clear since Freud's *Interpretation of Dreams* that man is inhabited by a law that he does not constitute but that constitutes him. He is 'inhabited by the signifier; he did not create it.'

It is true that the symbols of the Superego appear to be eternal and universal, uncaused but causative, timeless but operating within time. It is, however, the task of psychoanalysis not merely to describe these symbols and the manner in which they determine the character of individuals and of culture, but to show how they are formed by the psyche and projected outwards to appear as objective laws or divinities.

We have said that the Superego does not originate with the Oedipus complex but occurs during the earliest periods of the child's development, that every libidinous primacy produces its own Superego formation. While, therefore, the Oedipus complex produces a paternal Superego which is of fundamental importance to the culture of patriarchy, the seat of conscience and morality, it is, nevertheless, one of many Superego representations. The pregenital Superegos do not disappear but continue to operate unconsciously as a kind of underground movement of the psyche. The infantile fixations, pre-genital libido energies, which remain undischarged and continue to demand fulfilment, will spill over into later primacies and influence the character of the Oedipal Superego. Therefore the most important Superego formation retains

many components of earlier phases of development, many characteristics of the childhood of individuals projected upon Superego
images.

The oral primacies of the libido, with their sucking, swallowing, biting and attacking urges, produce symbolic representations
of all these activities. The oral-aggressive urges create a great
number of symbolic images such as distorted, angry faces showing their teeth and fangs and glaring eyes, figures in aggressive
and threatening postures with arms reaching out and grabbing with
their claws. In the large variety of such representations the primary organs of attack and the muscular impulses of aggression
are vividly expressed. On the primary level, that is to say, before
they become projected upon parental objects, these images are
usually seen in a dissociated manner, not as whole persons but
as part objects such as teeth and mouths, threatening eyes or
hands, etc. It is only when they are projected upon parental objects
that they become Superego symbols personified as witches and
demon figures. The open, incorporative, swallowing mouth of the
infant, on the other hand, finds symbolic representation in images
of caves in whose darkness objects and people disappear, bogs
which swallow up children, or whirlpools that threaten to suck
one into their unfathomable depths.

The sea, as the mouth and throat which draws men into its
abyss, is dramatically presented in Schiller's poem 'The Diver':

Wer wagt es, Rittersmann oder Knapp'
Zu tauchen in diesen Schlund?
Einen goldnen Becher werf' ich hinab,
Verschlungen schon hat ihn der schwarze Mund . . .

Who dares, soldiers and knights,
to dive into this chasm? (literally translated 'throat')
A golden cup I cast into it,
Already it has been swallowed by the dark mouth of the waters.

On his first attempt the heroic young man recovers the cup and
tells of his adventures in the horrors of the deep. But being

persuaded by the king's promise to give him his beautiful daughter for a wife, he dives again, never to emerge. This poem is also of great interest in that it shows how the symbols of the devouring mouth become associated, on the genital level, with the imagery of the devouring vagina. We shall visit this theme later.

In the imagery of Hieronymus Bosch, in particular his *Vision of Tondal*, a universe subjected to the terrible influences of mother and father is depicted by the mouth of a monstrous parent which represents the gates of hell. It is interesting to note that in patriarchal cultures the parent who devours the children is represented by the father, whereas in primitive Celtic and Finno-Ugric myths it is the mother-figure who devours her children. In Magyar mythology, the water-mother dwells in the rivers and lakes and lures people into the depths. There are a great many such water-mothers or water-sprites among those cultures, and if any of their people drank water in a strange village they would conjure away the possible malevolence of the water-goddess with this prayer 'Do not attack me, select someone else for your satisfaction,' often adding as an afterthought, 'preferably a Russian.'

In the pathology of individuals we find a multitude of psychosomatic disturbances relating to the incorporative and swallowing organs. One of the most common amongst them – anorexia nervosa – is, as I have mentioned before, related to the oral-aggressive type of incorporation, which becomes repressed and arouses severe constrictions in the throat and oesophagus, making swallowing painful and difficult. People suffering from this malady are obsessed by fantasies of aggressively distorted mouths threatening to attack and swallow them.

The anal stage of the libido produces fantasies and dreams of dirty, slippery floors, overfull lavatories, rooms and landscapes covered with faeces or mud. Animal figures representing faeces, such as scaly snakes, worms and gnomes of all kinds, will populate the fantasies and emerge as mythological figures. Gnomes represent straining defaecators, their bodies and faces expressing preoccupation with anal functions, their faces close to the bottom, so to speak, and their mind preoccupied with their dirt – the dirty, the unclean, the tortured people. The unfulfilled and unaccepted libido spills over into all their activities and converts them into faecal preoccupations, besmirching their hands and bodies, causing anxiety and confusion and frequently inhibiting productive work. Such inhibitions and confusions result from an inability to sublimate the anal drive by transforming faecal matter into more acceptable and interesting substances.

A young man of twenty-two suffered from an irresistible obsession to comb his hair, to make sure that it was perfectly groomed, that no hair was out of place. This obsession dominated practically every waking moment of his life, and all his attention was focused upon this preoccupation, making it impossible for him to engage in any activity or to relate to people without being acutely anxious that his hair might be out of order and constantly forced to groom it. At his work place or in a pub or on any social situation he had to absent himself and go to a lavatory or somewhere where he wasn't seen in order to put his hair in order. When he was with a girl he could think of nothing else but his anxiety and that he had to get away as quickly as he could to comb his hair. If he resisted this obsession he would feel unbearable anxiety. Needless to say he gave the impression of being acutely self-conscious, and was extremely sensitive that people would consider him very odd, would ridicule or reject him, to a point when it amounted to acute paranoia. While in fact he is a strikingly good-looking young man, he felt dirty, 'unkempt', and never properly acceptable. He was extremely meticulous, both in his behaviour as well as in his dress and general appearance, but was beset by the fear that he looked a mess and would spoil everything he did.

In analysis he became aware that he really wanted his hair to be wild and out of order, to be a wild person in complete contrast to his fastidious demeanour. When gradually he felt that he was permitted to be wild and to have his hair swept by the wind, he began to feel his pleasure in getting his hair in disarray and allowing himself to be a bit dishevelled. He then became aware that he wanted to touch things, and play with them and handle them and to make something with them, even though he was afraid that he would mess them all up. Under hypnosis he felt a strong, libidinous urge in his hands but became anxious and disturbed when he did not know what to do with his hands, what he wanted to touch, how to touch a person or to handle or manipulate any material object. I asked him to take some plasticine and mould and shape it into an apple. In his hypnosis he did this, and felt an enormous pleasure in making this apple and painting it red and yellow, making it look most attractive. I then told him to show it to a girl he knew, and she was very surprised and impressed that he could produce such a wonderful apple, and showed her pleasure. I then asked him to show it to his mother, and he spontaneously regressed to being a little boy showing this apple to his mother. She reacted in a kind of correct manner, and said that it was very attractive but remained cold and unexcited and distant. Indeed, she gave him the impression that he should not really have done it and rather suspected his motivation for presenting this apple to her. Gradually the patient discovered that really she was very embarrassed. Soon we were led back to the boy being on the pot and feeling the pleasure of defaecation and wanting to touch his faeces while he was looking at his mother with a kind of pride at what he had produced and wanting her response. But to his distress she did not respond, rather she remained aloof and appeared anxious, somewhat embarrassed and showed signs of disgust. The most important impression the boy gained was her embarrassment and not knowing how she should respond to his offering and his pride. I asked him how he reacted to her response, and he became aware that he himself became increasingly embarrassed and did not know what to do. The whole situation was very puzzling to him, and he wished he had nothing to do with it. He became tight, and wanted to hide himself or pretend he did not exist or show his mother anything at all, for what he had to show appeared embarrassing and disgusting.

This patient's urge to show his prowess as an anal producer was connected with a strong narcissistic urge to be admired and to be special, and the two libido primacies interacted. When he wanted to show his anal products to his mother in order to receive her attention and admiration, it was also his narcissistic self that demanded admiration, that wanted to be admirable and beautiful and special. His mother's rejection of his anal-narcissistic libido caused him to withdraw and to hide it. He saw her as being embarrassed and disgusted by his exposure of himself, he identified

145

with her and caused himself to be disgusted and embarrassed by his own desires. He felt himself to be disgusting and embarrassing, and he had constantly to rectify and undo his (disgusting) exhibitionistic desires by means of his obsessive acts. He felt himself dirty and had to clean himself at all times and make himself perfect.

Neurotic obsession and compulsive acts can be transferred to collective obsessionalism, by which they acquire social approval, as for instance in religious ceremonials and rituals. The obsessive ceremonials of undoing, i.e., overcoming the dominance of the unacceptable libido, apply both to the oral-aggressive as well as to the anal impulses, and they will frequently combine. For instance, the Jewish law of the kosher (kashrut) is concerned, in the first place, with the taboo upon biting the nipple during the act of sucking the milk. While you drink the milk you must not devour the flesh, you must not draw blood and mix it with the milk. So a believer has to go to great lengths to keep the two different activities separate. At the same time this ritual is also concerned with cleanliness. Laws concerning cleansing hands and person, as well as washing of cooking utensils, play a large role in Jewish ritual. On the oral-aggressive level, the taboo upon blood imposes rituals of killing animals in such a manner that blood is drained from the animal's body before it is fit for consumption. Not only has the milk to be separated from the flesh, but the flesh has to be separated from the blood, the blood being taboo as well as holy at the same time. Blood is reserved for God only, and in the animal sacrifices of the early Jews the blood of animals had to be given to God and was forbidden to humans. The art of sacrifice and the secret knowledge of its rules was the preserve of priests and made them holy people. The taboo on blood-letting created a profound defence against human blood-sacrifices among Jews, and set up moral injunctions against killing and the taking of human life long before such taboos emerged among other nations. In this respect we can see how the taboos imposed upon the oral-aggressive and anal urges have produced some of the most significant concepts of morality and hygiene.

In the chapter on the anal libido we have observed the symbolic transformation of excrement into a great variety of substitute objects such as earth, clay, sand, mud, and eventually that of gold and money. We have also seen how the narcissistic libido strives to finds its representations in such anal-projective objects as images of the self. Thus the anal and narcissistic libido merge and create externalised self-images in the manikin and in all kinds of precious objects. Moreover, the quest for immortality, the urge to preserve the narcissistic self from the ravages of time have led men to identify with indestructible objects. Stones, in particular, representing something that is whole and permanent, provide perfect images of identity which remain unchallenged by time.

Since earliest times men have collected stones and have apparently felt they contain living energy and soul. The ancient Germans, for instance, believed that the spirit of the dead continued to live in their tombstones. The custom of placing stones on graves may spring, as Jung observed, from the symbolic idea that something eternal of the dead person remains which can most fittingly be represented by a stone. The urge, which we find in practically all civilisations, to erect stone monuments to famous men or on the site of important events most probably stems from this belief. The stone that Jacob placed on the spot where he had his famous dream, or certain stones left by people on the tombs of local saints or heroes, show the nature of the human urge to express the desire for the continuity of the soul by a stone symbol. Many religious cults use a stone to signify a place of worship in which the Spirit of God resides. The holiest sanctuary of the Islamic world is the Kaaba, the black stone in Mecca to which all pious Moslems intend to make their pilgrimage.

While stones symbolise the substance and continuity of the self, gold, jewellery and money embody the narcissistic desire to attract attention and to be recognised. The sparkling, shining, shimmering qualities of gold and of precious stones arouse interest, a sense of wonder and admiration. He who has gold and jewellery and money will gain recognition, he will not be ignored by the world; he will be seen as somebody special – the centre of attention. The people who are favoured by the world are born with silver spoons in their mouths, they are the golden boys, the bright children and the people who shine amongst men. In gold and jewellery the anal and narcissistic libido merge and gain realisation of the infant's perception of its anal product – shiny, golden and wonderful representations of the self.

On a higher level of the narcissistic phase of the libido, when the concept of the self finds personalised representations, the image of the self appears as an important or gigantic superhuman being who embraces the whole cosmos. As, during the narcissistic primacy, the self is invested with large amounts of libido, it becomes the centre of the child's attention, and acquires a sense of omnipresence and omnipotence, of being the centre of the world, transcending the limitations of space and time. Its symbolic representations are of a gigantic human being who embraces and fills the whole cosmos. These images are the prototype of the manic self whose thoughts and desires are omnipotent and over-rule time and space, the laws of nature and the limitations of human beings. It is, therefore, not surprising that the figure of the 'cosmic man' appears in many myths and religious teachings.

In Western civilisation the images of the 'Cosmic man' have attached themselves to the symbolic figure of Adam, the first man. There is a Jewish legend that when God created Adam, he first gathered red, black, white and yellow dust from the four corners of the world, and thus Adam 'reached out from one end of the world to the other'. When he bent down, his head was in the east and his feet in the west. According to another Jewish tradition, the whole of mankind was contained in Adam from the beginning, which meant the soul of everybody who would ever be born. The soul of Adam, therefore, was 'like the wick of a lamp composed of innumerable strands'. In this symbol the idea of a total oneness of all human existence, beyond all individual units, is clearly expressed. (M.-L. von Franz: 'The Process of Individuation' from *Man and his Symbols*, ed. C. G. Jung)

In ancient Persia, the same original first man called Gayomart was depicted as a huge figure emitting light. When he died, every kind of metal sprang from his body, and from his soul came gold. His semen fell upon the earth, and from it came the first human couple in the form of two rhubarb shrubs. In the east, and in some gnostic circles in the west, people soon recognised that the cosmic man was more an inner psychic image than a concrete outer reality. According to Hindu tradition, for instance, he is something that lives within the individual human being and is the only part that is immortal. This inner Great Man redeems the individual by leading him out of creation and its sufferings back into his original sphere. In the symbolic myths of Old India, this figure is known as the Purusha, a name that simply means man or person. The Purusha lives within the heart of every individual and yet, at the same time, he fills the entire cosmos. In the West, the cosmic man has been identified to a great extent with Christ, and in the East with Krishna or with Buddha. In the Old Testament this same symbolic figure turns up as the Son of Man, and in Jewish mysticism he is called Adam Cadmon. Certain religious movements of late antiquity simply called him Anthropos. It is significant that Adam, as the cosmic figure, is punished by God for his manic ambitions, and through this punishment his mania is transformed into depression when he has to face reality. From being the Lord of Creation and God's special pride, the focus of His attention and the master of paradise, he was condemned, and God said to him: 'Because you have listened to your wife and have eaten from the tree which I forbade you, accursed shall be the ground on your account. With labour shall you win your food from it all the days of your life. It will grow thorns and thistles for you, none but wild plants for you to eat. You shall gain your bread by the sweat of your brow until you return to the ground; for from it you were taken. Dust you are, to dust you shall return.' The perfect statement of the punishment meted out to those maniacs whose narcissism transcends the boundaries of reality and challenge the Superego. The Superego revenges itself by making the Ego shrink into depression. The manic-narcissistic individual wants to annihilate the Superego and to take its place, whereas in the state of depression the Superego annihilates the Ego or at least punishes it severely.

When the child reaches the phallic primacy of the libido, the narcissistic symbols are to a great extent transferred to the genital, and it acquires an aspect of omnipotence. It becomes the centre of the child's attention and, in turn, the child imagines it to be the centre of attention of those who love him. Its narcissistic imagery, and the sensations of its powers, play a large role, not only in the fantasy life of children but in many myths as well as in the fabric of society. The feeling of the erect penis not only becomes the centre of the libidinous sensations absorbing the child's interest and attention, but finds symbolic expression in a wide range of artefacts. High towers and spires dominate the landscape as well as the city and symbolise the importance of churches and civic monuments. The child plays with swords and arrows, and he handles all kinds of elongated objects, which give erotic gratification and a sense of power. Tools and weapons acquire phallic significance, and the pleasure which their use provides reflects the excitement of the phallic libido. There is no boy who does not love to wield a sword or a spear or shoot an arrow, who does not want to play with trains and engines; there is no man who is not fascinated by motor cars – not only by the length of its bonnet but the whole body of the car and its potential speed that penetrates and overrides the barriers of distance – as well as by guns, rockets and missiles.

While the phallic symbol represents aggressive self-assertion, power and dominance, it is usually self-centred and relates to the community in a self-assertive manner. It conquers and penetrates the environment but does not merge with it. Thus the Renaissance merchants built towers to assert their status, and the height of their towers gave an indication of the power of their owner. The church steeple, while phallic, is meant to serve the community which surrounds it, gives it leadership and protection and symbolises its unity. It is indeed a symbol of God's penis which provides an enhanced self-image, a sense of belonging as well as spiritual identity of those who identify with it. The secular town hall and even the factory chimney reflect the civic virtues and productive ability of the community. The citizens of Sydney, for instance, were inordinately proud of a huge factory chimney which belched smoke close to the harbour bridge, for it symbolised their productive manliness. High-rise blocks, on the other hand, represent the phallic-narcissistic satisfaction of the engineer and his technology, which ignores the need of the community and forces its members to live in a state of isolation submitting only to the megalomania of technology. Indeed, the conflict between the phallic and the genital primacies, which play an important role in the development of personality, are reproduced in the cultural

setting. Whether a culture is dominated by genital, that is, productive, protective, caring and co-operative values, or whether it
is dominated by the values of self-assertion, aggression, competitive selfishness and manipulative exploitation depends largely
upon the achievement of genital primacy as the predominant form
of libidinous self-expression as distinct from a fixation upon the
phallic primacy.

The symbols of genitality express the sensation of merging
with another person, of breaking down Ego boundaries and barriers which separate one person from another. The sensations of
union, of giving oneself up fully to another without any reserves
are the most intense and exquisite experiences of pleasure given
to human beings. It is as if nature invested the most difficult act
which it demands of the individual for the purpose of reproduction, namely the giving up of the self and even the momentary
loss of self, with the greatest possible pleasure sensation and sense
of fulfilment. This self-giving and unreserved merging with another person is accompanied by mental images of union with the
universe, the merging with nature, the cosmos or God. And nature
becomes flooded with the sensations of the loved object to whom
one gives oneself and who receives one in a universal embrace.
This oceanic feeling is expressed by the mystical yearnings which
underlie the concepts of religion and the imaginings of poetry.
In the loss of the sense of self the Ego partakes in a wider union
with life itself, a sensation whose spiritual quality religions and
artistic creations attempt to recapture. The limitations both of
narcissism and of phallic assertiveness are transcended in the joy
of self-giving and merging with another person or, on the spiritual
level, with nature or the universe.

Just as the human infant experienced the pleasures of the breast
as a universal fulfilment, so man and woman once again experience the genital fusion as a universal event of fulfilment. Human
imagination has always found representations of sexual experiences in the images of nature. The earth which is opened by the
plough to receive the seed, to be embraced and nurtured by her
are part of our genital communion with another person, with
nature and with all that lives:

Freude, schöner Götterfunken,
Tochter aus Elysium,
Wir betreten Feuertrunken,
Himmlische, dein Heiligtum,
Deine Zauber binden wieder,
Was die Mode streng geteilt:
Alle Menschen werden Brüder,
Wo dein sanfter Flügel weilt.
Freude heisst die starke Feder
In der ewigen Natur.
Freude, Freude treibt die Räder
In der grossen Weltenuhr.
Blumen lockt sich aus den Keimen,
Sonnen aus dem Firmament,
Sphären rollt sich in den Räumen,
Die des Sehers Rohr nicht kennt.

Friedrich Schiller, *Ode to Joy*

But there are harsher sounds to be heard. When taboos are imposed by repressive cultures, when joy is tainted with the dread of sin and the wings of elation trimmed by the chains of bad conscience, and the expansive forces of life are blocked, then the soul of man regresses to infantile forms of self-expression. Then genitality once again becomes overwhelmed by phallic aggressiveness, the Ego which has experienced a measure of self-transcendence in the experience of joy and empathy with life becomes narcissistic once more, retreats behind its boundaries, and can only communicate by competition. Above all, the joys of the body become subjected to the restraints of fear, the muscles tense and the open embrace is transformed into aggressiveness. Sadism displaces love; attack becomes the only form of contact; instead of showing themselves joyfully to each other, men hide themselves and are unable to look into each other's eyes, only seeing their own sense of sin reflected in them. Then people become isolated from nature, they lose their empathy with life, and have to manipulate, attack and dominate nature and their fellow men.

The expansive lips that drink in the cosmic energy will become tense and hard, their yearning for pleasure and love will become a source of embarrassment, and the teeth will want to bite and attack in order to feel a sense of aliveness. Sado-masochistic primacies will come to dominate the libido and will constantly attempt to gain expression either in criminal behaviour or in madness, or will seek channels of discharge through sacrificial mythologies, religions and ideologies. The genital libido which is blocked from discharge creates anxiety which is bounded by muscular tensions, and these, in turn, produce rage and aggression, that is to say, the tensions can only be released by sadistic forms of self-expression, but they again have to be repressed by an authoritarian Superego. The patriarchal Superego, which produces aggressive urges, in turn has to repress them, and to do so assumes authoritarian powers. It justifies these powers by pointing to destructiveness as the essence of human nature, without, however, drawing attention to the fact that it is largely responsible for it.

It can be argued that without the repressions imposed by patriarchy and the blocking of libidinous gratification, the intense drama of its religions and the white flashes of genius would never have occurred. The question, however, remains whether patriarchy can provide sufficient sublimatory outlets for the instinctual energies which it has held in check, whether its cultural-spiritual achievements and satisfactions can provide discharge for the energies whose direct gratification it denies.

4. INITIATION RITUALS

We have seen that in matrilineal societies the incest taboo is, generally speaking, as powerful as in patriarchal societies. However, it is not enforced so much by the father as by the mother's brother, who becomes the representative of social authority. There is no doubt that in matrilineal cultures the mother comes to represent the Superego as well as the centre of love and protection. But we can say that the harsh aspects of the Superego which impose the taboos of incest are split off from the mother and projected upon her brother, and it is he who has to enforce those taboos. This frees the mother from the onus of having to reject the young boy's advances, and allows her to remain the object of affection and love. The actual father adopts the role of friend and helper, without much power over the son and without any sense of rivalry with him. In patriarchal cultures, on the other hand, the community of mature males claim authority and power over the women and children and the right of paternity. The son is regarded by the father as his heir and successor, it is through him that the father sees his possessions and his soul perpetuated. At the same time the son is his rival. We find therefore in patriarchy a battle being acted out on two fronts. First, the battle for succession. The husband wrests from his wife the right of paternity and the perpetuation of his totem through his offspring, who acquires his name, worships him as ancestor and secures the immortality of his soul. In the second place, the bonds between mother and child, and particularly between mother and son, have to be severed. As soon as he reaches sexual maturity the son must forgo his desire for mother. The libidinous bond between mother and son must be de-sexualised and the boy must be enabled to free himself from his erotic dependencies upon her. At the same time, some of the libido de-cathexed from the mother must be vested in the father for the purpose of identification and loyalty towards him. It is upon the success of these processes, which Freud called 'the resolution of the Oedipus complex', that the whole edifice of patriarchal culture rests.

These transformations, which must occur during the second puberty, can however draw upon deep layers of identification which have occurred during the latency period. Indeed, one can say that the identification with the father has been a dominant feature of the latency period but is overwhelmed by the renewed sexual attraction for the mother, which occurs once more during the second puberty. As the incestuous attractions are much more intense during the second puberty, the taboos against them become much more severe. The full force of father's authority has to be evoked in order to achieve repression. This time, however, the father has the full backing of society and culture behind him, as the transformation from incestuous to exogamous sexuality, the transformation from childhood to manhood, is not merely an individual matter concerning father and son but the concern of society. The whole of society is intent that the young man forgoes his mother fixation and achieves identification with the males. Indeed, one might say that with every transformation of puberty the battle between mother and father domination, matriarchy and patriarchy, is re-enacted, and society must ensure that the young male becomes a member of its culture and affirms it in his own life. By becoming a member of the male group, the boy becomes a fully-fledged member of society, and only then is he considered capable of establishing sexual relationships with a woman, a woman, moreover, who is clearly exogamous, a member of another family or another tribe. To ensure this transformation and imprint it upon the mind of each young man, all patriarchal cultures entertain initiation rites at the age of thirteen or thereabouts, when the boy's transformation from child to man is enacted.

These rites are celebrated by a variety of symbolic actions whose meanings depend upon the psycho-cultural constellation of the group and are deeply felt and understood by its members. In these rites the boy has to submit himself to the will and powers of the males, and in so doing show his readiness to accept their authority. By means of the initiation tests the boy becomes aware of his own strength and weaknesses, his limitations and capacity of playing a full role as a member of his community; he acquires a valid Ego consciousness which equips him for the tasks which life demands of him. This readiness to exchange the life of childhood for that of maturity and to submit to the social Superego also has masochistic connotations. For the initiation is also a test of his readiness to submit himself to punishment and to bear pain. By being ready to be punished for his incestuous desires and, above all, his Oedipal wishes, he takes the side of the grown-ups against his own infantile Ego. The sado-masochistic aspects of initiation, the wide range of mutilations, injuries and pains which the boy has to undergo without complaint, prove that he is on the side of the Superego, against his own Oedipal wishes which threaten the authority of the elders.

Among the most interesting ceremonial rites still widespread in primitive cultures is the symbolisation of rebirth. After the usual tests of courage and endurance, followed by singing and dancing in the evening, the dancers form a circle, and suddenly the mother appears in the middle of the circle and by means of a ritualised sleight of hand the boy emerges from between her legs and goes through the symbolic motions of being born. The mother gives birth to the boy again, but this time she hands him to the males who take charge of him, and they form a new dance in which the boy participates. The mother has now relinquished the boy to the males, and from now on he belongs to their world. He is reborn as a man once he has shown the courage and capacity to withstand pain and is ready to relinquish the ties of childhood. It is interesting that among Australian Aborigines and many tribes of Southern America grown men frequently submit themselves to renewed initiation ceremonies in order to ensure their continued identification with the tribe and its godhead.

The transformation from childhood to adulthood, from the world of the mother to the world of the father, is rarely entirely successful, however much parents and cultures are determined to make it so. The fantasies of childhood do not disappear entirely but continue in the underground of the unconscious, challenging the claims of maturity and the demands of society, and forever straining to defy the Superego. The child in the man asserts itself in the dreams and memories of childhood, dominated by the illusion of an all-bountiful and all-loving mother who does not require the tests of courage and the evidence of success but who loves without condition. On the other hand, images of the mother forsaken by the boy and defeated by the man, the *mater dolorosa*, create feelings of sweet melancholy and a loyalty to her which often brings forth a resolution to defy maturity and the demands of the male world and to fight for her in order to avenge her. The heroic fantasies often remain unstilled and undefeated by the initiation, and continue to exult in romantic images of rebellion and conquest. And, indeed, the mother is often reluctant to hand her son over to the fathers.

If the son cannot relinquish his libidinous ties to his mother, then his Oedipus complex will remain unresolved; he will enter the male world in a state of defiance as well as guilt, he will be plagued by anxiety and will feel himself an outsider, unwanted, rejected and isolated from society.

I have mentioned some of the difficulties of the socialisation process during the first puberty if the boy cannot achieve a measure of identification with the father. The problem becomes even more acute during and after the second puberty when the boy encounters the social representatives of paternal authority. I shall illustrate this problem by the case of a young man, which I believe is typical of a great number of young people in our time.

Mr L. B. was sixteen when he was first brought to me. He could not get up in the morning, and would stay in bed till three or four in the afternoon. He was unable to pursue his school work, being absent from class more often than not, and failed all his exams. He was actually a rather bright young man with artistic potentials, and if engaged in an intelligent discussion could be alert and enthusiastic. For most of the time, however, he was morose, cynical, defiant and depressed. His mother tried everything she could to encourage him to get up to go to school, to work and show some sense of responsibility for his development, but without avail. His parents separated when he was twelve, and his relationship to his father was very ambiguous. He felt a deep sense of loss, a continued feeling of shock that his father had left him, and at the same time he was angry and outraged. His love and need for him turned into hatred and he gained some satisfaction in denigrating father and in regarding him as a failure. His own disappointment was projected on the father, and he saw him as a disappointing man. In turn, he introjected this image of the useless and disappointing father and felt himself a disappointment and a failure. The loss of his father provoked a regression to his infantile oral-aggressive libido, which was very pronounced and found gratification in the castration, emasculation of his father and of himself.

He felt the world did not accept him, and therefore there was no good reason for him to accept the world with its rules and demands for effort and discipline. His only satisfaction lay in denigrating his father and all father-figures and in denigrating himself as a man. He had no vision of a goal which he could expect to achieve, and any disappointment was evidence for the futility and hopelessness of all endeavour. He suffered from an acute sense of inadequacy, of being underdeveloped as a man and his relationships with girls were bedevilled by fears that his penis was too small and he would be unable to please them. In fact he felt himself as a helpless, angry child who could not take his place in the world of men. He thus withdrew into depression, passivity and sleep, and once this attitude came to dominate the Ego it became an involuntary reflex difficult to break.

This syndrome of passivity, defiance of rules and withdrawal from manhood, an obsession with manic-narcissistic fantasies which appear to be constantly thwarted, is a widespread malaise among young men, particularly of the middle-classes, where the fathers appear distant, uninterested, devoid of empathy with their sons, and have lost their significance as a model and guide. The process of introjection is severely impeded and leaves many teenagers bereft of a sense of purpose.

Let us return to the 'normal' process of maturation in patriarchal cultures and its development from the rites of initiation. In the 'rebirth', the boy introjects both the taboos as well as the imperatives and duties of the grown-up males. He will repress his incestuous desires, and a large part of his libido is directed to the fathers and other boys and young men. (We can see this process in the high cultures of patriarchy, as for instance in the flowering of the arts and of the intellect during the sixth and fifth centuries BC in Athens, and also in the somewhat different manifestations of religious passion during the Early Middle Ages.) The libido transferred to the group of males is devoted to the exploration of the wonders of nature, to learning its secrets, to glorifying and worshipping the gods, and, on the more mundane level, acquiring the skills of a practical kind; they form into gangs to engage in sports and all kinds of adventure, and find collective discharge for their aggression by games of group or tribal warfare, and provide excellent material for the army.

These sublimatory activities are encouraged by the establishment as they promote the highly prized virtues of discipline, courage and perseverance. The development of these qualities trains the young male to accept the gratification delay which is fundamental to the existence of patriarchal civilisations. It is the age of the long-houses, schools, colleges, youth clubs and all kinds of youth organisations or gangs to which the boy transfers his allegiance and which become the centre for his identification. While in matriarchal cultures young people spend the years of early adolescence in bisexual communities – the long-houses being mixed – preparing for social maturity which includes the practice and experience of sexual relationships, in patriarchy the sexes are segregated and sexuality is repressed. It is this repression of the sexual drive precisely at the time when it is most powerful which creates the hot-house atmosphere of cultural sublimation, which has caused the unparalleled outburst of religious and intellectual activities, the explosive growth of civilisation as well as its conflicts and sufferings.

But despite the intensity of sublimatory activities, the narcissistic and sexual drives continue to press their claims, and being thwarted produce aggressive urges directed against the denying culture. Fantasies of destroying the school, the church, the college, the factories or offices in which they work or the towns in which they live can be so powerful that it becomes difficult for some adolescents to study and so submit to the discipline necessary to incorporate the knowledge of their culture. I have mentioned such situations in the context of the first puberty, and they emerge once again, and even more powerfully, during and after the second puberty. In order to cope with the important residue of unsublimated aggression, the Superego employs further psychic mechanisms in order to deflect the danger from itself.

Patriarchal Paranoia

1. OUR GOD AND THEIR GOD

We have seen that the parental images which the child introjects so that they operate within the Ego as the Superego – the internal watchman observing, guiding and threatening the Ego – are by no means a realistic representation of the parents. They usually assume highly distorted and bizarre forms, and act within the Ego with far more severity than the actual parents. The study of these distortions is perhaps one of the most important tasks of psychoanalysis as they are at the root not only of many personality disturbances but also of the irrationality of cultures; they provide the driving force for the aggressive, paranoid and generally morbid behaviour of societies. Such a study is also a necessary corrective for the widely held concept of the Superego as the internal representation of social norms, summed up by Durkheim's dictum: 'Not only does every individual exist in society but society exists in every individual.' Durkheim stressed that the individual, as a member of society, is not wholly free to make his own decisions but is constrained to accept the orientations common to the society of which he is a member. He tended to identify society, as such, with a system of moral norms, and stated explicitly that society exists only in the minds of individuals.

Talcott Parsons, the doyen of American sociologists, considered Durkheim's concept to be at the centre of a process of congruence between sociological thinking and Freud's discovery of the internalisation of moral values as it links in a most dramatic way fundamental ideas of sociology with the depth psychology of individuals. However, the process of internalisation is seen by Parsons, and most other sociologists, as being relatively straightforward, namely, the internalisation of existing social norms. The norms and imperatives of society, in this view, are seen to operate inside the Ego and direct the behaviour of individuals. Even Wilhelm Reich and Erich Fromm in their early studies on the relationship between psychoanalysis and society considered the structure of society, its economic foundations and its social relationships as objectively given, and held that the conflict between the norms of society represented by the Superego and the demands of the instincts were the proper field for psychoanalysis. They repeatedly emphasised that the psychological processes of man in society and, in particular, the unconscious structures are themselves the product of objective, historical, socio-economic processes. It is still a widely-held fallacy that we introject the social norms and that it is the function of the Superego to provide an internal representation of external reality. This view, based on a kind of naive realism which considers the mind as a photographic plate reflecting reality, has to be corrected, for it has contributed much to our helpless dependency upon our man-made environment. It is not the actual reality which is taken inside the Ego in the process of Superego formation but a highly distorted and often quite fantastic image of reality. Indeed, it is of considerable importance to recognise that our Superego represents not so much a realistic image of the world but a representation of our sexual and aggressive fantasies superimposed upon the real environment.

It is precisely these distorted Superego images which shape our concept of social reality and motivate our behaviour. The very structure of society is fashioned by our fantasies; they are projected upon society, and society in turn embodies these fantasies. We tend to create a social structure which makes our fears come true, makes our apprehensions reality, in the same way as neurotic individuals project their infantile fears and fantasies upon the environment and produce situations in reality which reflect and reinforce their fears. We have observed the processes of introjection, projection, splitting and re-introjection as they occur from earliest childhood, and can observe them on the level of male Superego formation.

With the onset of heterosexual genitality, the pre-genital fantasies give way to a more personal image of the Superego. However, this image will still retain pre-genital components as no one is actually free of pre-genital fixations. The aggressive urges aroused by the Oedipal rivalry will contain many aspects of the oral-cannibalistic libido. For instance, processes of incorporation which play a large role in the identification with father during the genital period frequently turn into aggressive-destructive-devouring fantasies. Just as oral-incorporation can be dominated by the expansive-sucking libido or by aggressive-incorporation so the processes of identification with the father can be of a loving or an aggressive-destructive kind – the good incorporation or the bad incorporation. The former creates images of the father who wants to be accepted by his sons and gives himself to them so that they can acquire his powers and his skills, to learn from him and perpetuate his name; and on the other hand there can be the urge to mutilate or destroy the father, producing images of the devouring, mutilating and castrating father. Oral aggression, which has previously been directed towards the mother and made her into a witch, is now directed towards the father and makes him into a threatening monster. But this monster is in constant conflict with the loving and protecting father. The two images become split off from each other and fight for dominance, and the manner in which they are split and the drama of their struggle characterises the Oedipal conflicts.

It is easy to see that the need to preserve the image of the good father necessitates the splitting-off of his aggressive and pre-genital aspects and their projection them upon alien godheads. Our father who loves us must be protected from the father of the other tribe who threatens to destroy us. Thus the battle between the good and the bad father, the conflict between the impulses of love and hate is transformed into a conflict between the own and the other tribe. But in the same way as the repressed sexual and aggressive energies constantly press for entry into consciousness and thus become a threat to the Ego and a source of anxiety, so the alien tribes and their gods, upon whom we have projected our own repressed urges, represent a constant threat to our tribe and to our God. The Superego then has to be protected from the attacks of the 'others', it has to be glorified and affirmed, made more and more powerful and defended against the enemy. And all the spiritual powers, the powers of the will and of the faith, as well as the material powers at the command of a civilisation, all the weapons and arms provided by technology must be devoted to this task, no matter whether a civilisation calls itself scientific or theocratic or anything else. For in the same way as the repressed Id impulses attempt to gain access to the Ego and threaten to break through its defences, so the enemy Superego representing those Id impulses will constantly strive to penetrate the defences of the tribe or the nation and attempt to take possession of its soul and its territory. The tribe will, therefore, constantly feel threatened by the enemy and inevitably become paranoid. This 'tribal paranoia' is a universal condition of patriarchy.

Just as the sons have to defend the father and his representatives on earth, the ruler, the king or the party against the enemy without, so they have to defend God the Father against the enemies within, the sinful thoughts and the evil that resides in the soul: 'I acknowledge my transgressions and my sin is ever before me' (*Psalm* 51,3). We appeal to the omnipotent being to release us from our guilt and our wickedness, and we glorify him and sacrifice ourselves to him that he should be pleased and convinced of our repentance: 'Hide thy face from my sins and blot out all my iniquities' (*Psalm* 51,9); 'To the Lord our God belong mercies and forgiveness, though we have rebelled against him' (*Daniel* 9, 9); 'O Lord, correct me, but with judgment; not in thine anger, lest thou bring me to nothing' (*Jeremiah* 10,24); 'Our Father which art in Heaven, hallowed be thy name. Thy kingdom come. Thy will be done in earth as it is in heaven. Give us this day our daily bread. And forgive us our trespasses, as we forgive them that trespass against us. And lead us not into temptation; but deliver us from evil: for thine is the Kingdom, the power, and the glory, for ever and ever. Amen' (*The Lord's Prayer*); 'Dearly beloved brethren, the scripture moveth us in sundry places to acknowledge and confess our manifold sins and wickedness; and that we should not dissemble nor cloke them before the face of Almighty God our heavenly Father; but confess them with an humble, lowly, penitent and obedient heart; to the end that we may obtain forgiveness of the same, by his infinite goodness and mercy.' (All these prayers are quoted from the *Book of Common Prayer* of the Church of England.)

But it is not enough for us patriarchal sinners to beg God's forgiveness in prayer: we have to defend him from the external enemy and take up arms against the heathen, the non-believers, who are eternally determined to destroy him and his representatives on earth. The unity of the cross and the sword, submission to God and unbending strength in face of the enemy are the dual characteristics to which patriarchal man aspires as the highest virtue and the undeniable duty. Of course, there are an enormous variety of totems and gods, tribes and nations, religions and ideologies. They all represent the same fundamental duality: patriot and revolutionary, puritan and libertarian, rebel and disciplinarian, all have their gods whom they worship and enemies whom they have to fight.

It is hardly necessary in our time to provide evidence for this schizophrenic compulsion, for it dominates all too visibly our social and political life. But I cannot resist giving just a few examples of the reality of the arms race and contemporary men's readiness to engage in unparalleled destruction in pursuit of their patriarchal paranoia. 'It is generally assumed that the most devastating war instrument known to man in our time is the hydrogen bomb. But a secret briefing of Congressmen by the Army in 1969 revealed that the U.S. stockpile of nerve gas can kill the 3.4 billion people on earth many times over. One estimate given by an army official was that there was enough to destroy no less than 100 billion people, thirty times the planet's population.' (*Chicago Sunday Times*, March 5th, 1969). Associated Press reports: 'In 1960 the nation has spent 2.5 billion dollars on gases and germs, and some 5,000 technicians and scientists are engaged in testing and developing poisoned chemicals, some of which are odourless, tasteless, and invisible and can kill a human being in a matter of seconds.'

From 1946 to 1967, according to the statistics of Senator J. William Fulbright, 'the Federal Government spent 904 billion dollars or 57% of its budget for military power and only 96 billion or 6.08% for social functions, such as education, health, labour and welfare programmes, housing and community developments. Both the public and Congress rubber-stamped an arsenal of horror that began with the 20 kilotonne Hiroshima atom bomb and escalated to a stockpile of multi-megaton hydrogen bombs equivalent to billions of tonnes each; that began with a modest bomber plane of limited range and escalated to inter-continental bombers, then unmanned missiles, and finally multi-weapon missiles independently targeted; that began with a capacity to kill a few million people and grew in a single generation with hydrogen bombs, missiles and chemical and biological weapons to a capacity to kill all living things on this planet dozens of times over.' (Sidney Lens: *The Military Industrial Complex*, Kahn & Averill, 1970)

Since then production of inter-continental missiles with independently targeted warheads, strategic missiles and laser-directed death rays, as well as chemical weapons, has multiplied, and the amounts of money spent on them increased accordingly. Those states who can least afford it are seeking to advance their military technology and production quite spectacularly, and we saw in the days of the Soviet Union that their spending on 'defence' took a much larger proportion of their gross national product than the amount spent by the Americans in proportion to their overall production.

What then is the nature of the enemy who compels nations to produce weapons of destruction which are capable now of completely destroying the planet? More precisely, what is the psychic image of the enemy who terrifies nations and makes them sacrifice their citizens to the slaughter of wars? What is the nature of the fantasies which makes nations afraid of each other and clouds the lives of men with fearful apprehension of the next bloodshed? One of the most deep-seated characteristics of the paranoid fantasy of the enemy is that he would threaten to take the land of one's nation, slay the king and tyrannise its people.

He would destroy the Superego and replace it with an alien Superego. The enemy would take over the home, kill the father and take the mother for his wife, abuse her sexually, maltreat the children and force them to submit to him. He would rob the mother of her husband and the children of their father, deprive them of everything they love, and bring his own children into the house and treat them as favourites.

This rudimentary scenario of patriarchal paranoia reflects the boy's own unconscious desire to kill the father, to chase him out and humiliate him and take the mother for his wife, become the head of the house, the mother's favourite and superior over his brothers and sisters. The primeval Oedipal wish is projected outwards on to a powerful stranger who then enacts the boy's desire, the perennial robber, the alien king, who breaks into the home and takes possession. He represents the boy who wants to invade the parents' bedroom and climb into the parents' bed and possess mother. There is no need to point out the differences between bed, bedroom, house, city or nation, but in the unconscious they are interlaced symbols. The boy crawls under the blanket to enact the infantile union between himself and his mother, and at the same time to keep out the hostile forces lurking in the room. The bedroom can be a territory in which the enemy is lurking, threatening and invading the bed, the house inhabited by enemies threatening to invade the bedroom, a community a danger to the house, a city a danger to the community, the country hostile to the city, the world a threat to the country, the earth populated by aliens and dangerous foreigners, and the cosmos a constant threat to the earth – the oasis of life in a lifeless universe. Outside is death – Thanatos; inside is life – Eros, that needs to be protected. When a Frenchman finds himself in America he becomes aware of himself as a European, and when he goes to Russia he becomes aware of himself as a member of Western society, and when in Africa he feels himself as a representative of modern civilisation which includes Europe, America and Russia.

When boys leave the maternal home and venture into the world, the world of adventure, promise and danger, they form gangs in order to replace the father-dominated family group. The new community will quickly re-establish the sense of 'us and them'; they will play-act the dangers of enemy groups and pretend to be threatened by 'the others', and will wage gang warfares so as to defend the new group Superego against the perennial enemy. And as boys grow up they become members of a multitude of tribes which interrelate in a hierarchic order, from the gang of adolescents, football gangs, racial gangs, university, trade union, business concerns, to political party, church and nation. All these are experienced as tribal units subordinated to the even larger unit of Western civilisation, culminating in the consciousness of humanity. But the ideals of humanity, the dreams of progress and of religion are constantly defeated by the ancient powers of tribal compulsions which refuse to relinquish their hold over the minds of men. The adolescent gangs give way to the larger tribes of church, political party and state, and they become the supreme claimants for tribal loyalty. Indeed, they appropriate the ideals of humanity and claim to be their supreme representative. Communist parties and nations consider themselves to be the representatives of the brotherhood of man, possessing the key to its ultimate realisation, while the capitalist nations claim to be the defenders of freedom and humanity. Thus the ideals of the perfect society become an instrument of propaganda serving the interests of our own nation, our own party or our own race, even our own God, constantly being thwarted by the 'others'. The destructive and perverse side of 'human nature' which we have repressed in ourselves continues to be in control among the 'others', dominating their lives and making them not only inferior but dangerous to ourselves, to our culture, race, religion, etc. They represent the return of the repressed which constantly challenges our defences.

This fearful challenge of the unconscious represented by the other tribe makes people who teach tolerance intolerant, who preach the ideals of humanity inhuman towards the outsider, who uphold the purity of their race determined to besmirch the others and to eliminate them from the world. Indeed, one might say that all the collective aspirations for perfection hide their own imperfections and recognise them with distaste and horror in the 'others'.

2. PARANOID PSYCHOPATHY: NAZISM

Hitler maintained that the Jews were poisoning the blood and soul of the Aryan race. For him, the Aryans were the epitome of everything that is superior and pure and had to be defended against the enemy who represented everything that was impure and infectious. He considered himself to be the chosen individual to save his people from the contaminating influence of the Jews and to resurrect the true soul of Germany. The Jews were only one of the foreign races who threatened the German people, albeit the most dangerous. The threat of the Capitalist-Bolshevik-Jewish world conspiracy, robbing the German nation of the fruits of its labour and poisoning its economy with their international financial manipulations, had to be liquidated.

But the Jews represented a rather special category of enemy transmitted down the centuries by Christian indoctrination. They are the original father murderers, the nation of sinners eternally condemned for their act of deicide. This nation of sinners, however, is everywhere, its tentacles are spread across the world, manipulating the nations and threatening to destroy them. On this people, the Jews, Western man has projected his own pre-genital and repressed fantasies, the rapacious aggressiveness and greed of the oral-sadistic libido, the narcissistic image of the universal self which fills the Earth from one end to the other, the anal projections of filth and poison, the seducer of respectable women and, above all, the Oedipal sin of father murder. No wonder then that they have proven to be the ideal object of hatred which caused not only Germany but much of Europe to forget all rational consideration and all moral compassion.

Instead of begging forgiveness from the Jews for the persecutions perpetrated on them for two thousand years, which hardly left a generation of Jews unscathed by mass murder, when whole communities were exterminated and others subjected to torture and insult and made into victims of a lie that was propagated incessantly from all Christian pulpits, Christians at best, and in their most charitable mood, were prepared to forgive the Jews.

The Christian image of the Jew bears witness to the fantasies

of the evil and destructive adversary, the embodiment of the paranoid imagination of patriarchal man. It will be of interest here
just to give a few historical examples to show that this is not just
a neurotic quirk in men's minds, not merely a myth but a very
real aspect of social existence, a madness that became reality.

The fantasy of the Jews as a brotherhood of evil was first
conceived between the second and fourth centuries, and seven to
eight centuries later in Western Europe it developed into a coherent and terrifying demonology. From the twelfth century onwards
Jews were seen as a conspiracy of sorcerers working on orders
from Satan for the spiritual and physical ruination of Christendom.
This was the period when Jews began to be massacred on charges
of killing Christian children, of torturing the consecrated wafer,
of poisoning wells. (Norman Cohn: *Warrant for Genocide*, Harper
& Row)

There is no doubt that the collective fantasy of the Jews is the
most glaring and unequivocal expression of the Oedipal conflict,
insofar as they have come to embody in the myths of Christianity
the vengeful father-figure threatening to castrate or poison the son.
These fantasies about the Jews are of particular interest as they
have occupied a parental relationship to Christianity. As such they
became the representatives of the bad parental images, the incarnation of ruthless, cruel power, utterly untempered by love or
concern. From the Middle Ages onwards they appear in popular
art as extremely old men who are also devils, more particularly,
old men who unsuccessfully hide their devilish nature, creatures
with enormous beards, with expressions of terrible cruelty, often
with horns, and tails just visible. One only has to look at any
medieval picture illustrating a ritual murder story to recognise the
unconscious content of the fantasy: a small boy – it is, significantly, always a boy – is surrounded by a group of old men who
are torturing and castrating him and drawing off and collecting
his blood. The same unconscious content is clearly recognisable
in the other, constantly recurring accusation which was of torturing the consecrated wafer. Here too the illustrations show bearded
Jews attacking the wafer with nails and pincers, and as though
to uncover the true meaning of these stories we are sometimes

told not only that the host gushed blood but that at the height of the torture Christ appeared in the wafer as a small child, bleeding and weeping.

While the oldest and most terrible charge held against the Jews is that of deicide, we find that at the same time the Christians identify themselves with the young son who suffers the most cruel punishment from the angry and vengeful father. For Christians, the crucified Christ has the significance much more of a son than that of a father. If, therefore, as is constantly asserted in Christian teaching, the Jews are collectively guilty of the death of Christ, they are both parricides as well as slayers of the son and, at the same time, gain new strength by drinking his blood and castrating him. And nobody who has ever watched a passion play can doubt for a moment that that is how medieval people really did interpret the Jewish part in the crucifixion. The Jew had the image of a father killer imposed upon him, and at the same time he represents the bad father who in his rage sets out to destroy and annihilate the sons. The Christians identify themselves with the sons, with the young life emerging from the tyranny of the old, and then re-enact the primal crime, the father murder, by the torture and slaying of the Jew. There can be little doubt that the enormous popularity of Christianity has its roots in the justification it provides for the cathartic re-enaction of the Oedipal fantasy by presenting the Jew as the evil father-figure who has denied the Father in Heaven and killed his Son, his incarnation on earth, and thereby is guilty of deicide. He is the outlaw, the embodiment of the evil and corrupt father, envious of the sons who are loyal to the Almighty Father in Heaven and receive His blessing.

The Jews, therefore, deserve to be maligned, and their destruction is a virtuous and justified act of parricide.

E. H. Erikson considered Hitler to be an adolescent who never even aspired to become a father in any connotation, nor, for that matter, a Kaiser, a president. He is the Führer, the leader of a group of brothers who determined to kill and replace the father. He is a gang leader who keeps the boys together by demanding their admiration and by shrewdly involving them in crimes from which there is no way back. And the central crimes are those performed against the bad father incarnated in the Jew. But not only is the Jew seen as the old terrifying father with a knife, intent upon revenging himself upon the boy, but he is also the poisoner, he himself is a sort of poison.

This fantasy took shape at the same time as the fantasy of ritual murder. The first occasion when the disappearance of a young boy was attributed to Jewish blood lust was in 1144; the first time that Jews were burnt for plotting to poison the Christian population was in 1161. By the fourteenth century such accusations were commonplace. In France in 1321 it was reported that the Jews were employing lepers to poison all the wells in Christendom. At the time of the Black Death in 1349 it was widely believed that the Jews had caused the plague by poisoning the wells with a mixture of Christian flesh, hearts and blood obtained by ritual murder, and spiders, frogs and lizards. On that occasion some 300 Jewish communities in Germany, France and Spain were exterminated. Martin Luther, in his later years, was expressing the general view when he wrote: 'If the Jews could kill us, they would gladly do so, ay, and often do it, especially those who profess to be physicians. They know all that is known about medicine in Germany; they can give poison to a man of which he will die in an hour or in ten or twenty years; they thoroughly understand this art.'

The 'Protocols of the Elders of Zion' accuse the Jews not only of giving Gentiles poisonous drinks to undermine the physique of Gentiles but actually of inoculating Gentiles with disease. In Nazi propaganda this idea is carried to the point where the Jews were habitually called the 'world poisoners', and were even equated with bacteria. Norman Cohn has pointed out: 'To imagine that the Jews have poisoned the water supply or are corrupting people's blood is to ascribe to them truly uncanny powers. And it is likely that when anti-Semites kill not only Jewish men but also Jewish women and children, when they see the extermination of all Jews as an indispensable cleansing or disinfection of the earth, they are moved by terrors stemming from the earliest stages of infancy.' (Norman Cohn: *Warrant for Genocide*, Harper & Row)

There is another peculiarity among leading exponents of anti-Semitism and their followers that reminds one of paranoid schizophrenics: their megalomaniac sense of mission. When it comes to describing their role, the medieval Jew-killers as well as Nazi leaders employ apocalyptic imagery taken straight from the Book of *Revelation*. They see themselves as the angelic hosts over-throwing the power of darkness, even as a collective Christ over-throwing Antichrist. No army engaged in a real war against a real enemy has ever indulged in such self-exultation as Jew-killers engaged in their one-sided struggle against an imaginary con-spiracy. To hear them one would think that killing unarmed and helpless people, including small children and old women, is a very brave and risky undertaking. It is a phenomenon which only begins to make sense when one recalls that a paranoic murderer too can feel terrified of his harmless victims. For what these people see as the enemy is in fact the destructiveness and cruelty in their own psyche externalised. And the greater the unconscious sense of guilt, the more fearsome the imaginary enemy. The sense of guilt, originally engendered by the murderous impulses felt by the small child towards his parents, is enormously intensified in the world of grown-ups with its real violence which is deployed against its victims. Yet it is not experienced as a sense of guilt but as a sense of danger, of a threat and of blind terror lest the wronged ones – the parents killed in fantasy and the parent sur-rogates killed in reality – arise and exact retribution. This alone can explain the extraordinary paradox about the Nazi massacres, that as the Jews became more and more helpless as they were killed in ever greater numbers, so they were felt to be more and more powerful, malignant and dangerous. It also accounts for the fact that a man like Goebbels, for whom anti-Semitism was at first little more than a technique of vote catching, ended his days raving about the omnipotent Jewish rulers of the world. It was his own guilt-ridden unconscious that made of the imaginary elders of Zion a power more terrible than the Nazi regime itself.

3. PARANOID PSYCHOPATHY: STALINISM

While the image of the Jew as the father-murderer and, at the same time, the vengeful and omnipotent father has provided the central and most clearly defined manifestation of the patriarchal

172

Oedipal conflict, it is by no means the only one. The fantasy of the *eternal adversary* has found its expression in many guises, with the most fateful consequences upon the political life of nations, and it was responsible for the transformation of socialism into Stalinism and its politics of mass deception. The Stalinists corrupted the minds of their citizens by an organised falsification of history, and taking those lies as their justification exterminated not only thousands of pioneer Bolshevists but millions of ordinary citizens. They did irreparable harm to the image of socialism, transforming it from a vision of human liberation into a tyranny that bears its name.

When the facts of the Stalinist brutalities and Stalin's own paranoia became known, the rulers of Russia did not apologise for their misdeeds but continued to indulge in accusations against the enemy and to foment international conspiracies. They continued to justify their dictatorship with the same Stalinist lies about the relentless manipulation of the capitalists determined to destroy the fatherland of socialism and threatening to nullify its glorious successes. The rulers of the Soviet Union continued to torture the 'representatives of the enemy', the so-called agents of capitalism, in their detention camps and psychiatric hospitals. This mode of torture and detention was all the more horrible as it operated under the guise of helping the inmates to overcome a disease which had overtaken them like an intellectual poison, a dangerous germ by which they had become infected by exposure to capitalist propaganda. So this system no longer claimed to rely on torture or killings but on the purification of errant souls through scientific means and for their own benefit. While this was rather reminiscent of the reasoning of the Spanish Inquisition (which also claimed to save the souls of those who refused to accept the Kingdom of Christ by killing them), it created a sense of confusion and disorientation among the masses. But this kind of confusion was deliberately produced in order to make people unable to discriminate between right and wrong, between sanity and madness, between freedom and oppression. This type of political tyranny reveals a combination of sadism and omnipotence employing paranoic fantasies for its own purpose as well as being the outcome of a paranoia which operates at the highest levels.

Erich Fromm has discussed the sadistic components in the feelings of omnipotence. He suggests that the core of sadism, common to all its manifestations, is the 'passion to have absolute and unrestricted control over a living being, whether an animal, a child, a man or a woman. Sadism has essentially no practical aim; it is not trivial but devotional. It is the transformation of impotence into omnipotence, it is the religion of emotional cripples.' (Erich Fromm: *The Anatomy of Human Destructiveness*, Jonathan Cape, 1974) Fromm could have added that sadism includes the passion to have absolute control not only of another human being but of large numbers of people, whether they be members of a party or a nation.

Controlling the Ego of another person or masses of people, making them submit to our will and to our whims and, above all, forcing our way through their resistances, cutting through their armour and penetrating into their inmost being and forcing them to submit to us, is the core and aim of the sadistic impulse. We have seen the roots of this syndrome in the oral-sadistic-cannibalistic phase, but it is one of the tragedies of human existence that this drive continues to exercise a profound influence upon the life of adults and, in particular, on the structure and dynamics of societies. Stalin himself, in his person, is a paradigm of the sadist overwhelmed by a passion to control others and to manipulate them.

One aspect of Stalin's sadism was his habit of arresting the wives and sometimes children of some of the highest Soviet or Party functionaries, and keeping them in a labour camp while their husbands had to carry on with their jobs and bow and scrape before Stalin without even daring to ask for their release. Thus the wife of Kalinin, president of the Soviet Union, was arrested in 1937. Molotov's wife, and the wife and son of Otto Kuusinen, the leader of the Comintern, were all in labour camps. Stalin asked Kuusinen why he did not try to get his son freed. Evidently there were serious reasons for his arrest, Kuusinen answered. According to a witness, Stalin grinned and ordered the release of Kuusinen's son. Kuusinen sent his wife parcels to her work camp but did not even address them himself but had his housekeeper do it. It is reported that she was tortured by investigators until she signed statements compromising her husband. Stalin ignored them for the time being – he wanted them as a basis for the arrest of Kuusinen and others whenever it would please him (statements by Medvedev).

It does not require much imagination to visualise the extreme humiliation of these high functionaries, who could not quit their positions, could not ask for the release of their wives or sons, and had to agree with Stalin that the arrests were justified. As Erich Fromm remarks: 'Either such men had no feelings at all, or they were morally broken and had lost all self-respect and sense of dignity.'

A drastic example is the reaction of one of the most powerful figures in the Soviet Union, Lazar Kaganovich, to the arrest of his brother Mikhail, who was the minister of aviation industry before the war. Mikhail, who himself was responsible for the repression of many people, was accused of taking part in an underground Fascist plot and of having agreed to become the vice-president of the Fascists if the Hitlerites took Moscow. When Stalin learned of these depositions, which he obviously expected (as he most probably inspired them himself), he phoned Lazar Kaganovich and said that his brother would have to be arrested because he had connections with the Fascists. 'Well, so what!' said Lazar. 'If it is necessary, arrest him.' At a politburo discussion of this subject Stalin praised Lazar Kaganovich for his 'principles' and for agreeing to his brother's arrest. Shortly afterwards Mikhail Kaganovich shot himself. The whole episode is all the more preposterous as Mikhail Kaganovich was a Jew.

However, the most important aspect of Stalin's path to power was his cultivation of the image of a relentless enemy determined to smash the revolution and the Soviet Union, by inventing a powerful opposition within the state who were the agents of the capitalist enemy, infiltrating the party, undermining socialist solidarity and threatening the very existence of the workers' state. There is no better illustration of the manner in which Stalin and his henchmen created a paranoid fantasy to justify the relentless persecution and eventual liquidation of the 'internal enemy' than to quote from the *History of the Communist Party of the Soviet Union*, the communists' bible, largely written by Stalin himself.

Writing of the 15th Party Congress (December, 1927), he states that: 'The opposition has ideologically broken with Leninism, has degenerated into a Menshevik group, has taken the course of capitulation to the forces of the international and home bourgeoisie, and has objectively become a tool of counter-revolution against the regime of the proletarian dictatorship . . . Of course, at that time the party did not yet know that Trotsky, Rakovsky, Radek, Krestinsky, Sokolnikov and others had long been enemies of the people, spies recruited by foreign espionage services, and that Kamenev, Zinoviev, Pyatakov and others were already forming connections with enemies of the USSR in capitalist countries for the purpose of collaboration with them against the Soviet people.'

For Marx and Engels the establishment of a dictatorship of the proletariat was always justified as a necessary but transitory stage on the road to socialism; the socialist society, once established, would no longer need the state, as it is an instrument of oppression by the ruling class and it would gradually wither away. However, once Stalin took over complete power, it could never again be claimed that the state would wither away, nor could it be denied that what did wither away were his opponents and that a brutal and complete dictatorship had been established over the people. The whole of Stalinism's political and social structure was designed to strengthen the power of the dictatorship, to safeguard its permanence and to justify it by constantly holding before the public eye the existence of an external and internal enemy against whom the state and the party had to protect itself. In order to 'defend the revolution', the state apparatus and the party had to maintain constant vigilance against the manipulations and conspiracies of the enemy, and had to consider every member of the state as a potential enemy.

In a circular letter to all organisations, dated May 13, 1935, on the subject of the registration, safe-keeping and issuance of party cards, the Central Committee instructed all organisations 'to make a careful verification of the records of party members and to establish Bolshevik order in our own party home.'

In connection with the results of the verification of the records of party members, a plenary meeting of the Central Committee of the party adopted a resolution on 25 December, 1935, declaring that this verification was an organisational and political measure of enormous importance in strengthening the ranks of the CPSU (Communist Party of the Soviet Union). In resuming the admission of new members to the party, the Central Committee instructed party organisations to bear in mind that hostile elements would persist in their attempts to worm their way into the ranks of the CPSU. Consequently: 'It is the task of every party organisation to increase Bolshevik vigilance to the utmost, to hold aloft the banner of the Leninist party and to safeguard the ranks of the party from the penetration of alien, hostile and adventitious elements.'

Purging and consolidating its ranks, destroying the enemies of the party and relentlessly combating distortions of the party line, the Bolshevik party rallied closer than ever around its Central Committee. 'In 1937, new facts came to light regarding the fiendish crimes of the Bukharin-Trotsky gang. The trial of Pyatakov, Radek and others, the trial of Tukhachevsky, Yakir and others, and lastly, the trial of Bukharin, Rykov, Krestinsky, Rosenholz and others, all showed that the Bukharinites and Trotskyites had long joined to form a common band of enemies of the people operating as the "Bloc of Rights and Trotskyites". The trials showed that these "dregs of humanity" in conjunction with the enemies of the people, Trotsky, Zinoviev and Kamenev, had been in conspiracy against Lenin, the party and the Soviet state ever since the early days of the October Socialist Revolution.

'The trials brought to light the fact that the Trotsky-Bukharin fiends, in obedience to the wishes of their master, the espionage services of foreign states, had set out to destroy the party and Soviet state, to undermine the defensive power of the country, to assist foreign intervention, to prepare the way for the defeat of the Red Army, to bring about the dismemberment of the USSR, to hand over the Soviet maritime region to the Japanese, Soviet Byelorussia to the Poles, and the Soviet Ukraine to the Germans, to destroy the gains of the workers and collective farmers, and to restore capitalist slavery to the USSR.

'These contemptible lackeys of the Fascists forgot that the Soviet people had only to move a finger and not a trace of them would be left. The Soviet court sentenced the Bukharin-Trotsky fiends to be shot. The People's Commissariat of Internal Affairs carried out the sentence. The Soviet people approved the annihilation of the Bukharin-Trotsky gang, and passed on to the next business. And the next business was to prepare for the election of the Supreme Soviet of the USSR, and to carry it out in an organised way.'

For 'Soviet people' read 'Stalin', and he gloried in the fact that he had only to lift his finger and not a trace of his opposition would be left. After having annihilated the opposition, the next business was to prepare the election of the Supreme Soviet of the USSR, and carry it out in an organised way so that Stalin's power reigned supreme. He assumed the image of the sole and undisputed Superego with universal powers, and his glorification knew no bounds while millions of Soviet citizens perished in labour camps.

It may be said that since the horrors of two wars and the experience of Hitler and Stalin the social consciousness of the modern world has purged itself of the attractions of such paranoid, sadistic fantasies, and that its defences against them are now more powerful than before, as if the collective Ego of civilisation, having had the devastating experience of a madness that has overtaken nations and their leaders, will never again allow itself to fall victim to it.

Everyone who has been subjected to the terrors of Nazism or Stalinist communism, or has come to know about them, is impelled to ask what made millions of civilised people, capable of rational thought, submit to the neurotic fantasies of those rulers, what it was that gave them the power to pervert the minds of people, turn nations into prison camps and continents into battlefields.

The Process of Maturation

1. THE QUEST FOR IDENTITY

Before we can answer the obvious question how a nation which has prided itself on being in the vanguard of the European Enlightenment, the embodiment of what is best in European philosophy and its scientific achievements, can succumb to delusions of madness, and how it is that socialism, which has prided itself on representing the highest stage of enlightenment and of the rational mind, the practical fulfilment of the aspirations of humanism and of the scientific spirit, can regress to a medieval dictatorship and become enslaved to the manic, paranoid delusions of a Stalin, we must enquire how people deal with their infantile fantasies and how they normally manage to resolve them. In other words, we must look at the maturation process as it occurs in individuals as well as in cultures.

But if we speak of the maturation process, a host of questions immediately spring to mind. What do we mean by maturity or normal, or indeed what do we mean by being grown-up? The problem does not arise in animals. When an animal is grown-up it has generally achieved the capacity to carry out the genetic programming of its instincts, it is able to fulfil the task presented to it by the genetic-biological constitution of the species to which it belongs. Unless it has suffered from some profound injury, it is mature when it is grown-up. In human beings this is not so simple because due to the vastly increased importance of the pre-frontal areas of the cortex their behaviour and attitudes are very largely determined by psychological and mental processes; mind, to a large extent, has taken over from instinct as the determining factor of human evolution. And it is the Superego which acts as our guide and judge and attempts to control our behaviour; it acts as the internal representative of the expectations and demands of our culture, and we judge people by their ability to fulfil these demands and to adjust to them. However, while psychologists and sociologists in times past could blithely speak of social ad-justment, and consider a person mature if he was adjusted to his cultural environment, we can no longer accept such criteria. Having lost our confidence in the sanity of our culture, we can no longer accept that maturity simple means the capacity for adjustment. A convinced Nazi was the perfectly adjusted citizen in Nazi Germany; a member of the communist party who un-questioningly supported the dictates of the Stalinist regime, whose greatest achievement was to rise in the communist hierarchy, and who was prepared to denounce and torture his fellow citizens, was called the true representative of Soviet man. Anyone who refused to 'adjust' was either sent to the gulag or liquidated or, later, during the more 'liberal' years, was sent to a mental hospital and considered to be insane.

It is one of the characteristics of human beings which distin-guishes us from other animals that we are not endowed by nature with a secure sense of our identity. We do not, as it were, belong to our instincts, and they do not suffice to assure us who we are as individuals, how we are to relate to our environment, how our environment sees us, and what is expected of us. We have to dis-cover these things, and constantly strive to gain an acceptable image of ourselves.

We have seen that the libido attaches itself to a number of tasks necessary for self-preservation and the perpetuation of the species. The task of identity-seeking is at first stimulated by the narcissistic libido, followed by what I call the anal-productive libido and then identification with father by the boy and with mother in the case of a girl. However, we have seen that we can also identify with the other sex, and our sense of identity will to a great extent be determined by whom we identify with. There is a measure of feminine identification in the boy and male identification in the girl, which led Jung to postulate the existence of a female spirit (the anima) and a male spirit (animus) in every person. But it is never just one or the other we identify with but a variety of characteristics of male or female images which we introject. Identity seeking is also related to our membership to a group, tribe, religion, race, country, social class, political party, and our identity is to a great extent influenced by which of these groups we belong to, or want to belong to.

One could make a study of a person's development of certain skills and talents according to the predominance of certain pregenital primacies, as, for instance, the talent for music and singing due to a strong urethral libido, craftsmanship or hoarding dispositions to anal productive or anal retentive libido, the tendency to analyse things or to look below the surface to oral-aggressive drives, etc. These primacies become sublimated during the latency, and enable the child to acquire a wide range of skills and knowledge.

At this stage, from about seven, boys and girls don't mix easily; there is a reluctance to show their nudity to each other, and their play relationships become inhibited and somewhat embarrassed. Each sex adopts a gender-conscious pride, wanting to assert their sexual identity. In progressive kibbutzim in Israel, where parents encourage the sexes to mix freely and without shame, one finds that from the age of seven or eight boys and girls are reluctant to share the same showers or to undress in front of each other. Individuals who were born and reared in those kibbutzim remember that as small children they enjoyed mixing and playing freely with the other sex, but 'for some reason' strong inhibitions appeared among them almost suddenly and spontaneously at the age of about seven or eight. Children form gangs of the same sex, and boys show the first signs of wanting to be independent from mother, but as they are still children and dependent their striving for independence is limited and confined to short periods. However, generally speaking the latency period is devoted to the repression of sexual drives and regression to pregenital impulses, and their sublimated transformation into socially required skills.

The repression of the sexual drives of the first puberty is necessary for the human being for reasons I have outlined earlier, namely, the enormous amount of skills and disciplines accumulated by man's cultures which have to be acquired and learned by each individual. He has to repress the sexual drives as he is still a child and unable to assume responsibilities of reproduction. It is a time of exploration and identification with his culture and the world of men by means of learning, experimentation, and acquisition of skills.

In patriarchal cultures girls also have to acquire the skills and the knowledge necessary for preparation in citizenship, but a large part of the learning process will be related to female skills and identification with the mothers and the world of women. I should remind the reader here that the process of identification with their own sex and the differentiation of skill acquisition is not entirely due to an environmentally enforced role playing, by which boys are given bows and arrows or guns or machines to play with, and girls given dolls and dolls' houses and are taught how to dress up and play at cooking and sewing, as if this were an artificial, entirely socially determined imposition. Instinctual, biological and psychological forces play a large part here, and are felt to be natural, and have been seen as such for perhaps hundreds of thousands of years. In the evolution of the human being the development of a division of labour has been essential for the survival of the species, as it is indeed in most other animal species. The notion of sexual equality as meaning sameness between the sexes simply contradicts the psycho-biological disposition of the sexes, which differentiates them from each other in many ways, even though this differentiation is not rigid and absolute and, as I have said, what we call male and female characteristics are in various degrees shared by both sexes. There are many men with strong female dispositions, and many women with male dispositions, and, indeed, it is essential for the sexes to share in some degree the feelings of the other sex, in order to understand each other and to partake in each other's activities. It is a question of emphasis, and it is natural that in boys masculine drives are emphasised and in girls feminine drives. These drives are reinforced by the process of identification with the same sex. Indeed, it is quite astonishing how many little girls behave like grown-up ladies and strongly imitate their mothers. (These somewhat exaggerated forms of identification are doubtless due to a compensatory process for wanting to eliminate the mother, take over from her and claim father for themselves.)

2. THE HOMOSEXUAL PHASE

At the end of the latency period, with the full emergence of sexual puberty with its hormonal and psychological transformations, when boys begin to grow a beard, their voice changes and their genital libido is activated, the Oedipus complex and rivalry with father once again flare up, and this time with far more intensity than before.

While on the one hand the boy sees his father as a rival, he now needs him, and becomes more dependent on him than ever. It is important for the boy to be proud of his father; he needs to feel his interest in him, he needs to know what father expects and wants him to be, and above all he needs his father's love and participation, his comradeship and sympathetic leadership. In other words, he needs his father's love in order to be able to love himself and to feel lovable as a man.

We have spoken of the practically universal initiation ceremonies, which include the barmitzvah among Jews and confirmation among Christians, when mother relinquishes the boy and hands him over to the community of males. He is initiated into male ways, he is accepted as a man amongst men, and he has to play his role amongst them. But the love of men is not unconditional. To be a man the boy not only has to acquire the skills and knowledge as well as the rituals of his culture, but he has to prove his capacity of accomplishing the tasks set before him. These tasks include the capacity to bear pain and injuries, so necessary for success in the battles of the hunter (a way of life which has predominated over far the longest period of man's evolution). He is required to show courage and a degree of fear-lessness, he has to obey the rules and disciplines of work, of trade, and of rational inquiry, he has to understand the interrelationship between effort and reward. He has to learn the value of com-petition in the male world to achieve status and respect. All this he has to imbibe from the father and father figures, and his libido has to be directed to these ends so that he can enjoy them and experience some pleasure in their pursuit. In the same way as libido flows into the various, vitally necessary primacies in the development of the individual, we may be justified in thinking the libido will flow into male identification and produce the satis-factions and pleasures of male bonding. In other words, a degree of homosexual relationship between the son and the father and father substitutes as well as between boys will emerge during this time.

These homosexual bonds will be repressed in various degrees and operate as a latent force on the pre-conscious level. Fathers want their sons to take an interest in what they are doing, to share their skills with them and to show them off. They will also take an interest in boys' sexual needs, and help them to understand and instruct them about the ways of men. It is very important for boys to experience this need in their fathers, and their libidinous bond promotes both a sense of identification as well as love and respect for their individuality, their problems, their aspirations and their doubts. We as humans, however, cannot quite behave in the open, natural and generous ways of our nearest animal relative, the gorilla, whose young offspring often jump onto the back of their father while he is having intercourse, and participate in his rhythmic sensations. We have lost the uninhibited experiences of gorillas, but on a deep level of the psyche every boy has the urge to do just that.

There is intense curiosity among boys about the father's sexu-ality, and they want to look at men and to be looked at by them. Boys want to be proud of their father's penis so that they can be proud of their own, and they want to share in their father's mas-culinity.

However, there are many fathers whose own homo-erotic drives were rejected by their fathers and who have to repress those needs, and react with fear to their sons' desires for them. Having had to repress their own feelings towards their fathers, they will want the son to repress his feelings towards them, and adopt critical and often aggressive attitudes to him. It is not so much here the question of jealousy towards the son's heterosexual urges but of the father's fears of his own homosexual needs which he cannot tolerate in his son. These conflicts can be found in many male patients, and I shall mention one very typical example.

Mr. S. P., a young man of twenty-eight, suffered from bouts of profound depression and paranoid anxiety, intense inferiority feelings, inability to mix socially without experiencing agonising fears and a paralysing sense of inadequacy. During analysis he became aware of an intense rage towards his father, who always criticised him. He could not do anything right. Whatever he tried to do was met with impatient criticism and ridicule. In his imagination he saw himself attacking his father violently and then being overwhelmed by self-condemnation.

During an hypnotic session, he felt very frightened 'I'm frightened, my anger frightens me, it's all bottled up. I'm tight, I can't breathe, I'm choked. It's not just that father is angry, I am angry. I want to tear everything to pieces. Knock all the walls down – it's a prison.' I ask: 'What is the opposite of the hate you feel?' 'It's love, sweetness – I never dared to show it, I can't show it to father. I am angry because I could never admit my love for father, he would attack me, make me feel I am a fool, a namby pamby, a pansy. I think all men would ridicule me if I dare show my love. It would be horrible. I can't face men or look at them because they would see I want to love them. I want their affection but I can't show it, I want to show them and talk to them but they would laugh at me. I am going to explode, I want to explode out of the barrier I made myself. I am angry at my self-made frustration. If I could only trust people. But I can't trust my own feelings.'

It would be easy to say that this young man is a repressed homosexual, but this would not be correct. He is not a homosexual in the grown-up sense of the term; he does not fantasize homosexual relationships but yearns for affection and acknowledgement from men, for sharing and showing mutual interests. His homo-erotic needs during puberty were angrily rebuffed by his father, and his relationship to men and to his own manhood appeared to him forbidden and dangerous. His masculine self-image, his capacity for work and his relationship with women remained blocked and profoundly impaired.

Another man of about forty, separated from his wife, with two sons, suffered from a similar difficulty. His relationship with his sons was disturbed due to his own inability to let them show their need for his love. He too was rebuffed by his father.

We notice here that the fear of homosexual feelings is perpetuated from father to son, from generation to generation. Psychotherapists nowadays frequently encounter men who are unable to work, who are withdrawn in a depressive sense of inadequacy and futility, and it becomes apparent that they suffer from a lack of empathy with their father, or rather an inability or refusal on his part to empathize with the son. The father remains a stranger, who does not show much interest in his son and does not include him in his world. In such cases the boy's male identity, his masculine narcissism is diminished and he feels unaccepted, helpless and unable to participate in male activities, the world of work, ambition and creativity, and any attempt to enter into it appears futile. The world seems to be against him, and defeats all his attempts to assert himself in it. Such young men often retreat into passivity, which nowadays is reinforced by drug taking; they seem lazy and devoid of ambition. There is often an acute sense of disappointment with the fathers' lack of power to assert themselves in the world and an identification with their failure. Having projected a degree of manic expectations upon the father, the son feels disappointment if father has failed his expectations of him, and, indeed, has failed his expectations of himself. Much will depend upon the boy's attitude towards his mother and her attitude to him. if the boy admires his mother and feels her love and admiration and her hopes for him, then it can happen that the boy will be fired with the desire to prove himself a better man than his father, take great heroes as his alternative male models and try to emulate them, and he will attempt to show himself worthy of his mother's trust in him. He will sense that his mother has made him her hero to compensate for her disappointing husband,

and he will enter into the world with great hopes. He will see himself achieving great things and overcoming all the obstacles which would defeat lesser men like his father.

If, on the other hand, the boy's mother does not appear to be his ally, if she seems to support the father rather than the son, he will feel betrayed and his courage will be undermined. Hope will be displaced by anger, and he will enter the world of men with defiance and hostility.

The point we have to bear in mind is that before the young man can enter into satisfactory heterosexual relationships, before he can 'have a woman' out there in the world and have the confidence of approaching her and feel wanted by her, he has to experience homo-erotic bondings which provide him with an adequate, narcissistic, male self-image. It frequently happens that the boy does not experience satisfactory homo-erotic relations with his father, nor establishes libidinous relationships with boys' games or idealised heroes. Then his homosexual needs are left unsatisfied, they cannot find sublimated outlets, and he continues to search for them. In other words, he is on the road to becoming homosexual.

This usually happens when the mother dominates the family, is in competition with the father; the father then is unable to draw the boy into his orbit and free him from his bondage to the mother. The boy will then remain tied to her and tend to identify with her. But here a paradoxical thing tends to happen: he will, on the one hand, remain emotionally dependent upon her as the most powerful person around him but, at the same time, will resent her powers over him. He will need her protection but at the same time hate and resent her for not relinquishing him from her power and for tying him to her. He will sense that she does not give him the space and the emotional freedom to transfer his libido towards the world of boys and of men. He will find himself uneasy with boys' activities and find it difficult to mix with them, to partake in their exuberance and keenness to prove themselves in gangs, in sports and all kinds of activities, and above all he will not be able to enter into sublimated libidinous relationships with them. Such boys develop images of a devouring mother, of dangerous female genitals, and all kinds of horrible fantasies about them will populate his mind. The demanding, oral-aggressive images of the vagina which appeared during his early childhood will re-emerge, the vagina with teeth and claws wanting to take possession of the boy, devouring and castrating him, will fill his pre-conscious fantasies and he will want to escape her. And still his hunger for the love of the male will remain. He will need the love of a man to reassure him of his maleness. The female organ – the genital without a penis – will evoke fears of being castrated, and he needs a penis to assure him of the security of his own. Such men are obsessed by an over-emphasis upon the penis, they will desire it and their libido will hunger for its presence. They spend hours in public lavatories looking at other men's penises, showing their own and hoping that another man will want it. Their sexual desires centre upon being wanted by a penis, and their anus very often assumes the libidinous urges of the vagina. They have an anal vagina and a penis at the same time, they can be active and passive, man and woman to other men, and this is very reassuring to them. When young, they often acquire feminine characteristics of sensual passivity which attracts older men, who also look for the feminine person with a penis. But above all they will fear the female as a dangerous predator who will want to take possession of them, dominate their lives, and in the sex act devour them and make them helpless. The more active and usually older homosexual will identify with a younger man whom he sees as himself as a boy, receiving the love and reassurance of a male which he has not received from the father, and as a protection against the predatory mother.

It is often considered paradoxical that homosexuals are very much at ease with women and manifestly like their company. This is usually the case as long as they do not have to submit to their sexual demands. Having reassured themselves that women do not threaten them with castration, and as long as they are safe in their sexual relationships with men, they can be at ease with women and indeed find that they have much in common. For, after all, they want the same thing. But underneath the ease the aggressive image of the woman reveals itself in a disposition to bitchiness among homosexuals and an easily aroused rage. In short, as I often say to homosexual patients, the problem is that they have not been homosexual enough when they were young. At first they usually stare at me in amazement when I say this, but quite quickly they recognise what I mean.

If the boy's narcissistic needs are denied by his father, then his homo-erotic drives regress to the unsublimated level and become sexual. By means of sexual contact with males the boy experiences the libidinous contact which was denied to him. But these homosexual forms of identification are the exception. What much more frequently develops out of the disturbed identification processes is the Oedipus complex. We may say: Narcissus denied by the father turns into the Oedipus complex. 'If you don't love me, I hate you!' Conversely: 'If you let me be one with you, and share your male identity and your powers, then we do not need to be rivals, and I can love you.' Thus it is the failure of identification particularly during the second puberty which perpetuates the Oedipus complex.

3. FATHER'S LOVE DENIED: THE OEDIPUS COMPLEX

It is often forgotten that the Oedipus story begins with Laius' determination that his son should not be born and his subsequent rejection. It is true that the oracle warned Laius that any child born of Jocasta, his wife, would become his murderer: 'Do not beget a child, for if you do, that child will kill you.' Laius 'therefore put Jocasta away, though without offering any reason for his decision, which caused her such vexation that, having made him drunk, she inveigled him into her arms again as soon as night fell. When, nine months later, Jocasta was brought to bed of a son, Laius snatched him from the nurse's arms, pierced his feet with a nail, and, binding them together, exposed him on Mount Cithaeron' (Robert Graves, *Greek Myths*, Volume 2, 1955).

The boy is rejected by his father, and his feet are pierced by a nail and they are deformed. We know that in the unconscious mind the feet need a secure and supportive contact with the ground, a strong and healthy relationship with the boy's background. The feet deformed by the father means that his foundations are lacking, that he has no parent to support him, he is without home and without identity. Indeed, Oedipus wanders abroad and constantly searches for his origins and for his identity. But these searches are defeated by a web of ignorance and deceit. He is unable to secure true self-knowledge and the knowledge of his father.

For Freud, the 'real' meaning of the myth is that every boy of a normal family wishes to kill his father and sleep with his mother. While this has become one of Freud's central concepts, we must also point to his statement that the Oedipus complex is resolved or dissolved by the renunciation of the boy's incestuous sexual wishes and by an identification with the parent of the same sex. The boy no longer wishes to eliminate his father but to be like him. Thus the erotic bonds between mother and son have to be transferred to some extent to the father in order to establish in the boy a sense of his male identity, enabling him to renounce his incestuous desires, become exogamous and play a satisfactory role in the world. The catastrophes which Oedipus brought upon himself and upon his empire were the consequences of a denied identity.

With the onset of the sexual maturation of the second puberty when the boy experiences the powerful, almost irresistible sexual urges, he needs the father's guidance and reassurance, and his know-how. He needs to receive and introject his father's male libido and to learn how to be a man, how to relate to the society of males and to women. The relation to the father is not in the first instance sexual but narcissistic. His father is the object of his narcissistic needs, and we can speak here of a narcissistic identification process, in the same way as a child during his narcissistic primacy needed the mother as an object of his narcissistic needs and for his Ego formation.

Of course there are as many forms of identification as there are people, each influenced by a large variety of fixations, childhood experiences and personality traits, among both fathers and sons, but we can discern five basic forms of identification:

(i) The classic scenario as described by Freud. The jealous father confronts the son as his antagonist and rival, as the representative and enforcer of sexual taboos. By denying his son's sexual needs, he also denies his narcissistic needs, for in the second puberty, unlike the first, the boy wants to feel grown-up and recognised as a male. Maleness, and not only sexual gratification, is now at stake. By not acknowledging the boy's sexual rights, the father denies his rights as a man.

The father, to whom the boy turns for the nourishment and affirmation of his male identity, comes to represent the armoured and unyielding breast, as he is unresponsive to his son's needs. But the father who does not share his libido but is repressive and authoritarian will inevitably arouse aggressive urges against him. The son will want to attack the father's penis and take it away from him. The castration urge will be very real on the principle that 'if it is not given to me I have to take it away from him, cut it, tear it off in order to incorporate and possess it and experience its powers.' But the introjected penis – that is, father – will become a renewed source of fear and of remorse, producing the ambiguity between aggression and submission; the typical Oedipal situation will re-emerge and remain unresolved. We may take into consideration that this is to a large extent a re-enactment during puberty of the infant's oral-cannibalistic-sadistic drives, when the unyielding nipple had to be attacked in order to derive the libido from it, now transferred to the father. As the mother had appeared to the small child as a frightening witch, so the father now appears in the boy's pre-conscious fantasies as the threatening, attacking monster, vividly described by Freud, and discussed by Fromm in his studies of the authoritarian family and the authoritarian personality.

(ii) In this scenario, the authoritarian father yields to the son's remonstrations and anger at being rejected. He understands the boy's needs, and his aggression will be rewarded. Periods of responsiveness and affection will occur between them, a rhythm of aggression and love, enabling the boy to feel proud of his aggressive strength. He feels that his father does not 'really' reject him and is not hurt by the boy's aggression, but understands him and responds to his needs if prompted vigorously enough. As W. R. Bion expresses it (in his rather esoteric language), referring to the mother/child relationship: 'The infant projects into the breast his anxiety and inchoate, primitive, concrete elements. A mother capable of containing projective identification unconsciously processes these projections and responds adequately to the infant's needs. When this happens, the infant can re-introject his projections, modified by understanding, and he also introjects the breast as a container capable of dealing with anxiety. This forms the basis of his own capacity to deal with anxiety.' (W. R. Bion: 'Attacks on Linking', *International Journal of Psychoanalysis*, 1959, pp. 308–15). In other words, the mother or father responds to the child's needs even if expressed aggressively (and aggressiveness, as I have pointed out, is always a reaction to anxiety). Aggression is understood by the parents as the child's reaction to their depriving attitudes, and they are able to respond positively. Then the child's aggressive impulses are not blocked by guilt and renewed anxiety of losing his parents' love.

(iii) This mode of identification, which we might consider to be particularly important, is simply a loving bond between father and son, when the father responds to the boy's libidinous needs and is happy with them. However, the love of the father for his son is never quite unconditional, for it is a sign of the father's love that he wants to teach the boy the rules of masculine duties and responsibilities which are required by his culture. He is the transmitter of his culture, and it is his duty to lead, to teach and to admonish. However, he would have empathy with the son's personality and allow him the space to develop his own views and interests, and encourage him to do so. In this way, the Superego of the culture represented by the father develops into an Ego ideal, encouraged by the father's respect for the son's Ego development, confidence and trust in his own unique personality, his ideals, expectations and hopes. This does not rule out conflict, but any conflict is understood and respected. It helps to sharpen the young man's sense of his own right to be different and to transcend the limitations of the fathers. We may call these conflicts between fathers and sons as benign rebelliousness, ultimately based upon the secure ground of their father's love and their pride in the son.

(iv) This scenario presents a relationship which appears to be perfect but in fact is very problematical: it is the unconditional love between father and son.

Rather than presenting the boy with a model of masculinity to which he can aspire or can emulate, the father submits to the boy's wishes and impulses without exercising a sense of discrimination; he provides approval and acceptance without affirming his own values, views and beliefs. To some extent this equals the love of the mother, but the boy is deprived of the guidance and model of masculine feelings and values. There are many variations in this type of relationship. The father may compete with his wife for the boy's love, and do so by satisfying his every whim, and thoroughly spoil him. Men like this often project their own infantile, narcissistic fantasies upon the young son, and spoil him as they expected to be spoilt as children and still wish to be spoilt as grown-ups. Their own narcissism is often frustrated by their wives and by the world in which they live, and they compensate for its loss by projecting it upon the son. They identify with their son, and behave towards him in the same way as they desire the world to behave towards them, namely, by feeding and satisfying his narcissistic and manic urges. But by doing so they will deprive the son of an education for manhood, they fail in their duty to communicate a sense of self-restraint and responsibility towards others, the learning of rules and skills of his culture. Even if they teach skills and encourage the acquisition of knowledge, this acquires the characteristic of self-glorification and neglects the capacity for relationships. Many men of this kind want to replace the mother and themselves play her role towards the son. Young men who emerge from this type of identification will become either manic-narcissistic or ruthlessly egocentric, with little respect or appreciation for the personality of others; they cannot tolerate or understand a view other than their own, and consider their environment merely as a means for their own immediate gratification; their capacity for gratification delay will be severely impaired, and they tend towards outbursts of rage or tantrums if thwarted.

(v) Another form of identification which has become widespread as a result of the breakdown of patriarchal values is the father's indifference to the son. Out of his own sense of spiritual impoverishment the father feels he cannot be a model or guide to the son; he will feel hostile to his demands and adopt rejective attitudes. He will sense that his son needs him and makes demands upon him but will feel inadequate to satisfy them. He has no convictions, no image of masculinity to give or to share, and his male libido will feel vacuous; he will renounce his paternal duties, remain aloof and distant from his son, or disappear altogether. In the maturation process of the young man much then depends upon his relationship to his mother. Often he will experience a strong bond with her, identify with her, and later seek women who are dominant or masculine and represent the quality of the father for whom he is seeking. He sees a masculine mother in every woman, becomes over-dependent upon her and arouses her resentment and frustration, or he will resent the demands of women and become frightened of them. In his search for a male image, he will be drawn to aggressive groups of young men who seek to gain their male identity by acts of violence. This can be seen as a self-assertive, aggressive form of revenge upon the world of the fathers who seem to have disowned the sons and failed to feed them with a male libido. It produces social as well as psychological breakdowns and leads to widespread drug and drink addiction where any remaining inhibitions on aggression are neutralised. Indeed, we see here a renewed eruption of the Oedipus complex on the socio-cultural level as well as the individual level, the anger against the neglecting fathers, and the urge to attack civilised values and their social representatives. The waning of the father, of which much is spoken and written about, does not resolve the Oedipus complex but, paradoxically, intensifies it. Freud was frequently puzzled by the fact that people with weak or much absent fathers develop a particularly powerful Oedipal conflict, and here we see its manifestations on a large scale.

4. THE IDENTIFICATION PROCESS IN GIRLS

This process is in many ways similar to that of the boy but is in fact immensely complicated by a duality of identifications which in patriarchal societies girls have to undergo. Girls have to identify both with their mothers and also with their fathers in order to enable them to enter into society and play an active role in it. There is also the problem with girls that, as I have pointed out before, there are in fact two processes of identification, due to the duality of their genitals, a clitoral and a vaginal identity.

The identification process serves not only to overcome the girl's rivalry with her mother but also to liberate her from the fears of her own aggressive urges and sadistic fantasies; it serves the quest of the vaginal primacy which is directed towards the incorporation of the penis. The vagina as the mouth wants to re-experience the satisfying sensations of the infant upon receiving the nipple during its infancy. We have earlier pointed to the equation: mouth—vagina, nipple—penis. While at first the mouth is the organ that receives the nourishment and the libido necessary for the preservation of the self, and the nipple is the fountain to provide it, so the vagina is the mouth that receives the nourishment necessary for the preservation of the species, and the penis the fountain, the instrument to provide it. Both man and woman, moreover, identify narcissistically with these functions; not only do they provide the most intense pleasure for which they yearn, but the good feelings which accompany these functions make them feel good as persons. The good sensation of the mouth-vagina overcomes the infantile fears, and enables women to enter into the world as life-affirming persons with the potential for gratification and fulfilment of their needs. The acceptance and enjoyment of vaginal sensations spreads over the whole body, influences a woman's posture and self-image and her relationship to the world. The skin will radiate a certain warmth, the musculature will be free from chronic tensions and able to relax, the pelvis capable of rhythmic movements.

The exhibitionistic urges are probably more strongly pronounced in girls than in boys for the simple reason that a girl's genitals are not as visible as those of a boy. Her whole body, therefore, becomes more libidinised, more sensitive than that of a man. Its adornment is also meant to evoke men's responses and to draw them towards the fulfilment of their duty towards the preservation of the species.

Freud has shown that some of the differences that exist between the Superego formation of the girl and that of the boy are associated with anatomical sexual differences. (Sigmund Freud: 'Some Psychological Consequences of the Anatomical Distinction between the Sexes', 1927) These anatomical differences affect, as Melanie Klein has pointed out, both the development of the Superego and the Ego in various ways: 'In consequence of the structure of the female genitals, which marks their receptive functions, the girl's Oedipal tendencies are more largely dominated by her oral impulses, and the introjection of her Superego is more extensive than in the boy. In addition there is the absence of a penis as an active organ. The fact that she has no penis increases the greater dependency the girl already has upon her Superego as a result of her stronger introjective tendencies.' (Melanie Klein: *The Psychoanalysis of Children*, 1969)

Therefore introjection of the Superego is more extensive than in the boy in the process of identification. She is highly sensitive to her mother's own sensations and her attitudes to her, on both the narcissistic as well as the genital level. There is the need in the girl to feel the mother's good feelings, her satisfaction with herself, and her approval of the girl in order to assure her of her own goodness.

We must remember that the psycho-biological goal of the girl's maturation lies in the attainment of a pleasurable and satisfying vaginal libido, which in turn is reflected in a positive feminine self-image. The inability to achieve this goal will lead her to hate her mother, as she feels that she has introjected her unsatisfactory, immature characteristics. The hatred towards her mother will be projected upon her, and the mother will be seen as an aggressive and malevolent witch. This in turn produces anxiety and guilt feelings and the need to restitute her by adopting subservient and dependent attitudes. The girl will need to protect her mother from her own aggression and sadistic desires to hurt her, and needs to reassure her and protect her. Feeling that her mother mistrusts men or is hostile to them, she identifies with her and often adopts an aggressive, phallic-clitoral personality trait in order to revenge her mother and herself upon the men who have treated them badly. She sends out the message to men which says: 'As you don't love us, I hate you. Moreover, if your penis does not desire my vagina or makes it feel unacceptable or inadequate then I shall have a penis of my own, and either regard yours as of no importance and unnecessary or I will compete with it.' The anger in the vagina will find a measure of release by the affirmation of the clitoris as an assertive and aggressive weapon. The vagina is largely denied and considered as unimportant or inferior. The vaginal urge of yielding and giving oneself to the man will be blocked as it is considered to be a sign of submissiveness, subservience, of weakness and stupidity; femininity itself will be considered as an embarrassment from which one needs to escape.

Such women are frequently highly intelligent, ambitious and competitive; they often succeed in the 'man's world' in which their less assertive sisters often fail or, more usually, do not really wish to enter. The connection between the oral and the vaginal libido is frequently brought home to me when, under hypnosis, I regress such women to early childhood and to oral primacy and suggest that they feel their lips and enjoy the sensation of the mother's nipple. They quite frequently become very disturbed when their mouth starts to make sucking movements and begins to salivate and they experience what are in fact the intense pleasures of oral gratification. They frantically try to pull themselves out of the hypnotic state, often sit up and remonstrate vigorously that I shouldn't do this to them. When I tell them to lie down again and relax, and ask why they are so disturbed and angry about this experience, they invariably say that it makes them feel terribly stupid and weak as well as intensely embarrassed. When, after I have woken them up, we discuss this, they usually say that this sensation of slobbering and enjoying some primitive pleasures makes them feel like stupid women, without dignity and self-respect, and that they behave in a way many stupid women do. It then emerges that they indeed despise the 'average' woman, sometimes followed by diatribes against those women who allow themselves to be dominated by men, have no guts and no individuality, etc. I then sometimes bring the conversation around to their mother and what they feel about her; it becomes evident that they despise her or are sorry for her for being weak and allowing herself to be subservient to the father, to be dominated by him and generally badly treated. Often they become aware that they would want to love their mother but couldn't and that they don't want to be like her, and then frequently they start to cry. They cry because they feel sorry for their mother as well as for themselves having been deprived of something in their lives; they cry for the pleasures and satisfactions which have been denied to them, for having to repress their feminine desires in order to gain self-respect and an acceptable sense of identity. There is often a deep-lying sense of isolation and loneliness amongst them, which they have to overcome by being assertive, vigilant and mistrustful.

There has been a widespread propaganda among 'women liberationists', which based itself upon Masters and Johnson's findings, that the vagina does not have any innate sexual sensations but that it is the clitoris which is the centre of orgastic experience. The idea fostered by Masters and Johnson that all orgasms are alike (the only difference being the number of orgasms that a woman may experience in intercourse or masturbation) was largely based upon the concept of the difference between sensory experience and motor experience, the distinction being between the sensation as stimulus and involuntary motor discharge. Involuntary discharge, i.e., orgasm, being a motor reflex, is considered the same in all cases. I have discussed this in considerable detail in my book *The Failure of the Sexual Revolution*, and observe in conclusion: 'This is not correct. The motor discharge does, in fact, show very considerable differences in people according to the amount of psychic inhibition and muscular rigidity, which sets a limit to the full movement and bodily convulsions in orgasm. What Masters and Johnson consider multiple orgasm in women, induced by the stimulation of the clitoris by means of masturbation, is usually no more than a series of orgasmic spasms which do not involve the whole body and not even the vagina. These spasms, of which a woman can have many in quick succession, do not lead to a full discharge of tension, to the "pleasant bodily and psychic relaxation" that signifies an orgasm. Many female liberationists have taken up Kinsey's statement that the vagina has no feelings at all and that vaginal orgasm is a myth. But it can be observed that after the experience of clitoral orgasm or rather orgastic spasms many parts of the woman's body will remain tense, the libido needs will remain unfulfilled and only physical exhaustion will put a stop to the pursuit of gratification. The stimulation and excitement which they receive are more or less confined to one area which serves as stimulant, but the rest of the body does not respond in orgastic contractions nor in the release of tension. Orgastic clitoral spasms as such often generate a sense of irritation and frustration, while orgasm which involves the vagina is accompanied by deep pleasure, gratitude and relaxation. Women who deny the vagina and are unable to acknowledge it often suffer from paranoic fantasies of being attacked, raped, and from a disposition to hysteria. Indeed, hysteria is not so much a disturbance caused by the desires of the uterus and vaginal libido but, on the contrary, is based upon the exaggerated and false assertiveness of a woman's masculinity. The psychosomatic symptoms of hysteria are the woman's unconscious attempt to produce a penis, which she, however, suspects of being unreal, her assertiveness false.'

An example of a negative fixation upon a competitive and assertive mother, who tried to impose her aggressive and sadistic attitudes upon her daughter, causing her many acute conflicts between a desire to be loved and an inability to believe that she can be lovable, has been supplied by a woman patient, aged 28 when I first saw her, a person of exceptional intelligence and high academic achievement. The following are extracts from two sessions, partly under hypnosis, as written down by the patient shortly after the sessions:

'I've been in a bit of a state this week; lots of feelings of wretchedness and guilt and tremblings. I couldn't think what it was – then I remembered that when I was last at George's, he said to me that I was getting better (or something to that effect) ... and all I heard was that I wasn't perfect yet. This made me very depressed.

'I was very upset that there was something that I had to do before I was quite better, and that not only wasn't I doing it, but I didn't even know what it was I was supposed to be doing! This gave me an immense feeling of insecurity.

'George asked me to make the face of the Superego – and I found myself thinking of being held at arm's length in disgust. I was smelly. I saw daddy making me always feel somehow that I had hurt him; and then I realised that when I get in these terrible states, I want to eat. And yet my mouth and my stomach are not connected. My mouth wants the food, but my stomach doesn't feel fed and contented when I give it to it.

'George hypnotised me, and told me to be a very tiny baby and feel my lips. They were all big and luscious and they made a wonderful picture of how the breast ought to be. The picture that my lips made in my brain of how the lovely breast was going to be was all shattered by the cold, hard, marble-like breast that actually came. I felt my lips all shimmering round the edge, falling apart, losing their sense of shape and identity as they lost the picture which they had created and which was essential to them. When I felt my essential picture being shattered, I had the strongest possible impression that the breast was attacking me. Then I saw my brain also shattering apart, flying to all parts of the room and embedding itself in tiny fragments in the wall. I had lost my wholeness. It was awful.

'But I wasn't prepared for this to happen to me. I found myself clenching my teeth, holding myself in; then I felt a tightness in my pelvic region, as my bottom also held itself in. I didn't like the tightness, but inside I could feel that it was all alive. Even if it was blocked up, that didn't mean it was dead. I was so excited and pleased; I had been afraid that it might be dead in there . . . but it wasn't. I was very proud of the fact that I was not surrendering the good picture. For though it wasn't at all a nice shape because I was held in from the outside, my holding myself in was meant to keep the good picture inside me, where mummy couldn't get at it and destroy it. I was very proud of myself for keeping it safe.

'George told me to be three or four months old and look at her again.

'I looked at the baby to see what she felt like. My teeth were now all clenched together further back in my mouth. I didn't know what to do with them, or how to release the tensions in the other parts of my body. There was a kind of stopper in my anus, and it felt all sore like the acidity in the oesophagus when I was sick. It was horrible. I could also feel a tension in my solar plexus, which seemed to stop off the mouth from the stomach. I was a bit puzzled by this, as the food *did* get into my stomach – but George said that it was the libido which got stopped off; that made sense, because I'd often felt that I couldn't *use* the food that went into my mouth. That now all figured.

'George told me to see the breast again. I could see it in my mouth, and it was all big and held-in itself; absolutely bursting with milk that it couldn't let out because it had stoppers in it. I was overwhelmed by a frenzy of desire to get the milk out of this breast – to suck and suck until it burst and hurt and gave itself to me. I was going to beat the hell out of it – or suck the hell out of it. It wasn't going to be real sucking, though, because the mouth movements were all in the wrong place – lots of pressure on my tongue and my cheeks, and none to speak of in my lips.

'I was a bit upset by all this. Couldn't I get the milk any other way? I watched myself suck the breast nicely, coaxingly, suckingly ... but then nothing came out of it at all.

'George told me to be five months old and feel my teeth just below my gums and feel their power. I suddenly realised how impotent I had felt while I could feel my teeth at a younger age still, but couldn't use them. I looked at her face, and saw that she wasn't clenching her jaws any more, but had her front teeth clenched together, ready to bite. Then I watched her at the breast, and she started nibbling at it, seeing how much she could scratch – or how much she needed to scratch – before the milk could come. And mummy liked this game. I saw me at her breast, and her eyes shining and her teeth gleaming with excitement. I scratched a bit more. And she still liked it.

'I was very pleased that at last we had made contact. Our earlier encounters with each other had ended in each of us going off to our own separate corners without ever having related libidinously; in a kind of dazed aloneness. Now we were relating. Yet at the same time as I felt this immense pleasure, I felt also a terrible, devastating sadness. For now she had become part of me, and that part of me which I was holding back from her so that she couldn't invade it was perhaps at risk. I hated her. Although the tension in my jaw was now better, and even the tension in my bottom, my vagina seized up in outrage; I had betrayed it and it couldn't bear it. I was so upset; I sank my teeth into her to kill her because I couldn't bear her to be me or me to be her. I wanted quite desperately to kill her.

'She hurled me away, whimpering with self-righteous aggrievement. I had hurt her. I was a bad girl. She wanted me to die. And without her I would die. But I didn't want to die. What could I do?

'I looked at myself having a tantrum . . . and suddenly I thought "good for her!" I was proud of her spirit, proud of her refusal to capitulate to mummy and take her in and let her invade me, proud of her biting and her anger and her judgement that mummy deserved to be killed. I wasn't screaming so that mummy would be sorry for me and come and make it better (which was what I had always feared I might be doing), but to assert my Self in the face of her desire to cast me out into the wilderness and let me die. I wasn't going to let her make me die. And I was proud. I wasn't like her, and I wasn't going to die.'

Next Session:

'I lay down, and George asked me what I'd like to look at. I felt terrible inside – guilty and bad. I said that I'd like to look at why I always did everything wrong.

'I could see me sitting in the corner, all drooping and sad. I looked almost like a monkey, with my face pointing downwards and long arms and sad, lethargic fur. I had a terrible pain inside me, and I could see myself cutting myself open to show what was inside, to prove that it wasn't bad; that there was nothing bad in there. Yet I was so sad and demoralised because anything I did was going to be misinterpreted and used against me. The safest thing seemed to be to do nothing – or as little as possible. Then

I remembered the three monkeys: see no evil, hear no evil, speak no evil . . . and I realised why I was a monkey.

'But what was going on? I saw myself, about two or three years old, squatting down, making a sausage. But it was all rather complicated. I didn't know whether or not I wanted to let this sausage out. There was a tension in my anus as the pressure to let it out became exactly equal and opposite to the pressure to hold it in. We reached a stage of complete equilibrium. Except that it wasn't really equilibrium; it was more like paralysis. My bottom – and my brain – were completely paralysed. Not only didn't they know what was going on, but they didn't know how to work out what to do next. It was very strange. But there was a kind of pressure in the struggle, and that was interesting.

'George asked me what would happen if I let it out. I wanted to let it out, because that would give me enormous pleasure. Yet I felt a tension also in my womb as he spoke, because I could see a picture of myself having a baby and mummy killing it. Then I realised that all this lovely golden stuff inside me was also like a baby, and that mummy would kill it. Yet at least I could see that it *was* lovely and soft and golden; I wanted to protect it from her aggression. George asked me what it was like when it was outside, this sausage. It was hard and brown and armoured, with nobbles and crags in it. He told me to see mummy and see how she reacted to it. I could see her looking disgusted, but at the same time rather pleased with herself because she was going to have pleasure from the destruction which her disgust was going to make her wreak.

'Then I looked at what she was actually doing. There she was with a kind of pickaxe. My first thought was that she was chopping the faeces up . . . but in addition to that, she was, as it were, using the pickaxe to mountaineer her way up it, taking possession of it as one might of a mountain. I felt that she was taking over my world, and making me enter into hers. There was a certain pleasure in the relationship – at least we were relating! – but at the same time I felt a horror of being involved in her sadism and destructiveness.

'George suggested that I might look at the sausage itself. I watched it stand up on its end, as if it had legs. It had very pugnacious jaws, and sharp, libidinised teeth and nails; its back was arched, and its shoulders held in a position where one was further forward than the other. I felt that it was forearming itself against the inevitable attack. It was all very sad that it had to be like this; a tragedy underlay it . . . yet at the same time, I felt a kind of pleasure in its spirit and its strength and its hard, craggy exterior. I was rather surprised to find myself liking it so much . . . but there it was – I did.

'Then George said that he'd like me to look at the paranoid sausage. Well . . . that was really interesting. I could see it with ranks of serried shields almost like a Greek hoplite army; it was absolutely *surrounded* by these shields. And from all directions were flying spears which its enemies were throwing at it. It looked like a veritable hedgehog with all these spears lodged in its enveloping shields. And yet . . . the sausage was having the most enormous pleasure out of all this. It was strong and powerful, and able to resist all these dreadful attacks, and to stand up for the good things even when under this terrible threat. It was immensely proud of itself for not being a wimp and collapsing under the strain, or bowing to the pressure. It stood up strongly and nobly and sprang around on its feet, parrying all the shots, from however unexpected a quarter. It was quite fascinating. I suddenly understood why I spent so much of my time looking for difficult situations so that I could fight them: there was a *pleasure* in it! The fear was an unfortunate side effect . . . but the pleasure was extremely important. I liked being strong and firm in the face of adversity.

'But what about the soft one? I had seen it crying at the tragedy. What should it do? George said that he thought there had been a confusion; that the soft one had identified with the hard one and then got in a muddle. And that was right; I suddenly realised that the soft one was pleased with the hard one, because the hard one was going out there fighting for them both, fighting to protect the soft one from being destroyed by mummy, standing up for goodness and rightness. But then it had become worried that maybe that made *it* aggressive as well, and then it didn't know whether it was nice or not. Now it could make a distinction, and that was nice.

'George told me to go back to the little girl. I could see her with all the faeces round her ... and mummy didn't like it. So the little girl decided to make it all right for herself, to affirm what was hers and try and give it a reality. She took it in her fingers and put it in her mouth. This would make it better. The trouble was that it didn't make it better, because her anxiety gave it a rancid smell and taste, so she wasn't really so confident after all that it was nice ... and in any case, by taking it in, she made it disappear, and that didn't solve any problems!

'He told me to see a big steaming heap in front of me and to smell it. I couldn't smell it, though, because I had such a pain in the muscle that controlled my clitoris. He said that this was because my clitoris was standing up like a spear, asserting its right to exist, and my right to exist. He said that this was what it had had to do every time I had wanted to *do* anything ... but that I didn't need to do it any more; it could just be. Yet I was afraid that mummy would bite it off. George asked me what I would do to my clitoris. I realised that I would suck it ... and yet I didn't quite distinguish between my way of taking it into my mouth and mummy's way. But George said they were quite different. I didn't really quite understand what was meant at the time, but what he said calmed me down enough for me to go back to the heap.

He told me to smell it. It was very nice. Now, he said, put your hands in it. But then he explained to me why that wasn't right. He said that monkeys eat their faeces because they are vegetarians. But humans are carnivores, and therefore, even though we all still want to play with our faeces, we have to learn how to do something else instead. I was fascinated by this; by the idea that we could want it, but not do it because it wasn't sensible as humans – *not* because it was bad. It made me proud to be human, and proud to find some other way of doing things which was appropriate to my status as a human. I suddenly *wanted* to learn how to sublimate my desire. And that was wonderful.

'I went into the garden to find some mud, and play with that instead. I made two things: a big round pot and a statue of a lady. Oh, she was beautiful! She had a big tummy, but it wasn't big high up like my tummy had been when I was being a defiant little

205

girl; it was big and round on her abdomen. And she had beautiful breasts which were happy and alive – and strong, wonderful shoulders . . . not aggressive, but looking as if they knew how to be themselves without having to be aggressive. I was so pleased with her. Then I saw myself crawling up her vagina and spreading all through her and becoming myself through her, expressing myself nicely. I was so excited; I felt that this was a more profound image than I had the words to describe; I felt that I finally understood how to sublimate, and how to make a relationship with what I made. Then sublimation wasn't giving up what I really wanted, but expressing it in a different way. I still had the pleasures, and could even understand that they were, in many ways, actually *better* pleasures. I had never understood that before; I had thought that sublimation meant getting palmed off with some cheap substitute.

'I was so pleased with what I had done. But I was a bit puzzled; how did all this relate to the little one earlier, the one having a tantrum? After all, she was only about a year old, while I was now about two years old. How did I create the continuum between the two of them? George told me to let her come into the garden as well, and to give her a piece of mud, too. She was very pleased. She put it straight in her mouth! Then she smeared it round her face. But I didn't tell her that that wasn't right . . . and soon she looked at what I'd done and started bonking her piece of mud up and down on the ground, trying to make a shape out of it. She was very pleased with herself . . . and so was the bigger me, because I'd seen how to let her learn for herself that there were other pleasures.

'Yet what would happen if mummy saw us? I saw her . . . and suddenly, I felt that mummy had an emotional age of about one. She didn't understand what we were doing at all; she sat on the grass with her genitals in the shape of a huge black hole, and played with her pubic hair. She was interested only in herself. *Then* I saw her getting angry and wanting to destroy what we'd made – but it was a reaction of impotence and lack of understanding; jealousy for something she vaguely understood was better than what she had, but which she couldn't achieve herself. And then I realised that it *wasn't my fault* that she hadn't been able to relate to me and understand me and the continuity of my person . . . because she didn't understand how to relate outside herself with anyone. And my clitoris relaxed, and I felt wonderfully better, overwhelmed by a sense of relief and pleasure.

'When I woke up, I felt as if someone had left me a legacy. I suddenly was empowered to *do* things . . . and that was marvellous.'

We see here a particularly intense conflict between the need to take in, to introject the primary object and in doing so acquire its characteristics, and the patient's attempts to refuse them. She has split the mother between the good object, that corresponds to her own innate urges for a loving and expansive libido, and the bad object, represented by the mother's aggressive and sadistic libido which threatens to invade her. Her oral needs command her to incorporate the mother's libido despite all protest, her rancid milk, the cold and sadistic sensations of her breast and, later, of her personality, for if she refuses to do so she has no mother, she kills her, and in her isolation she will lose herself. But if she takes her in, she will be invaded by her mother's characteristics, and we see the struggle between the innate, positive oral and vaginal libido trying to maintain its identity against the mother's sadistic, destructive libido. If she attacks the mother in order to rid her of her sadism and defend herself against it, then she behaves like mother, she herself becomes sadistic, and if she accepts her in an expansive and loving manner then she is invaded by her and becomes like her. This appears as an insurmountable conflict.

But we can also see that if her Ego can gain enough independence to affirm her innate, positive drives and the memories of a loving libido, she becomes nourished by them and does not need to take the mother in and identify with her; we also see the conflict of the good and the bad self-image represented by her anal product, and her success in recreating her good identity. By discovering her good desires and their acceptability, she learns to trust her femininity.

As is the case amongst boys, there are a great number of possible scenarios in the girl's process of maturation, and I shall present a few of them here:

(i) The most widespread in our culture is the mother who is insecure in her sexual and narcissistic relationship to her husband, and considers the daughter as a rival, imposing a repressive and angry model upon her daughter and making her feel guilty about her erotic needs.

If the mother represents the jealous Superego, angry and punishing towards the girl's sexual urges, then her genitality will feel bad, a source of shame and sin, and her vagina will be pulled backwards and desensitised in order to neutralise her guilt feelings and her anxieties. This affects a wide area of other somatic tensions: the anus will be pulled upwards, and the pelvis become immobile and rigid, the back tight, the shoulders pulled up. Her narcissistic libido also tends to hide itself by tightening the chest; the aggressive urges will cause her jaws to become tight in order to inhibit them, and the forehead disposed to a more or less perpetual frown, which manifests the bad conscience.

As we said before, the urge to identify with father is more pronounced in girls than the boy's urge to identify with mother, for, after all, he represents the great world of man where everything happens. She will want father to compensate her for the bad libido introjected by her mother, and liberate her from the guilt and anxiety which she experienced. She will want him to show his libido towards her, make her his favourite and defeat the mother's aggressiveness. She wants father to be her hero who frees her from her bondage to the mother, from the chain that ties her to the dragon, to overwhelm it with his spear, and swing the girl onto his masculine steed and take her to his castle where she can reign supreme in his love. The symbol of Saint George and the dragon represents the collective unconscious, which dominates the dream world of girls, and also of the boy, who emerges from his own insecurity to enter the world of masculine strength and freedom. Every man wants to liberate the woman from her inhibitions, and in doing so liberate himself.

(ii) But all too often the father fails to live up to his daughter's expectation, and is incapable of overcoming the mother's inhibiting powers. The mother who is herself not released by the love of her husband from her Oedipal conflicts, who does not admire him as a sex object (men are sex objects to women as much as women are sex objects to men) and as a person, adopts disparaging attitudes towards him and communicates them to her daughter, and undermines the girl's love for her father. The father will appear to her as a man dominated by the mother, his masculine libido defeated and unable to assert itself towards the daughter. She will feel him to be inhibited and afraid of her advances. His more or less consciously rejective attitudes will make her feel rejected and cause her to adopt withdrawing or rejective attitudes towards her own libidinous feelings. She will despise him in her disappointment, and will be unable to free herself from dependency upon mother, and remain fixated upon her infantile conflicts, her Oedipus complex unresolved.

There are many possible variations in the scenario of the weak or apparently weak father. He may withdraw from his masculine role in the family and devote his energies to his career and to a life outside. He may be absent for long periods or indifferent, a stranger to his daughter. The girl may feel unwanted by him and become convinced that it is her fault that he does not show his love for her. If the father repulses her advances or shows his fear of them, she will feel unwanted and her desires a danger to man. She may feel that her desires are too powerful, and she will constantly be on guard against them, suspicious and mistrustful of herself and unable to 'let go'.

Many fathers who are insecure in their sexuality become afraid that if they allow themselves to be stimulated they would be unable to control their urges. Such men usually show their love and affection towards their baby daughters, but when they become five or six begin to withdraw from them, hide their own libido and adopt aloof attitudes, and their inhibition becomes particularly pronounced when the daughter enters into her genital puberty. They become cool and reserved towards them in order to avoid their own arousal, being afraid of their own feelings and particularly of the jealousy of their wives. Many girls experience this behaviour of their father, feel that he rejects them, or is in some strange way hostile and mistrustful towards their libidinous feelings, and they subsequently come to believe that there is something wrong with them, that they are unattractive and that their libido is unacceptable. They, so to speak, imitate their father's withdrawal, and withdraw their own libido, hide it, as it were, they mistrust their own desires and desires of others. A mixture of inhibition and aggression, defensiveness and anger will come to dominate their personalities. Such girls will feel trapped in their own defences and frequently search for the father they wanted, identify with the imagined ideal father and adopt masculine attitudes; they will in their own person enact the strength which they wanted to see in their father, they will, so to speak, set an example to him by behaving how he should behave and in their fantasy liberate him from his inhibitions. They will forever want to improve men, seek out weak or inadequate men who they can make strong and capable, or men with potential, whom they can teach and help towards their fulfilment. Such a quest can lead to constant disappointment, to a critical and resentful disposition, always blaming men for their inadequacies and for her unfulfilled life, or it can lead to the kind of female personality who is an inspiration and encouragement to a man, the sort of woman of whom it is said that behind every successful man there is a strong woman. Or again, in her attempts to enact the successful male as she wants him to be, she may transfer this desire, not so much to the man but to her own Ego. Such a woman will become ambitious, enter into the male world and compete with men on their own territory. She will often be a successful, professional person, determined to dissociate herself from her dependence upon men and meet them as equals. She will assert her independence and jealously guard it, but consider her feminine urges a threat to her independence and attempt to deny them. She will frequently despise women, and on the one hand idealise men and at the same time mistrust them, and enter into relationships which are frequently torn by arguments and competition for power.

(iii) Here we want to point to an ideal scenario in the girl's maturation process. This is the girl whose mother has herself overcome her infantile conflicts and fears, fully enjoys her sexual desires and finds them satisfying, and the father who expresses his male libido towards his family, who can love and share his love and is a source of joy and confidence to his children and to his wife.

The girl's mother will look with pleasure at her own parents, she will not feel jealous of them or see them as a threat to her own libido but as an enhancement. The daughter will introject the good breast and the good vaginal feelings which the mother presents and wants to share with her daughter, and feels happiness in doing so. The mother is not frustrated by her man and will therefore show to the daughter her admiration and love for him, and the daughter will feel that she has the right to admire and to love him also. The father will show his pride in his masculinity, in his sexuality and the pleasure he derives from it. He will not be afraid to embrace his daughter and show his joy of her, and while he will not feel any need for sexual contact with her, will not be embarrassed by her advances. She will be proud of his masculinity and of the masculinity of men she comes to love, and will be secure in the feeling of their admiration for her and for her female desires.

On the basis of trust and confidence in her own libido, she can cultivate her talents in whatever direction they may lie, and while accepting her female needs can feel equal to men without having to compete or be afraid of them. And when she becomes a mother, she will be what every baby wants her mother to be, namely, a happy woman, and mother and child will establish the link in the chain of mature personalities, unencumbered by the infantile and Oedipal conflicts which bedevil much of our culture but which, as I have shown, are not inevitable.

The World of Grown-Ups

1. PSYCHE AND SOCIETY

In his *Group Psychology and the Analysis of the Ego*, Freud wrote:

The contrast between individual psychology and social or group psychology, which at first glance may seem to be full of significance, loses a great deal of its sharpness when it is examined more closely. From the very first individual psychology is at the same time social psychology as well.

This is particularly true of adults whose relationship with the world is no longer confined to the circle of their family but extends to society. It would be absurd to study a child's development without considering its parents and other members of the family, and it would be equally absurd to study a grown-up person's psychological experiences and behaviour without reference to the society in which he lives.

If we intend to apply psychoanalytic concepts to the study of social relationships it is not enough to consider how people react to the demands of the social world but also how psychological forces operate in societies. We shall be obliged to show that society itself is an embodiment of psychological processes and what we call reality is frequently a kind of socialised neurosis or even an institutionalised madness. We have seen this in the psychopathy of Nazism and Stalinism which was experienced as real, all too real, by its citizens and victims. While in previous chapters we have observed how neurotic and psychotic processes develop in individuals, how loving and embracing as well as aggressive, sadistic, defiant, fear-ridden and paranoid symptoms and character structures develop, now we have to examine how these traits, these psychic facts are transferred to society to become social facts, objective conditions.

We can say that the culture and structure of a society is the objectified manifestation of the complexes and conflicts which grown-ups have repressed, split off from their Ego and projected upon society where they once again come to life and demand their satisfaction. The libidinous drives which individuals have developed during their infancy and childhood, and which continue to operate unconsciously, return to the surface and are re-enacted in society. What the adult has to repress acquires validation when expressed in society, what is not permitted to the individual is permitted to society (as Plato observed). Manic fantasies, paranoid obsessions and phobias are institutionalised in society and perceived as objective conditions, the subjective unconscious becomes objective reality. A culture can be seen as the mirror which reflects people's unconscious fantasies, but they don't know this; they consider what they see as reality, as objective conditions outside themselves.

While in his childhood a person's libidinous drives are totally absorbed with his family, the grown-up transfers his libido, together with its complexes and conflicts, to the wider world of society.

When we are considered grown-up and ready to fight our own battles and prove ourselves in the world and are, to some extent at least, liberated from the confines of our parents' beliefs, prejudices, convictions or delusions, we encounter new Superego symbols towards whom we tend to adopt the same attitudes as we have adopted towards the earlier Superego. The same rituals of identification, projection, submission or rebellion, self-assertiveness or dependency are enacted again.

Socially orientated psychoanalysts like Reich, Fromm and the exponents of the Frankfurt school of social research defined the task of a psychoanalytic sociology as having to investigate how the socio-economic conditions of a society influence the structure of drives and the largely unconscious attitudes of individuals. The pre-eminent question, as they saw it, is how and when the social condition is transferred to the individual, how the objective becomes subjective.

I have shown many examples of how cultural and social conditions influence the attitude of parents to the child, determine their expectations and taboos, their concepts of right and wrong, their own self-image in society and their image of the child's role in society, and in this way produce subjective processes in the child and adolescent which have a major influence upon the psychological structure of the grown-up and his role in society.

However, we have to face not only the question how the conditions and values of society are transferred to the psyche of individuals, how the objective becomes subjective, how the psyche comes to reflect the social and cultural reality, but also how the subjective psychological processes are transferred to society and its culture. For it is fallacious to consider socio-cultural reality as objectively given, developing independently and outside the psyche of men. In other words, we have to study the psychological processes which operate in society, seeing it not merely as a structure of objective conditions but as the embodiment of psychological processes. How then are we to describe the processes of projection and transfer from psyche to society?

In our study of the psychological development of an individual we have observed the various primacies of the libido and the emergence of fixations and complexes which determine a person's character and frequently produce neurotic symptoms. Each of these primacies directs the individual to pursue the necessary functions of self-preservation as well as the preservation of the species. But beyond these fairly specific forms of the libido, there is another, more fundamental libido drive which pervades all others and which I call non-specific. If there is one rule which we can consider to be fundamental in the life of a person it is that everyone is born with the need for love. He needs to give love and to receive it. And perhaps the most astonishing thing I have discovered in my long practice as a psychotherapist is the extent to which the infant is aware of its mother's libidinous attitude towards it, its extreme sensitivity for the quality of her love. It is of course extremely difficult to define the quality of love in empirical terms, and it is equally difficult to define the means by which the infant receives the messages of love from its mother. It receives sensations of the libido, and these can be felt to be good or bad, positive or negative or of a wide range of intermediate quality, but they all evoke a deep response in the child. As these communications of libido as well as the responses to them occur on a pre-verbal level, we lack the words to describe them and they are hard to explain in a rational manner. We may call them sensations, feelings, intuition, empathy or perhaps telepathy. They are not confined to any particular area of the body or any of the senses but may be considered a radiation which emanates from the mother.

There is no doubt that people radiate an energy, a libido, to which all of us react, usually without knowing it, and there is, moreover, in all of us an undefined longing for an intimate communion with our fellow beings and with nature. However, this fundamental drive, which has been called life-force, Eros, *élan vital* and orgone energy, undergoes many transformations in the life of an individual. Fundamentally these transformations serve the preservation of the individual and the preservation of the species, and we call them primacies. But these primacies, which we may consider biologically determined, undergo further transformations which are of a more specifically psychological kind as they are responses to the environment. In the course of an individual's development his libidinous drives encounter a wide range of frustrations, denials, hostility and rejection, producing defence mechanisms, inhibitions, displacement processes and fixations, which determine a person's character and frequently cause neurotic or psychotic symptoms. These processes are projected upon society where they are acted out in its culture. The conflicts of the psyche are re-enacted in the conflicts within and between societies.

2. CHARACTER AND CULTURE.

When we speak of the transfer from the individual psyche to the psyche of society, from the subjective to the objective world, we are dealing with the interaction between the character of the people who live in a society and the character of that society. Not only are a person's character and his responses to his environment determined by his fixations upon certain primacies of his libido and the pattern of his defences, repressions, compensations, anxieties and satisfactions he has adopted, but societies too have their character, which usually is called a culture, in which certain libidinous primacies are emphasised, encouraged or imposed. Every culture has a certain image of itself which acts as a model to its citizens, it represents a collective Superego which upholds certain values which are meant to express people's psychological needs and aspirations. By holding up a mirror to people in which they are expected to recognise their true selves, a culture exercises a powerful influence upon the collective self-image of its members and upon the formation of dominant character-traits. Individuals dominated by certain libidinous primacies will look for their representations in the social world. If, for instance, a person has a fixation upon an anal hoarding libido and finds his purpose in the pursuit of possessions and money, he will see the world of man dominated by this pursuit and will assume that the acquisition of riches is the basic law of life and will seek to promote a society which encourages this idea and gives it the best possible opportunity for fulfilment. Of course there are many possible combinations and reaction-formations of this primacy. For instance, this man may be a convinced liberal who opposes any authoritarian system that seeks to restrain him in his activity, or he may favour an authority that safeguards his right to amass money and protects him against those who threaten to curtail his freedom.

It would be impossible here to enumerate the almost endless combinations of psychological drives which find expression in people's social identifications and beliefs. We may, however, say that in every society there is a reservoir of a very wide range of characterological and ideological dispositions (as there is in each individual), each striving for domination. But, nevertheless, every culture upholds at its basis a consensus of some fundamental belief patterns which in turn give expression to certain psychological drives. The sheer multitude of psychological factors involved in the political, economic, ideological and religious life of societies, their values, obsessions, prejudices and the complex interaction between aggression and co-operation, between love and hate, have made it inevitable that observers of social affairs either confine themselves to specific investigations of certain areas only or write in general and abstract terms. In the following pages I want to give some examples of the way in which libidinous primacies and their conflicts determine the role which a person plays in society, and how they interact with and influence the character of his society.

An individual whose character is dominated by the oral-aggressive-sadistic primacies of his libido will feel the world to be selfish, mean, rejective and aggressive, and he will want to vent his aggression upon it and experience the satisfactions of sadism. He will, therefore, look to society to provide him with the opportunity to express his aggressive urges and to give them validation, and will find this in established authority of state or religion on whose behalf he can fight, or in a rebellious, terrorist subculture, which he can join to fight the establishment. Such an individual finds fellowship and homo-erotic satisfaction in the collective pursuit of aggressive goals, whether it be in the army, or the politics of terrorism or revolution or on behalf of religious fanaticism. There is no lack of agitators, Fascist, communist, religious or racial fanatics, who play upon the sado-masochistic dispositions which many people harbour in the unconscious areas of their minds, and bring them to the surface. Particularly in mass meetings and rallies they evoke an hysteric delirium of apocalyptic visions of destruction and salvation through destruction; the discharge of destructive-sadistic drives is an end in itself and there is no rational concern with the goal to be achieved. These experiences of collective aggressiveness allow infantile urges to erupt, short-circuiting, so to speak, Ego functions in the higher cortical areas, as can be seen in the incantation of slogans accompanied by obsessive movements such as raising arms, shaking fists, stamping the legs and in primitive dance movements. We have seen these expressions of oral-aggressive-sadistic drives in the fantasies and behaviour of infants, and we have also seen them acted out by adults in society. In the same way as we manage to diagnose the sado-masochistic processes operating in psychopathy or paranoia among individuals, we should also be able to diagnose them if they occur collectively and threaten to dominate societies. Such diagnostic understanding would strengthen the Ego defences of both individuals and nations against being overwhelmed by infantile drives and enhance the rational faculties in the exercise of discrimination and judgment.

When the expansive oral libido has retained a dominant role in a person's character, the urge to give love and to receive it will play an important part in his life. Such people will tend to be trustful towards their environment, anticipating responsiveness and sympathy for their needs and aspirations. They will reach out to others and communicate their pleasure feelings in doing so. As grown-ups the world around them will symbolise their loving and responsive mother, they will gain pleasure in looking at beautiful things and will see beauty and colour and a sense of aliveness around them, ready to empathise with nature and people. As Goethe used to say: 'The good man expects the world and people generally to be good, and he will not assume nor understand evil.' Such a man may also be endowed with a loving father-Superego image which encourages him in his expansive urges and helps him to develop his rational functions and to refine his judgments. People who suffer from pleasure anxiety and a contractive libido will consider such a man utopian and lacking in a sense of realism, whereas he himself will be inclined to the view that the good is real and evil an aberration, however frequently it may show itself.

On the anal productive level individuals want to create representations of their self-image by transforming material things into artefacts in which they can recognise themselves and be recognised. They have a close libidinous contact with material things, like to handle and shape them and to show what they have made. They frequently develop a talent for craftsmanship, or become artists if craftsmanship is combined with strong visual imagery; or they may be musicians when craftsmanship is combined with auditory (and urethral) sensitivity and imagination. They will assume that people are interested in their product, and that they will show appreciation and possibly admire them. If on the other hand such an individual has met rejection, disgust or displeasure upon wanting to show off his anal products or material objects which he has made, he will become inhibited and his productive urges will arouse anxiety and guilt feelings. He then adopts retentive attitudes and becomes physically as well as spiritually withholding. His sensitive hands will become tight or mean. He will want to amass material riches and hoard them, he will be pedantic, careful, prone to measure and weigh things in order to determine their value. The primeval gold which he wanted to produce and show off as an infant but which was debased and made to feel dirty has to be regained in the form of money. He will become obsessed with profit and financial gain, he will seek for the gold which was denied him, and the wealth which he can amass will make him feel clean again and respectable. But he will not want to dirty himself by the handling of things and with producing; he will pay others to do so and receive their products which he will carefully evaluate according to their monetary worth.

We see here a dialectic between the producer and the aristocrat or capitalist, the craftsman or the artist and the merchant. The love for gold and wealth, and the love of craftsmanship oppose each other as well as interact. In hierarchical class societies, the producer is the dirty one and the rich man, being freed from actually having to work, is clean and superior; he projects the dirty part of wealth and gold creation on to the lower classes, and the lower classes can only admire their products from the distance. But the sense of guilt among the producers for having to soil themselves in their work makes them feel that they belong to a lower order and often prevents them proclaiming their rightful and dignified place in society. The best they can do is to demand some more of the money which the capitalist receives from their product.

Individuals with an acquisitive, hoarding character will readily enter into the capitalist, acquisitive, profit-motivated system, and will happily play their role in it, and being positively motivated are likely to be successful. They will take any advantage which this society offers, whereas production-orientated persons who consider their work, their craftsmanship or their art as their main source of satisfaction and a source of pride will resent the businessman who exploits their product and considers it merely as a means for making a profit. They will feel demeaned by a culture devoted to the profit motive.

If the contrast between wealth and poverty, between the enjoyment of riches and a life of labour and deprivation is too pronounced, then the clean and the beautiful ones acquire the image of greedy exploiters and will be resented and hated by the people. However, in a capitalist system which not only promises to give everyone the opportunity to acquire possessions but encourages the acquisition of wealth, the possessive, acquisitive and manipulative primacy will tend to predominate. A culture of this kind will regard only material things as worthwhile and important, and will consider their statistical and numerical relationships the chief criteria for what is real and meaningful. We may call this the late, organised state of capitalism, where the world as well as people can only be understood in statistical and quantitative parameters. It is also called postmodern and one of its most powerful recent philosophical manifestations has been the movement of deconstructionism, which proclaims that there is no purpose behind the numbers and the statistics, there is only mathematical probability. There is neither a future nor a past to which one can ascribe real meaning, there is no such thing as mind and no centre to anything behind the world of facts, behind 'what is the case', as Wittgenstein used to say. And even language has no intrinsic meaning behind the word games in which we are engaged, as in the games of manipulating and amassing objects. As there is no connection between the soul, the libido of the producers and the world of things which they have produced, but only the statistical game of acquisition, so people's soul and even their minds, their personalities have no intrinsic meaning. This produces a widespread sense of isolation in many people which is evidenced in their restlessness, their compulsive need for activity which avoids the necessity of reflection, for there seems to be nothing to reflect about. Indeed, reflection would only threaten an encounter with a sense of void inside.

We can consider such a culture to represent a collective regression to the anal primacy, when, as I have pointed out, the
collecting, counting, measuring and weighing of objects becomes
a dominant preoccupation of children. There is the desire to
possess such objects as treasures, to count them and exchange
them. Piaget remarked that at this stage, between two and two
and a half, which is dominated by the acquisition of skills, logical
classes and logical relations, numbers and concrete relations in
space and time emerge. He subsumes these operations under the
term 'quantification'.

But while for the child this is an important preparation for his
Ego functions, a stage in the development of his personality, for
the grown-up these functions are only a part of his psychic
structure, which has to reach the genital stage of the libido in
order to make it possible for him to experience himself as a whole
person in relation to other people and to the world. He has to
develop a concept of selfhood, a self-image able to give love and
to receive love as a procreator and creator who contributes to
society, acknowledges his role and responsibilities in it and whose
role is recognised. Above all, he has to develop the concept of a
person whose erotic drives are transferred from his family to
society and who cathexes his libidinous urges upon it, by which
means the past is connected to the future by the purposiveness
of the present. But when society and its culture appear to be
meaningless, when people feel themselves alienated strangers in
the world around them, then their libido withdraws and the unifying forces of the mature libido, its quest for love, self-affirmation
and purposiveness, tend to atrophy. Cultures then undergo a collective regression to earlier primacies when the unifying processes
of the mature, genital libido give way to a preoccupation with
quantification, statistics and numbers; people are seen as objects
in the mass, as depersonalised, statistical units to be manipulated,
and means become ends.

We have spoken of the interrelation between the narcissistic
and the genital libido, of a person's need to be able to love himself
in order to love others; but in order to love himself he needs the
reassurance also of being loved. The narcissistic libido needs the

221

friendship and recognition of a community where a person is accepted and can play a valid role. During adolescence boys form into gangs which provide them with a sense of identity fed by the homo-erotic bonding with their peers, and as a gang they go out across the hill into the new territory of the social world, assert themselves and prove themselves and find 'the woman'.

Grown-ups continue to need a sense of acceptance and acknowledgment as valuable members of a community. The experience of homo-erotic relationships enhances a person's sense of self, the confidence of being wanted and appreciated, enabling him to reach out to others.

Again and again I find that a person's capacity to relate sexually in a fulfilling and gratifying manner depends on the fulfilment of his narcissistic needs and the role he plays in his community and in society.

Men's narcissistic libido often produces manic fantasies, which in previous times were projected upon the gods and kings and powerful individuals, and in turn people would identify with these manic images, thereby enhancing their self-image. But then the Oedipus complex, which, as I have shown, relates to both the manic-narcissistic as well as the sexual projections upon the father-figure, produces the enmity of the sons, the citizens, and they want to slay the omnipotent father-figure in order to acquire for themselves the power which they have vested in him. The slain father becomes the threatening Superego, a source of remorse and guilt; he is invested with anger which the citizens have directed towards him, he becomes the source of conscience and of fear; he then needs to be worshipped and served in order to propitiate him so that he will release them from their sins. He is given authority over the community and becomes the universal repressor, and men become afraid not only of the external representatives of their Superego, the religious and the secular establishments, but also of their own manic and sexual urges which have caused them to attack the father-figure; they develop a mistrust of themselves and the conflicts of pleasure-anxiety. We know of the phobias, anxieties, inhibitions, the guilt and the shame as well as the aggressiveness which result from the inhibition of our narcissistic and sexual needs. Pleasure-anxiety and mistrust, even fear of one's own urges are reproduced on the social level as mistrust and fear of others, a paranoic disposition of people towards each other, when they are afraid that others threaten to give vent to those urges which they have had to repress in themselves and consider taboo. There is this proneness to consider humanity sinful, driven by dirty, greedy, selfish, brutal and indiscriminate sexual desires, and the subsequent need to be protected from them by the repressive powers of religious and secular authorities. As we are afraid of our own fantasies and urges, and develop a complex system of defence mechanisms in our own mind to prevent them from gaining access to consciousness, so we have to secure ourselves by imposing social defences and repressions. The desire for repressive authorities and even dictatorships which has puzzled philosophers and social scientists can find its explanation in the psychological repression which people project upon their fellow men and upon society. They need to reinforce their own repressions through powerful rulers and authoritarian systems of government.

I have spoken of patriarchal paranoia and its fateful influence upon societies. But one also has to consider the pleasures which authoritarian systems can provide among people who are afraid of their own libidinous urges. Having projected many of their own repressed fantasies upon other members of their own community, they feel pleasure in seeing them punished for their transgressions. There is pleasure in righteousness and in being allied to the Superego, and at the same time excitement in seeing other people's misdeeds exposed. The inhibitions of emotionally repressed people contribute much to the establishment and the acceptance of authoritarian systems.

Individuals in whom an expansive, narcissistic and sexual primacy dominates and who have achieved a level of maturity as persons, find the forces and manifestations of repression puzzling, distasteful or outrageous. They will yearn for freedom and liberty and democracy, and dream of a world where people can be free to show their feelings to each other, people whose natural self is no longer a source of anxiety which has to be hidden, at a time when people no longer have to be ashamed of themselves or underhanded and mistrustful towards each other nor governed by the strong hand of authority.

The European Enlightenment had promised to return to people respect for themselves, freedom from guilt and fear, from servitude to religious or secular authorities; freedom, equality and brotherhood were at last to create the concept of humanity when a man's libido could reach out beyond the confines of family and tribe to the wider sphere of the human community. The joy of the expansive and embracing libido as well as the pleasures of production were to dominate reality, love no longer denied by a hostile and mistrustful world. But it was not to be.

The new world of the Enlightenment created new symbols of power which were to stand over man, it produced a new reality principle which claimed the right to determine men's behaviour and their intellectual orientations. The visions of an almighty God and the splendour of kings were replaced by the vision of an almighty technology and of science which would produce wealth, to be shared by all more or less equally.

But in order to fulfil those visions, men have to obey the imperatives of technology and the rules of its scientific priests and its administrators; they have to learn how to manipulate the machines, how to buy and sell and make profit in an impersonal, objective manner. They have to deny soul and internality in order to master soulless machines and the impersonal, statistical rules of economics and profit. They have to become objects in the world of objects, ruthless and unemotional in the grasping of opportunities. Did not Hayek, that prophet of modern capitalism, propagate the virtues of a market economy that is not inhibited by loyalty to the community or fellow feeling, to enable it to expand and spread its wings to the exploitation of ever new territories? New markets, new raw materials, new scientific and technological discoveries and their ruthless application for the creation of wealth have become the key principle of Western technological civilisations. The attitude towards people as objects to be used as means to further one's purpose of making profit, to be manipulated for self-advancement, the unemotional approach, is considered the most effective way of succeeding in this world.

State and business organisations have to manipulate and control people, use lawyers, personnel relations experts, management consultants and psychologists, to ensure that the system works in a more or less harmonious manner; educationalists and teachers have to train people into becoming capable operators of the machines or scientists to understand how the machines work and to produce ever better ones. An army of market researchers, public relations and advertising consultants are needed to promote market requirements; health administrators, social workers, behavioural engineers and counsellors are required to keep the workforce relatively contented and able to serve the industrial system, while banks, finance houses, insurance companies and investment consultants are required to provide the capital. Mineralogists, geologists, even nuclear physicists have to explore the planet and search for raw materials and find new forms of energy in order to ensure the supply of fodder for the machines and enable them to satisfy an apparently insatiable need for ever new commodities and possessions, for, after all, that is what we worship them for and why we give them our labours. The more we are deprived of our needs for community and fellow feeling, the more greedy we become for possessions to compensate for our narcissistic emptiness and sense of isolation.

Modern industrial societies have produced not only an expectation explosion but also an expertise explosion which has given birth to a vast number of specialised occupations. The sciences are split up into innumerable fields, each separated from each other and occupied by experts who, while claiming to be masters in their particular area of knowledge, do not expect to have mastery or knowledge in any other area, being experts only in their own, and able to communicate their findings only to their fellow experts, while not expecting them to be understood by experts in any other area or by the public in general. This division of work and of knowledge into a huge number of separate territories isolates people from each other and from the world as a whole, for they cannot understand or really know what people outside their own occupation are doing or how they think, nor do they expect to understand the world that lies outside their fence, their particular area of competence. The people 'outside' are anonymous shadowy figures whose inner life is beyond one's understanding or empathy. No wonder people are glued to their television sets and devour the scandals provided by mass circulation papers, for they provide their only view of people outside their own circle. We are increasingly separated from the world of others and separated from our own internality; we see each other only from the outside, objects amongst objects which are either useful to each other or they get into each other's way. Psychology has become behavioural engineering, philosophy the analysis of the meaning of words whose intrinsic and emotional meaning we cannot trust and therefore have to investigate as objects. No wonder that mind, soul and psyche have become taboo words. Even in psychoanalysis it is not the libido, the internal and often unconscious processes which are recognised as important but the study of relationships – 'object relations psychology'. In the Eastern European world, which was dominated by the deities of Marx and Lenin, the ideals of a rationally, scientifically organised central planning and governing apparatus led to total power over the people. It was only slowly recognised that they did not, after seventy years in power, succeed in realising the dreams of an enlightened, rationally controlled economy, but had established a tyranny which denied people their freedom and in the end failed to provide the commodities and the kingdom of plenty which they promised. Dictatorship, corruption and industrial inefficiency were the results of communism. All their means of coercion, their secret police, their political prisons, their Pavlovian brainwashing institutions, their hordes of propagandists did not succeed in making people's minds completely subservient to their rule. Since I wrote the first edition of this book, the Berlin Wall has been torn down and a great cry of celebration erupted all over Germany and other Eastern European countries, declaring the dictatorship of communist hallucinations finally discredited.

No doubt the West has kept its freedom, but what is the cost? Not just hard work – for this is no longer necessary as in the world of old because machines and machine technology have kept their promise of efficient production making man's labour physically much easier – but the increased objectivation and depersonalisation of people's mind and psyche. But perhaps most important of all is our attitude to the world around us, to nature and to the planet. In our frantic quest to generate wealth we have gone back to the habits of the ice ages when our ancestors considered nature as a hostile world to be fought with the utmost determination and courage and with all the means of aggression available to them. The means of production have in our time become increasingly aggressive, they serve to attack the world of nature and make it submit to our purpose, and increasingly this means for profit. The old instinct of defeating the natural environment and imposing our will upon it, the pleasure of sadistic attack to make it yield to our desires is once again given its primacy and justified in the name of practical realism. Tight-lipped, tight-jawed, aggressive libido has gained dominance in our approach to that object of our needs, that all-feeding breast, the planet. And the sadistic teeth, which are embodied in the machines we use and worship, are attacking the world and, as we can now see, are beginning to injure it. Nature is no longer the endless and limitless provider, no longer the boundless repository of our waste products: the air, the biosphere, the ozone layer, the rivers and the seas and the earth itself, the living organisms upon it, the vegetation and the animals are being destroyed by our voracious teeth, the machine system. Our powers of aggression are too great to be tolerated with impunity by nature, and her capacity to recover is now in question. The old instincts which up to now have assured our survival and have given us domination over all living organisms have almost suddenly become counter-productive: they are turning against us and threaten to bring about our destruction. The old masculine virtues which were decisive in the past for ensuring our survival have got to be transformed, they are no longer necessary or desirable. This of course leaves us with a new identity crisis: if not our ancient, well-proven instincts, if not our worship of power and strength, then what are we to aim at? This is not such a futile or ephemeral question as most cynics or knowers of 'human nature' keep asserting.

As we increasingly project our narcissistic and productive libido upon the machines and they govern our way of life, we are being deprived of our powers and of our narcissistic self-experience. The machines we produce become gigantic tools which dwarf the importance of the skill of our hands, deny us the pleasure of their exercise and of being what Kant called 'active agents in the determination of our lives'. Even our mind, and the exercise of our intelligence and imagination is being put in the shade by computerised thinking-machines, and we come to depend upon the giant tools and weapons to an ever-increasing extent. An analogy with the mammoth and the sabre-toothed tiger and the dinosaur may not be too far-fetched. Pressing buttons for immediate solutions and answers, being glued to graphs and statistics on the screen narrows and diminishes our psychic space to ten-second sound bytes, to thinking in terms of tabloid head-lines and staccato slogans which can be understood immediately and cause us to regress to infantile ways of cognition and reac-tions which short-circuit the functions of the higher cortical system. In other words, the more powerful our technological gad-getry the more helpless we become as individuals. Already mind, soul and personality are considered entities which our scientists find incomprehensible, and only the study of reflexes, reactions to outside stimuli appear worth bothering about.

As we become increasingly dependent upon the imperatives of technology which govern our lives, we have to be subservient to a technological bureaucracy which considers us as objects and which adopts a dismissive attitude to our psyche and the depth of our personalities. What goes on inside ourselves becomes un-recognised and irrelevant. We can see the regressive psychic processes which are produced by such conditions in the arts, where a cult of infantilism prevails. Dancing is reduced to spastic movements, music to the incoherent sounds and the babblings of infants – infantile sounds of desire and yearning on the one hand and de-sublimated aggression and brutalism on the other are considered entertaining. In the areas of politics and religion we are beginning to encounter a proliferation of religious fundamen-talist fanaticism, nationalisms and racial assertiveness. As more and more people are made to be anonymous entities in an in-creasingly complex technological world, which they can neither understand nor control, they will want to regain a sense of identity, and they will do so in the form of primitive protest movements which find their expression in vehement, hysterical and brutal forms.

Besides the discovery of which I have spoken at the beginning of this chapter, namely, the infant's awareness of its mother's libido in both its negative and its positive aspects, another is that aggression is a secondary drive, a reaction to the armoured, inhibited and life-negating mother and to a rejective environment. Children both introject their parents' inhibitions and fears and at the same time react to them aggressively, thus becoming aggressive towards their own inhibitions as well as to those of the world around them. They repress their libido, and then become aggressive against the repression which they feel both in themselves as well as in the outside world. In the first instance they become depressed and anxious, and in the second, aggressive. And they communicate their anxieties and their anger to their children, and an endless chain of pathologies is established from generation to generation. As analysts, of whatever school and whatever degree of competence, we attempt to break this chain.

In my work as a therapist I always come to a point when I ask people, usually under hypnosis, to see themselves as they really, deep down, want to be. And usually, sometimes almost immediately, sometimes after some visual experimentation, a new image of themselves appears which gives expression to deep libidinous urges. The soul, of which we have spoken, that deep repository of the true self, makes its appearance and transforms the image of the person. The tight and anxious lips begin to show their feelings and yearnings for love – they become sensitive and soft – and the whole body, which previously was tight and repeatedly deformed, relaxes towards libidinous sensations which radiate from it. I do not need to go into the details of these transformations which frequently are quite dramatic. But what is particularly revealing is that patients are inspired by these visions of themselves, and begin to realise what they want and how they want to be, and begin to believe in its possibility.

It is not difficult in our time to see the deformities, the anxieties and rages which pervade the social attitudes and postures of mankind, and it would certainly be most desirable that we obtain a vision of our collective potentials and come to believe in them: the vision where men are open to that primary libido, and under its embrace unite the world outside with the world inside, revealing to us that real reality which is waiting to be recognised. The planet needs to be a home, an internal world, and no longer present to us an external world to be feared, attacked and exploited without regard to its needs. The Ego of man has to relate to the Id instead of the Superego, and the Superego has to relate to the Ego and be transformed into an Ego ideal. In this way it may just be possible for us to liberate ourselves from infantile fixations and their phantasmagoric images and see each other with a new sensitivity and awareness.

To be really grown-up should mean that one is able to liberate oneself from infantile fixations if they are seen to be pathological. Of course it is easy enough to recognise a pathology, a neurosis or psychosis in individuals, but it is much more difficult to do so in cultures. However, the twentieth century and, indeed, much of our history can leave us in no doubt that there is a pathology in the social fabric which is increasingly dangerous. To be grown-up, not only in years but in maturity, should mean that individuals are able to recognise the deformations and the sickness in their society and strive for a vision of mankind's potentials.

Bibliography

Abraham, Karl: *A Short Study in the Development of the Libido*, Hogarth Press, 1927
— *Selected Papers on Psychoanalysis*, Karnac Books, 1988
Adorno, T. et al: *The Authoritarian Family*, Norton, 1969
Adorno, T. and Horkheimer, M: *Aspects of Sociology*, London, 1979
Alexander, Franz: *Psychoanalysis and Psychotherapy*, George Allen & Unwin, 1957
Bachofen, J.J: Myth, *Religion and Mother Right*, Princeton University Press, 1973
Berger, P: *Towards a Sociological Understanding of Psychoanalysis*, Social Research, 1955
Bettelheim, B: *The Informed Heart*, Penguin, 1986
Bernfeld, S: *Psychology of the Infant*, Kegan Paul, 1929
— 'Sigmund Freud', *International Journal of Psychoanalysis*, 1951
Bion, W.R: 'Attacks on Linking', *International Journal of Psychoanalysis*, Vol 40, pp.308-315, 1959
Bornemann, Ernest: *The Psychoanalysis of Money*, Urizen Books, 1976
Bowlby, J: *Attachment and Loss. Vol. 1. Attachment*, Hogarth Press, 1969
— *Attachment and Loss. Vol. 2. Separation, Anxiety and Anger*, 1973
— *Attachment and Loss. Vol. 3. Loss Sadness and Depression*, 1980
Breuer, J. and Freud, S: *Studies on Hysteria*, S.E., Vol 2
Brown, J.A.C: *Freud and the Post-Freudians*, Pelican Books, 1961
Brown, N.O: *Life against Death: The Psychoanalytic Meaning of History*, Routledge & Kegan Paul, 1959
Calvin, William H: *How Brains Think*, Weidenfeld & Nicolson, 1997
Campbell, J: *The Hero with a Thousand Faces*, Princeton University Press, 1971

Chodorow, N: *The Reproduction of Mothering: Psychoanalysis and the Sociology of Gender*, Univ. of California Press, 1978

Cohn, Norman: *Warrant for Genocide*, Serif, 1996

Damasio, Antonio: *The Feeling of What Happens*, Heinemann, 2000

Deleuze, G. and Guattari, F: *Anti-Oedipus: Capitalism and Schizophrenia*, Athlone Press, 1984

Deutsch, Helene: *The Psychology of Female Sexuality*, 1925

— *The Psychology of Women, Vol 2.*, Grune & Stratton, 1945

Deutscher, I: *Stalin: A Political Biography*, Oxford University Press, 1949

Dubos, R: *So Human an Animal*, Transaction Pub., 1998

Ellenberger, H.F: *The Discovery of the Unconscious – The History and Evolution of Dynamic Psychiatry*, Allen Lane, 1970

Erikson, E.H: *Childhood and Society*, Vintage, 1995

— *Identity: Youth and Crisis*, Faber, 1971

Fairbairn, W.R.D: *An Object Relations Theory of the Personality*, Basic Books, 1954

Fenichel, O: *The Psychoanalytic Theory of Neurosis*, Routledge, 1996

— 'A Critique of the Death Instinct', in *Collected Papers*, Routledge & Kegan Paul, 1954

Ferenczi, S: *Contributions to Psychoanalysis*, Hogarth Press, 1955

Foucault, M: *The History of Sexuality*, Vol. 1, Penguin, 1981

Frankl, George: *The End of War or the End of Mankind*, Globe Publications, 1955

— *The Failure of the Sexual Revolution*, Kahn & Averill, 1974

— *The Social History of the Unconscious*, Open Gate Press, 1990

— *Archaeology of the Mind*, Open Gate Press, 1992

— *Civilisation: Utopia and Tragedy*, Open Gate Press, 1992

— *Exploring the Unconscious*, Open Gate Press, 1994, 2001

— *Foundations of Morality*, Open Gate Press, 2000, 2001

Frankl, Victor: *The Will to Meaning*, Souvenir Press, 1971

Franz, M.-L. von: 'The Process of Individuation', from *Man and his Symbols*, ed. C.G. Jung, Arkana, 1990

Freud, Anna: *The Ego and the Mechanisms of Defence*, Hogarth Press, 1937

Freud, Sigmund:, 1900 *The Interpretation of Dreams*, S.E., Vol.43

— 1905 *Three Essays on the Theory of Sexuality*, S.E. Vol. 7

— 1908 *Character and Anal Eroticism*, S.E. Vol. 9

— 1913 *Totem and Taboo*, S. E. Vol. 13

— 1914 *On Narcissism*, S. E. Vol. 14

— 1915 *The Unconscious*, S. E. Vol. 14

— 1915–17 *Introductory Lectures on Psychoanalysis*, S.E. Vol. 15–16
— 1920 *Beyond the Pleasure Principle*, S. E. Vol. 18
— 192 1 *Group Psychology and the Analysis of the Ego*, S. E. Vol. 18
— 1923 *The Ego and the Id*, S.E. Vol. 19
— 1925 *Some Psychical Consequences of the Anatomical Distinction between the Sexes*, S.E. Vol. 19
— 1927 *The Future of an Illusion*, S.E. Vol. 21
— 1930 *Civilisation and its Discontents*, S.E. Vol. 21
— 1933 *New Introductory Lectures on Psychoanalysis*, S.E. Vol. 22
— 1938 *An Outline of Psychoanalysis*, S.E. Vol. 23
Fromm, Erich: *Escape from Freedom*, Holt, Rinehart & Winston, 1941
— *Psychoanalysis and Religion*, Yale University Press, 1950
— *The Sane Society*, Routledge, 1991
— *The Revolution of Hope*, Harper & Row, 1970
— *The Crisis of Psychoanalysis*, Jonathan Cape, 1971
— *The Anatomy of Human Destructiveness*, Penguin, 1977
Gedo, J. and Pollock, G.H: Freud: *The Fusion of Science and Humanism*, Psychological Issues, 1975
Glover, Edward: *Psycho-Analysis*, John Bale, 1939
— *On the Early Development of the Mind*, Alien & Unwin, 1956
— *The Birth of the Ego*, Allen & Unwin, 1968
Goethe, Johann Wolfgang von: *Essay on Nature*
Gould, Stephen Jay: *Ontogeny and Phylogeny*, Harvard University Press, 1985
Graves, Robert: *Greek Myths*, Vol. 2, Penguin, 1992
Groddeck, Georg: *The Book of the Id*, Vision Press, 1961
Guntrip, Harry: *Personality Structure and Human Interaction*, Karnac Books, 1995
— *Schizoid Phenomena, Object Relations and the Self*, Hogarth Press, 1968
Hartmann, H: *Ego Psychology and the Problem of Adaptation*, Imago Publishing Co., 1958
Horkheimer, Max, ed: *Studien Über Autorität und Familie*, Paris, 1936
Jahoda, M: 'Social Psychology and Psychoanalysis', Bulletin, Brit. Psych. Society
Jay, M: *The Dialectical Imagination*, University of California Press, 1996
Jones, E: *The Life and Work of Sigmund Freud*, Hogarth Press, 1953–7
Jung, C.G: *Symbols of Transformation*, Routledge, 1956
— *On the Psychology of the Unconscious*, Collected Works, Vol. 8, 1953

— *Modern Man in Search of a Soul*, Ark Paperbacks, 1984

Kardiner, A: *The Individual and His Society*, Columbia University Press, 1939

Kinsey, A. et al: *Sexual Behaviour in the Human Female*, W.B. Saunders & Co., 1953

Klein, Melanie: *Contributions to Psychoanalysis*, Hogarth Press, 1948

— *The Psychoanalysis of Children*, Virago, 1989

— *Envy and Gratitude*, Hogarth Press, 1975

Klein, M. et al: *Developments in Psychoanalysis*, Karnac and the Institute of Psychoanalysis, 1989

Kohut, H: *The Analysis of the Self*, Hogarth, for the Institute of Psychoanalysis, 1971

Koestler, A: *The Ghost in the Machine*, Hutchinson, 1967

Koestler, A, et al: *The God that Failed*, Bantam Books, 1970

Kolakowski, L: *Main Currents of Marxism*, Vol. 3., Oxford University Press, 1985

Lacan, Jacques: 'The Function and Field of Speech and Language in Psychoanalysis', *Ecrits*, Tavistock/Routledge, 1989

Laing, R.D: *The Divided Self*, Penguin, 1975

Lasch, Christopher: *The Culture of Narcissism*, Abacus, 1980

LeDoux, Joseph: *The Emotional Brain: The Mysterious Underpinnings of Emotional Life*, Weidenfeld & Nicolson, 1998

Lens, Sidney: *The Military Industrial Complex*, Kahn & Averill, 1971

Malinowski, B: *Sex and Repression in Savage Society*, Routledge & Kegan Paul, 1979

Marcuse, Herbert: *One Dimensional Man*, Routledge, 1991

— *Eros and Civilization*, Ark, 1987

Martin, Bernice: *A Sociology of Contemporary Cultural Change*, Blackwell, 1981

Masters, W.H. and Johnson, M.E: *Human Sexual Response*, Little, Brown, 1966

Mead, Margaret: *Coming of Age in Samoa*, Penguin, 1977

Mitchell, J: *Psychoanalysis and Feminism,* Penguin, 2000

Nietzsche, Friedrich: *Morgenröte*, Goldmann, Munich, 1980

Parsons, T: *Social Structure and Personality*, The Free Press, 1970

Piaget, Jean: *The Origin of Intelligence in the Child*, Penguin, 1977

— 'The Stages of the Intellectual Development of the Child', *Bulletin of the Menninger Clinic*, 1962

Popper, K: *Conjectures and Refutations*, Routledge & Kegan Paul, 1969

Pribram, K.H: *Languages of the Brain*, Prentice-Hall, 1971

Reich, Wilhelm: *Character Analysis*, Vision Press, 1951

— *The Function of the Orgasm*, Souvenir Press, 1983

— *The Mass Psychology of Fascism*, Penguin, 1983

— *The Sexual Revolution*, Vision Press, 1972

—*The Cancer Biopathy*, Vision Press, 1973

Reik, Theodor: *The Unknown Murderer*, Hogarth Press, 1936

— *Masochism in Modern Man*, Souvenir Press, 1975

Riesman, D: *The Lonely Crowd*, Yale University Press, 1961

Robinson, Paul A: *The Sexual Radicals*, Paladin, 1972

Roheim, G: *Psychoanalysis and Anthropology*, N.Y. 1950

Rose, Steven, ed: *From Brains to Consciousness* – Essays on the New Sciences of the Mind, Penguin 1999

Roszak, T: *The Making of a Counter Culture*, Faber & Faber, 1971

Sandler, J. with Freud, A: *The Analysis of Defence*, International Universities Press, 1985

Sandler, J., Ed.: *Dimensions of Psychoanalysis*, Karnac Books, 1989

Schopenhauer, Arthur: 'Transcendent Speculation on Apparent Design in the Fate of the Individual'

Schrödinger, E: *What is Life?* with *Mind and Matter*, Cambridge University Press, 1992

Sorokin, P: *Society, Culture and Personality*, Harper's Social Studies Series, 1947

Stekel, W: *Sadism and Masochism*, Liveright Publ. Co., 1939

— *Patterns of Psychosexual Infantilism*, Peter Nevill, 1953

Sterba, R: *Introduction to the Psychoanalytic Theory of the Libido*, N.M.D. Publ. Co., 1942

Stewart, W.A: *Psychoanalysis: The First Ten Years*, Allen & Unwin, 1969

Sullivan, H.S: *The Interpersonal Theory of Psychiatry*, Norton, 1965

Sulloway, F: *Freud, Biologist of the Mind*, Harvard University Press, 1992

Wheen, Francis: *Karl Marx*, Fourth Estate, 1999

Winnicott, D.W: *Collected Papers*, Tavistock Publications, 1958

— *The Maturational Process and the Facilitating Environment*, Karnac Books, 1990

— *The Family and Individual Development*, Tavistock Publications, 1965

Zilboorg, G: *Sigmund Freud: His Explorations of the Mind of Man*, Charles Scribner, 1951

— *Freud's Fundamental Psychiatric Orientation*, N.Y., 1954

Index

INDEX